Developing Sport Expertise

An athlete's road from 'ordinary' talent to elite accomplishment in sport is a long one. The emergence and fine tuning of high level sport skills takes place in increments over many years and is a journey that fascinates sport scientists, sport coaches and sport fans alike.

Developing Sport Expertise examines the science behind skill acquisition in sport and explores the application of science to optimal sports training and talent identification. The text also contains 'Coach's Corner' insets throughout to provide effective day-to-day coaching tips to take advantage of the material in the text. It includes discussion of:

- new approaches and their implications for training
- decision making and cognitive training in sport
- conscious and unconscious learning in sports
- play, practice and athlete development
- identifying and developing sporting experts, including coaches, athletes and officials

Edited by three of the world's leading scientists in sport skill acquisition and with contributions from both world-class coaches and cutting edge researchers, this textbook provides a comprehensive, authoritative guide to the field.

Damian Farrow is the Senior Specialist in Skill Acquisition at the Australian Institute of Sport.

Joe Baker is an Assistant Professor in the School of Kinesiology and Health Science at York University, Canada.

Clare MacMahon is a Lecturer in the School of Human Movement, Recreation and Performance at Victoria University, Melbourne.

Developing Sport Expertise

Researchers and coaches put theory into practice

Edited by
Damian Farrow,
Joe Baker and
Clare MacMahon

Routledge
Taylor & Francis Group

LONDON AND NEW YORK

First published 2008 by Routledge
2 Park Square, Milton Park, Abingdon, Oxon, OX14 4RN

Simultaneously published in the USA and Canada
By Routledge
270 Madison Avenue, New York, NY 10016

Routledge is an imprint of the Taylor & Francis Group, an informa business

©2008 selection and editorial content: Damian Farrow, Joe Baker and
Clare MacMahon; individual chapters: the contributors

Typeset in Perpetua and Bell Gothic by
Florence Production Ltd, Stoodleigh, Devon
Printed and bound in Great Britain by
TJ International Ltd, Padstow, Cornwall

British Library Cataloguing in Publication Data
A catalogue record for this book is available from the British Library

Library of Congress Cataloguing in Publication Data
Developing sport expertise: researchers and coaches put theory into
practice/edited by Damian Farrow, Joe Baker, and Clare MacMahon.
        p. cm.
  1. Sports sciences.   2. Physical education and training.   I. Farrow,
Damian, 1970–   II. Baker, Joe, PhD.   III. MacMahon, Clare.
  GV558.D48 2007
  796.01–dc22   2007020353

ISBN10: 0–415–77186–2 (hbk)
ISBN10: 0–415–77187–0 (pbk)
ISBN10: 0–203–93493–8 (ebk)

ISBN13: 978–0–415–77186–3 (hbk)
ISBN13: 978–0–415–77187–0 (pbk)
ISBN13: 978–0–203–93493–7 (ebk)

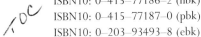

Contents

CONTENTS

Figures

FIGURES

Tables

Contributors

Bruce Abernethy is the Director and inaugural Chair Professor of the Institute of Human Performance at the University of Hong Kong and, concurrently, a Professor of the School of Human Movement Studies, at the University of Queensland in Brisbane, Australia. A first class Honours graduate and university medallist from the University of Queensland and a PhD graduate from the University of Otago, Prof. Abernethy is an international fellow of the American Academy of Kinesiology and Physical Education and a fellow of the Australian Sports Medicine Federation. He is the author of a large number of original research papers on skill acquisition and co-author of the texts *The Biophysical Foundations of Human Movement* and *The Creative Side of Experimentation*. Along with his students and collaborators, Prof. Abernethy has conducted a number of research projects on the characteristics of expertise and on the development of expert performance in sport, including projects funded by the Australian Research Council (ARC), the Australian Sports Commission, the Australian Football League (AFL), and Cricket Australia. In an earlier life, Bruce played first class cricket for the New Zealand province of Otago and as an Australian schoolboy was a national level 800m runner.

Joe Baker is with the Lifespan Health and Performance Laboratory in the School of Kinesiology and Health Science at York University. He is also a Visiting Research Fellow in the Carnegie Research Institute at Leeds Metropolitan University, UK. Joe's research considers the psycho-social influences on optimal human development, ranging from issues affecting elite athlete development to barriers and facilitators of successful aging. He recently co-edited a special issue of the *International Journal of Sport Psychology* on 'Nature, nurture and sport performance'.

Darren Balmforth has a long history as both a successful athlete and more recently a coach. As an athlete Darren started his Olympic dream as a reserve in 1996. In 1997 he was a member of world champion lightweight eights. Podium finishes followed in 1998 and 1999 before he won a silver medal as a member of the lightweight four at the Sydney Olympics. After retiring from competitive rowing Darren immediately began coaching. In 2003 he was coach of the gold medal winning under 23 men's single. In 2004 he became an Olympic coach overseeing the preparations of the women's double scull. From 2005 to 2007 he was the Tasmanian Institute of Sport rowing coach guiding the women's four to gold in the 2006 World Championships. In 2007 he became the Australian Institute of Sport (AIS) Assistant Women's Coach.

Sian L. Beilock is an Assistant Professor in the Department of Psychology at The University of Chicago. She received a BS in cognitive science from the University of California, San Diego, in 1997 and PhDs in both kinesiology (sport psychology and motor learning) and psychology (cognitive psychology) from Michigan State University in 2003. These dual degrees reflect Dr Beilock's interest in examining the cognitive processes governing performance across different task types, performance environments, and levels of expertise. Dr Beilock's research is funded by the National Science Foundation and the US Department of Education (Institute of Education Sciences) and she received the Young Investigator Award for distinguished research in sport psychology and motor learning from the International Society of Sport Psychology in 2005.

Steve Cobley is a Senior Lecturer in the Carnegie Faculty of Sport & Education at Leeds Metropolitan University, UK. Steve's research focuses on the factors that optimize and constrain expertise attainment in sport. Steve was recently awarded a Promising Research Fellowship from Leeds Met for his work on the relative age effect. As well as being a member of the British Association of Sport & Exercise Scientists (BASES) and the British Educational Research Association (BERA), Steve has experience in coaching and sport psychology consultancy, working with amateur, varsity, military, and elite athletes. In 2005–6, Steve was one of a team of scientists from Leeds Met Carnegie who provided support to the British Army's Everest West Ridge Expedition.

Jean Côté is the Director of the School of Kinesiology and Health Studies at Queen's University at Kingston, Canada. He holds a cross appointment at the University of Queensland, Australia and the University of Leeds, UK. Dr Côté is an associate editor for the *International Journal of Sport and Exercise Psychology* and sits on the managing council of the International Society of Sport Psychology. Dr Côté has been invited to present his research in various countries including Australia, Ireland, France, Brazil, Greece, Malaysia, Taiwan, Finland, Japan, and the United States. His research interests are in the areas of sport expertise, children in sport, positive youth development, and coaching.

Neil Craig is a veteran of 321 games with South Australian Football League clubs Norwood, Sturt and North Adelaide. He was a State-of-Origin captain and coached Norwood from 1991 to 1995. His association with the Adelaide (Crows) Football Club began in 1997 where he was the fitness coach during the Premiership years, before his appointment as an assistant coach in 2001. Neil was appointed as Senior Coach midway through the 2004 season and has taken the Adelaide Crows to consecutive preliminary finals in 2005 and 2006. Before his involvement with the Adelaide Football Club, Neil was a sport scientist (physiologist) with the South Australian Sports Institute and worked closely with the successful Australian track cycling team.

Barry Dancer played field hockey for Australia, winning the silver medal at the 1976 Summer Olympics in Montreal, and bronze at the Hockey World Cup in Buenos Aires in 1978. Barry became the AIS head coach, moved overseas to become the Head Coach of England's men's team before being appointed Head Coach of both the Kookaburras (Australian men's team) and the AIS Men's Hockey Unit in 2001. The highlight so far for Barry as a coach was winning the gold medal with the men's team at the 2004 Summer Olympics and then the 2005 Champions' Trophy in Chennai. He was inducted in the Queensland Hockey Hall of Fame in 2004.

Janice M. Deakin is a Professor of Motor Behaviour in the School of Kinesiology and Health Studies and the Dean of the School of Graduate Studies and Research at Queen's University in Kingston, Canada. A central theme of her research program continues to be the exploration of the constituent components underlying exceptional levels of performance. The influence of skill level has been examined in a variety of sport settings including figure skating, the martial arts, basketball, volleyball, and golf. Investigations into the relationship between the level of expertise in coaching and practice structure are recent additions to her research program.

Damian Farrow was appointed as the inaugural Skill Acquisition Specialist at the AIS in 2002. He is responsible for the provision of evidence-based sport science support to Australian coaches and athletes seeking to measure and improve the design of practice and other aspects of skill learning. He has worked with a wide range of sub-elite and elite level programs including: Australian/AIS Rugby (Wallabies); Australian/AIS Netball; AIS/Australian Football, AIS Swimming; Cricket Australia Centre of Excellence; and the Adelaide Crows Football Club. A former tennis coach and physical education teacher, his research interests center on understanding the development of sport expertise, specifically investigating the role of decision-making skill and implicit (subconscious) learning. He is also co-author of three general interest sports science books *Run Like You Stole Something*, *Why Dick Fosbury Flopped* and *It's True: Sport Stinks*.

Jessica Fraser-Thomas is an Assistant Professor in the School of Kinesiology and Health Science at York University, Canada. Jessica's research interests focus on children and adolescents in sport, positive youth development through sport, and coaching. Prior to pursuing a career in academia, Jessica was a junior high school physical education teacher and a member of Canada's national triathlon team. She continues to train and compete in triathlons, as well as coach and act as consultant to athletes in her community.

Jason Gulbin has worked as an applied sports scientist in the area of talent identification and development for well over a decade. He has led national talent identification initiatives at the AIS for over seven years, and currently manages the Australian Sports Commission's National Talent Identification and Development Program. Jason has been responsible for a number of innovative and evidence-based approaches designed to maximize the potential of gifted athletes. These include novel recruitment methods and a focus on mature athletes with the potential quickly to transfer their talents to Olympic level competition. Jason has a broad range of research interests and has published collaboratively in the areas of athlete profiling, exercise-induced muscle damage, biochemistry, genetics, and talent identification and development.

Terry Holland has served as a head coach for teams in sports ranging from skeleton, soccer, alpine skiing, and nordic skiing to track and field in skill levels ranging from beginner through to Olympic level athletes. His twenty-one-year tenure as a member of the US national skeleton team included numerous World Cup, World Championship and national level podium finishes. As lead business consultant for his company, Operations Advisory Group, Inc., he has accrued extensive experience providing business guidance in a variety of business ventures, primarily startups and turnarounds. Terry has also provided extensive assistance to a wide range of non-commercial ventures that run the gamut from community-based programs to international governing bodies in sport.

Sean Horton is currently completing his doctoral studies in Kinesiology and Health Studies at Queen's University in Kingston, Canada. His research interests, aside from coaching, include expert performance and successful aging. When he's not engaged in research, Sean can be found on the squash court or the golf course—two sports that he played at the intercollegiate level.

Patrick Hunt has coached over 350 games representing Australia and was Head Coach of the Canberra Cannons in the Australian National Basketball League in 1981. He was one of the initial coaches of the AIS basketball program and has been with the AIS from its inception in 1981, being Head Coach of the men's program from 1983 to 1992. An internationally renowned presenter and coach educator, Hunt has delivered coaching presentations around the globe. Based at the AIS Hunt is currently Manager of National Player & Coach Development for Basketball Australia and Head Coach of the National Intensive Training Centre Program. He serves as an executive member of the Fédération Internationale de Basketball Amateur (FIBA) World Association of Basketball Coaches (WABC) and President of FIBA Oceania WABC.

Robin C. Jackson is a Research Assistant Professor at the Institute of Human Performance, the University of Hong Kong. He is an accredited sport psychologist, chartered psychologist and founding member of the Division of Sport and Exercise Psychology (British Psychological Society). From 1999 to 2005 he worked extensively with Paralympic athletes, consulting in psychology and performance analysis with the Great Britain wheelchair rugby team at the 2000 and 2004 Games. He completed his BSc and PhD (psychology) at the University of St Andrews, Scotland, where he began conducting research into skill failure or choking under pressure. The primary focus of his present research is on the role of awareness in learning and expert performance.

Eddie Jones was a small mobile hooker who represented Randwick, New South Wales, and the Australian Barbarians before hanging up his boots and concentrating on his career as a teacher and school principal. Jones began his coaching career at Randwick Rugby Club in Sydney before taking over the Japanese national team in 1996. Jones then accepted an offer as Head Coach of the ACT Computer Associates Brumbies from 1998 to 2001, winning the Super 12 in 2001. Eddie was Coach of the Year two years running at the annual Super 12 awards. He coached the Australian Barbarians in 1999 and the Australian 'A' to victory over the British Lions in 2001. Jones was National Coach of the Qantas Wallabies, 2001–2005, making the 2003 World Cup final before losing to England in extra time. Eddie is currently a Coaching Consultant with Saracens Rugby Club in England.

Timothy D. Lee is a Professor in the Department of Kinesiology at McMaster University, in Hamilton, Ontario, Canada. His research has been funded continuously since 1984 by research grants from the Natural Sciences and Engineering Research Council of Canada, plus other sources. Research from the laboratories of Dr Lee and his collaborators has been published in over one hundred peer-reviewed journal articles and book chapters. He also collaborated with Richard Schmidt on the two most recent editions of the book *Motor Control and Learning: A Behavioral Emphasis*. In his spare time, Tim and partner, Laurie Wishart, enjoy spending time with their five children and their families. Tim also plays shortstop for his old-timer softball team and right wing for his old-timer hockey team, and competes frequently in golf tournaments.

Clare MacMahon is a Lecturer in the School of Human Movement, Recreation and Performance at Victoria University in Melbourne, Australia. She is also a research associate in the Centre for Aging, Rehabilitation, and Exercise Science, and a member of the Victoria University-Western Bulldogs Football Science Committee. She completed an undergraduate degree in Psychology at McGill University in Montreal and a Master's degree in Human Kinetics at the University of Ottawa. After completing a PhD in Human Biodynamics (Psychomotor Behavior) at McMaster University, she was awarded a postdoctoral fellowship from the Social Sciences and Humanities Research Council of Canada, which she held in the Department of Psychology (cognition) at Florida State University. Dr MacMahon's research and consulting interests focus on the acquisition and retention of complex perceptual–cognitive skills such as decision making, and how they are influenced by contextual factors.

Rich Masters gained degrees in Psychology from the University of Otago, New Zealand, and a DPhil from the University of York, UK. Rich is currently Assistant Director for Research at the Institute of Human Performance (University of Hong Kong), but previously lectured in applied psychology at the School of Sport and Exercise Sciences at the University of Birmingham, UK. He recently held a Universitas 21 fellowship at the University of Auckland, and is presently an associate editor for *Psychology of Sport & Exercise*. Rich is a weekend warrior with five happy kids and a superstar wife.

Nikola Medic is a Post-Doctoral Fellow in the Department of Kinesiology at McMaster University in Hamilton, Canada. His research interests focus on the motivational mechanisms of athletes across the lifespan. He teaches courses in sport psychology and quantitative statistics and acts as consultant to athletes of all ages and sports. In his spare time, he enjoys the company of his wife Dragana and daughter Danijela.

Greg McFadden took up the position as Australian/AIS Women's Head Coach in 2005 and is based in Sydney. In his first year as Head Coach the women's team won a bronze medal in the 2005 World League finals as well as a credible sixth placing at the Montreal World Championships. 2006 proved to be an exceptional year, with a gold at the World Cup in China where they defeated Olympic champions Italy in the final. Earlier in the year the Australian team also won gold at the Commonwealth Championships and a fourth placing at the World League finals. 2007 continued the success of 2006 with Greg being named AIS Coach of the Year and leading the team to a silver medal in the World Championships in Melbourne. Greg started his coaching career as the Scholarship Coach to the AIS senior men's program in 1990, progressing to Assistant Coach from 1992 to 1996. He then moved on to become the NSWIS Head Coach from 1997 to 2001 before returning to the AIS as the Head Coach for the men's program.

Sue L. McPherson is Professor in Motor Behavior in the Department of Physical Therapy at Western Carolina University, Cullowhee, NC. Her research interests focus on cognitive factors in children's and adults' motor skill acquisition in sport and rehabilitation contexts. She has developed several tools to capture performers' cognitive strategies and motor skills in natural environments. Her sport science articles and chapters concern knowledge development and sport expertise in tennis, volleyball, baseball, and track. Sue's research has appeared in the *Research Quarterly for Exercise and Sport*, *Journal of Sport and Exercise Psychology*, *International Journal of Sport Psychology*, *Journal of Sport Sciences*, *Quest*, and the *Journal of Experimental Child Psychology*. She is also active in several national organizations. Finally, her tennis background includes ten years of experience as a tennis teaching professional and coach.

Tim Nielsen has spent the last 18 years developing his people management and leadership skills in a range of fields. From playing ninety-nine consecutive cricket matches as a record-breaking wicket-keeper for South Australia, including captaining the State team for a short period, Tim has continually grown in his understanding of what makes elite athletes (and people!) tick. Tim spent three years as Assistant Coach of the South Australian Southern Redbacks under Greg Chappell and three years as Assistant Coach to John Buchanan with the Australian cricket team. His last two years have been spent leading a new era of Australian cricketers through the Cricket Australia high-performance development program at the Cricket Australia Centre of Excellence. With up to ten staff under his management, he has overseen the personal and professional development of 16–20 young, professional athletes aiming to make international cricket a career. All of this has culminated in his appointment as Coach of the Australian cricket team to succeed John Buchanan in May 2007.

Adrian Panozzo is the AFL's National Umpiring and Development Projects Manager including manager of the AFL Project CONNECT program in partnership with the Australian Sports Commission. Between 1999 and 2003 he was the AFL's Assistant Umpire Coach. Adrian holds a Master of Sports Business and Bachelor of Education (Physical Education) and in 1998 was a Queens Trust for Young Australians—Future Leader nominee. He is the current president of Reclink Australia, a not-for-profit organization that provides sport and recreation opportunities for disadvantaged Australians. He was an AFL field umpire between 1993 and 1996, and represented Australia as an age group competitor at the 1998 Hawaii Ironman World Championships.

Jae T. Patterson is an Assistant Professor in the Department of Physical Education and Kinesiology at Brock University in St Catharines, Ontario, Canada. Dr Patterson received his doctoral degree in Human Biodynamics from McMaster University in 2005. His research interests include practice factors facilitating motor skill acquisition and retention across the lifespan. Currently, Dr Patterson is examining practice factors facilitating the optimal levels of cognitive exertion facilitating the acquisition and retention of motor skills in older adults. In his spare time, Jae enjoys spending time with his two children (Daulton and Fynn), hiking on the Niagara escarpment, and spending long hours on frozen lakes ice fishing.

Henning Plessner is Assistant Professor of Social Psychology at the University of Heidelberg, Germany. He received his diploma in Psychology from the Technical University of Braunschweig in 1992 and his PhD from the Technical University of Chemnitz-Zwickau in 1997. From 1992 to 1997 he worked as Assistant Lecturer at the University of Hildesheim, and in 2004/05 as Theodor Heuss Lecturer at the New School University, New York. At the University of Heidelberg, he worked in various research projects funded by the German Science Foundation before he moved to his current position. His main research areas are judgment and decision making in sport, psychology of intuition, implicit attitude formation, and inductive reasoning. His strong relation to sport is evident, among others, in his many years of activity as gymnastic coach and licensed gymnastic judge.

Norma Plummer has an impressive netball playing and coaching history. A former Victorian State playing captain–coach and Australian captain, she retired from the court in 1981 but continued her coaching career from the bench as Head Coach of the Melbourne Netball Club now known as Melbourne Phoenix. Norma's national coaching appointments have included being the Head Coach of the Australian All Stars team, the Australian B team, and the Youth Cup team, winner of both World Youth Cup Series in 1996 and 2000. From 1999 until 2003 Norma was Head Coach of the AIS/Australian 21 and under netball program before accepting the position of the Australian Coach in 2004.

Markus Raab is Director and Professor for Sport Psychology and Movement Science at the Institute for Movement Science and Sport at the University of Flensburg, Germany. He worked at the Center for Adaptive Behavior and Cognition, Max Planck Institute for Human Development, at the Free University of Berlin and at the University of Heidelberg. He received a PhD in Sport Science as well as a PhD in Psychology for his research. His work is published in three books, numerous chapters and reviewed journals. The main areas he is interested in cover judgment and decision making in sports and beyond as well as motor learning and motor control.

Shannon Rollason is not your typical swimming coach. He's self-taught, strong-willed, prepared to push the boundaries of conventional theory on how to produce champions and he is still in his thirties. Shannon began coaching in 1990 and was Head Coach of the Chandler Swim Club from 1993 to 2004. In 2005 he moved to the AIS where he is now Head Coach of the swimming program. He was the Australian Swimming Coaches Association Coach of the Year in 2005. He has been a coach on Australian swim teams from 1995 to 1997 and 1999 to 2007. During these years more than twenty of his swimmers have represented Australia.

Janet Starkes is a Professor Emeritus at McMaster University, Canada. She is a lifelong devotee of sport and has enjoyed various roles as spectator, athlete, coach, referee, and researcher. She has served as President of the Canadian Society for Psychomotor Learning and Sport Psychology, the North American Society for the Psychology of Sport and Physical Activity, and the Canadian Council of University Administrators in Physical Education and Kinesiology. She is an international fellow of the American Academy of Kinesiology and a fellow of the Canadian Society for Psychomotor Learning and Sport Psychology (SCAPPS). Her research on sport expertise has had popular appeal and as a result she has been a keynote speaker in eleven countries around the world.

Bradley W. Young is an Assistant Professor in Sport Psychology in the Faculty of Physical Education and Recreation at the University of Alberta in Edmonton, Canada. His research interests relate to the long-term developmental pathways of expert athletes and coaches, and the use of self-monitoring devices to improve practice behavior. He currently teaches undergraduate courses on the theory and application of sport psychology, skill acquisition and motor learning, and the psychology of aging and physical activity. Dr Young has prior experience as a high school track and field coach, and served as Head Coach of the intercollegiate cross-country and distance track teams at McMaster University, Canada.

Preface

Some of the best films of all time tell the story of how an athlete 'made it'. As an audience, we want to get the inside scoop and see how Muhammad Ali or Nadia Commanechi became outstanding athletes. We are fascinated with how seemingly ordinary beginnings lead to extraordinary accomplishments. Sport scientists in particular have always had a special attraction to research pertaining to motor skill development and sport expertise. One of the most empirically sound conclusions from this research is that high-quality practice is fundamentally important for the development and maintenance of highly skilled performance. From ultra-marathoners to sprinters, gymnasts to volleyball players, proper training is an absolute necessity for the highest levels of performance.

Although applied scientists in the fields of physiology, psychology, and motor learning have amassed a significant literature detailing the factors that distinguish expert (i.e., elite) performers from their non-expert counterparts, and the type and amount of training necessary to develop these qualities, there is often a considerable lag between cutting-edge research and real-world application, particularly in the sports coaching environment. This book is designed to address this lag by having leading researchers from around the world provide a synopsis of their research programs and what their research results mean to coaches working with future or current elite performers as well as athletes striving to improve their own performance.

The chapters contained within are the result of an applied workshop convened by the three editors at the Australian Institute of Sport (AIS) in August 2005. The purpose of this meeting was to bring coaches, athletes, researchers, and applied sports scientists together to share information under the banner of Applied Sport Expertise and Learning. The researchers speaking at this workshop were asked to consider the following questions:

1. What does your research tell us about the development of talented/elite athletes?
2. How can the information from your research be used by coaches, athletes, and applied sports scientists to optimize athlete training and performance?
3. Do your research findings have any application to talent identification programs?

This book is divided into three sections based on the specialties of the researchers contained herein. After an introductory chapter by Bruce Abernethy, Section 1 considers issues related to the optimal environment for developing athletes. During the past 15 years there has been a resurgence of research investigating the development of expert sports performance, much of it the result of the seminal work by Ericsson, Krampe, and Tesch-Romer in 1993 on the importance of high-quality training (i.e., deliberate practice) to the development of expert performance. This section summarizes what is currently known about the environmental constraints to developing elite performers. More specifically, Chapter 2 by Jean Côté and Jessica Fraser-Thomas considers the role of play in the development of expert sport skills, and Chapter 3 by Joe Baker and Steve Cobley summarizes current understanding of the role of deliberate practice in promoting athlete development. Chapter 4 is written by Bradley Young and Nikola Medic and considers the importance of sustained motivation across an athlete's development. The final chapter in this section, by Jason Gulbin, considers the implications of this research for talent identification programs and whether future experts can be predicted during early stages of training.

Section 2 presents current research on conscious and subconscious processes that affect practice and performance of expert athletes. In Chapter 6, Sean Horton and Janice Deakin review their work examining what constitutes an expert coach, and in Chapter 7 Rich Masters considers the value of implicit learning. Chapter 8, by Rob Jackson and Sian Beilock, provides an overview of how conscious thought processes may interfere with skilled performance (i.e., paralysis by analysis), and the final chapter in this section, by Jae Patterson and Tim Lee, discusses research from the field of motor learning examining methods to improve the organization and design of practice.

Section 3 considers the perceptual and cognitive elements of skilled athletic performance. In Chapter 10, Damian Farrow and Markus Raab summarize current understanding of training programs designed to teach perceptual and cognitive skills to athletes, and, in Chapter 11, Sue McPherson examines research on the differences between skilled and unskilled performers in their use of tactical information. Chapter 12, by Clare MacMahon and Henning Plessner, examines a significantly under-recognized area—the sport official. This chapter discusses research on training for officials as well as factors that have an influence on decision making. Finally, the book closes with a chapter by Janet Starkes, who considers future directions in applied sport expertise research.

This book is quite different from other texts on sport expertise in that the researchers have presented their work in a manner that is applicable not only to scientists, but also to coaches and athletes. Furthermore, current top-level coaches have reviewed and commented on the researchers' findings (see the Coach's Corner segment of each chapter), and present real-world application of the concepts discussed. These coaches are either from the AIS or some of Australia's most competitive professional sports, and represent some of the finest professionals working in sport today. They work with a variety of sports and athletes at developmental, sub-elite, and Olympic or elite levels.

This book is designed for progressive coaches and athletes who are motivated to adjust their coaching or training programs so that they are making the most of current research on optimal training. Although the journey to expertise is a long one, and is often more mundane than depicted by Hollywood, we hope this book can provide some shortcuts and excitement along the way.

Damian Farrow, Joe Baker and Clare MacMahon

Acknowledgments

The editors would like to thank all the sport expertise researchers for their contributions to this text. Similarly, we thank all the coaches who provided their unique insights into the topics presented.

We would like to thank Megan Rendell for her assistance in proof reading and copy editing and Camilla Brockett for her organization of the 2005 workshop. Last, but by no means least, we would like to recognise the Australian Institute of Sport for supporting the Applied Sport Expertise and Learning Workshop in 2005, which provided the stimulus for the development of this book.

Permissions

Figure 5.4 Photo courtesy of the Australian Sports Commission.

Table 6.1 Reprinted with the permission of Edizioni Luigi Pozzi (Italy), publisher of the *International Journal of Sport Psychology*.

Figure 12.2 Reprinted with the permission of Edizioni Luigi Pozzi (Italy), publisher of the *International Journal of Sport Psychology*.

Figure 12.3 Reprinted with the permission of Edizioni Luigi Pozzi (Italy), publisher of the *International Journal of Sport Psychology*.

Figure 13.2c Figure printed by permission Elsevier Science.

Figure 13.2d Photos courtesy of Simi Reality Motion Systems, Germany.

Figure 13.2e Photos courtesy of Dr Joan Vickers, University of Calgary.

Figure 13.2f Photos of game and statistical analyses by permission of Simi Reality Motion Systems, Germany. France's attack analysis by permission of Z-Institute / SoftSport.

Chapter 1

Introduction
Developing expertise in sport—how
research can inform practice

Bruce Abernethy

In order for coaches to design practice sessions for the optimal benefit of their athletes and in order for sports scientists and administrators to develop sports systems that are most suitable to identify and nurture the development of sports talent, it is necessary to know the answers to some fundamental questions. It is necessary to know, among other things:

- what specific attributes are essential for expert performance
- how expert performers differ from everyone else in their control and learning of perceptual-motor skills
- what essential conditions need to be present during the developing years to improve the chances that acquisition of exceptional skill will occur.

Systematically determining the answers to questions such as these is the principal intent of the developing research field of *sport expertise*.

Although studying elite performers as a window into skill acquisition has a long history dating back to the late nineteenth century, the emergence of a consolidated field of study concerned with the scholarly description and explanation of expert sport performance is a much more recent development. The contemporary study of sport expertise originated in studies of expert pattern recognition and anticipation by ball sport athletes in the late 1970s and early 1980s. The modern study of sport expertise is concerned not only with attempting to understand the control processes that distinguish the experts from the less skilled but also with attempting to understand the processes through which expertise is acquired. As the many chapters in this book illustrate, this work is not only important theoretically, in terms of how it may contribute to fundamental understanding of perceptual-motor learning, but is also important practically. Expertise in sport is so highly prized, and so difficult and time- and resource-consuming to attain, that any means that can be found to accelerate the acquisition of expertise and to make skill learning more efficient will be exceptionally valuable to athletes, coaches, officials, and administrators alike.

In this chapter I attempt to 'set the stage' for the remainder of the text by providing some examples of how sport expertise research can inform sport practice and can cause us to question whether prevailing practice is necessarily best practice. The first section of the chapter provides a brief overview of some of the key findings from existing research on sport experts. Evidence is summarized, in turn, indicating that the experts' advantage is selective to only some components of performance, that experts use different sources of information (cues) to select and control their actions, and that the practice and developmental experiences of experts are different from those of non-experts. The second section of the chapter then provides examples of practical implications for the design of training sessions, junior sport systems and talent identification systems that can be derived from this evidence. Many of the themes introduced in the chapter are then expanded in greater detail in the specialist chapters that follow.

RESEARCH ON SPORT EXPERTISE: WHAT DOES THE RESEARCH TELL US?

The expert's advantage is selective to only some components of performance

There is a substantial body of evidence now available to help ascertain what particular attributes or components of performance are key contributors to the expert's performance advantage in sport. This evidence comes from studies that compare expert athletes with either less skilled or novice performers on a range of different sport sub-tasks. Although there is naturally some study-to-study variability, a reasonably consistent picture is beginning to emerge with respect to those attributes in which skill-related differences are typically seen and those in which an expert advantage is less frequently observed. Knowing what attributes distinguish experts from non-experts is important as it helps determine the limiting factor(s) to less skilled performance and can, hence, also provide some guidance as to what components should be given emphasis within training.

Pattern recognition and recall

Experts characteristically outperform non-experts on tasks that require specific patterns of play to be either recognized (from among other patterns) or recalled (in terms of the location of team-mates, opposing players, the ball, etc.). Tasks of this nature are usually presented via either short video sequences or briefly presented slides of images from the expert's particular sport. The expert advantage is typically pronounced for images showing sport-specific structure (for example, images showing offensive patterns for team sports) but either is diminished or disappears completely when the normal structure and relationship between players are disrupted (for example, when images are presented of players of different teams intermingling at the end of a match). This shows that the expert's advantage in terms of pattern encoding and recognition is due to specific rather than generic memory processes, although some recent evidence suggests that some transfer of pattern recall skills may nevertheless occur between related sports (such as basketball and netball). The expert advantage in pattern recall and recognition may also be an important contributor to expert superiority in decision making.

Multi-tasking and automatic movement control

When dual-task paradigms are employed, in which performers are required to perform two tasks simultaneously—usually a primary movement task from their principal sport and a secondary task such as a reaction time task or a memory task (e.g. counting backwards in threes from 100)—experts consistently outperform non-experts. This suggests that the control of movement by athletes becomes more automatic and requires fewer central processing resources as skills become better acquired. The superior ability to preprogram well-practiced movements and the reduced need to monitor ongoing feedback from these movements are probably responsible, in large part, for the experts being able to free attention from control of the primary movement task and create 'spare' attention that can be allocated to other concurrent tasks. The experts' more automatic movement control may, for example, permit them more spare attention to allocate to visual scanning and provide a wider functional visual field, with greater awareness of peripheral events, than is possible for less skilled athletes with less well-developed movement control. There is some recent evidence (for example, see Jackson and Beilock, Chapter 8) to indicate that requiring experts to consciously monitor their movement production may, in fact, interfere with their normal control and minimize or even eliminate their performance advantage.

At the neuromuscular level, expert movement control is characterized not only by more consistent patterns of movement but also by reduced co-contraction of muscles, the active recruitment of muscle only at those points in the movement where it is essential, and a greater utilization of external forces (such as those arising from gravity and ground reactions). Even at a micro level, experts are more efficient.

Sport-specific knowledge and tactics

Experts typically have more knowledge of both facts and procedures from their sport than non-experts, and this knowledge is organized in a more richly differentiated way. This permits the use of superior tactics by experts and, as a consequence, better success rates (see McPherson, Chapter 11, for more details). Declarative knowledge relates to knowing the relevant factual information about a particular situation (for example, *what* moves are permitted in a particular situation by the laws of the game) whereas procedural knowledge relates to knowing how to produce a particular action or generate a particular outcome (for example, *how* to produce the best outcome as a defender for the attacker's particular preferred pattern of play). Both declarative and procedural knowledge is extracted using verbal reports from the athletes. This method may be suitable for studying aspects of sport performance that are conscious and strategic but may be problematic, or even misleading, with respect to understanding aspects of skill that are performed automatically and controlled by processes largely below the level of consciousness.

Anticipation

For sports that are severely time-constrained there is clear evidence that experts are superior to non-experts at anticipating what is about to occur. In studies of ball sport situations such as receiving serve in tennis, defending the goal in soccer or hockey, or batting in cricket or baseball, experts are consistently shown to be better able to predict the forthcoming action (e.g. the direction of the serve or the shot on goal) than less skilled players. This anticipation typically involves extracting advance information from the movement patterns of the opponent and/or making use of probability information from previous experience against the same opponent. The predominant methodology for the study of anticipatory skills involves the occlusion of the opponent's action at variable times before, at, or after impact with the ball, using either video simulations in the laboratory or occluding goggles in the field. Earlier information pick-up allows experts either to commence their own movements earlier or to be relatively more accurate when they do (or must) initiate their response.

Coping with constraints

Many of the attributes that appear consistently to characterize expert performers, and differentiate them from the less skilled, are attributes that allow them to deal with the inherent constraints on skill that are built into their nervous systems and into the rules and requirements of their particular sports. For example, recognizing patterns helps alleviate known constraints on memory; automatic control of movement helps overcome constraints associated with conscious processing; and anticipation helps circumvent some of the constraints imposed by reaction time and movement time delays.

Eye movement behavior

Some attributes that might be expected to be critical for expert performance do not emerge as reliable discriminators of experts from non-experts. The evidence with respect to whether experts and non-experts use their eyes differently (i.e., have different visual search patterns) in sport tasks is not compelling. Although expert–novice differences are sometimes reported with respect to where performers look and how rapidly they move their eyes around the visual field, the evidence is generally non-systematic. For those studies showing some expert–novice differences, there are other studies in which the search patterns of experts and novices may be practically indistinguishable, even though their skill performance levels are markedly disparate. Visual search patterns are only a poor indicator of both where a performer's attention is directed and their capability to extract information from where they are looking. Consequently, it is probably not surprising that the evidence with respect to the relationship between visual search and expertise is mixed.

The specificity of expertise

Tasks that do not faithfully reproduce either the information content of the sport domain or the requirement to process this domain-specific information are generally incapable of reliably differentiating experts from novices. For example, experts do not consistently outperform non-experts in tests of visual attributes (such as acuity, contrast sensitivity, depth perception, and reaction time) that use standardized stimuli. Likewise, generalized tests of cognition and motor ability are also quite poor in their capability to distinguish experts from non-experts, suggesting that they are not measuring attributes that either are central to the expert advantage or act as limiting factors to the performance of the non-experts.

Experts may use different information to select and control their actions

A likely explanation as to why experts are able to 'read the play', respond 'apparently automatically' and appear to have 'have all the time in the world', as evidenced by their superior performance on pattern recognition, secondary and anticipation tasks, is that they may attend to different cues to those used by less skilled people. This may permit experts to pick up information from features or events either to which less skilled individuals do not attend or to which non-experts do attend but lack the requisite 'knowledge' to use or use effectively. Knowing what specific cues or sources of information experts use, and how these might differ for non-experts, is important for the effective design of perceptual training regimes and from the provision of supporting instruction and/or feedback to help learners become more expert. The chapter by Farrow and Raab (Chapter 10) explains this issue of effective design of training in more detail.

Experts' self-report

Sport expertise researchers have used a variety of different approaches in an attempt to determine what information experts and non-experts use and to address the question of whether experts and non-experts have learned to attend to the same or different cues. One obvious approach is simply to ask performers of different skill levels what cues they use in given situations to 'read the play' or to guide their selection and subsequent control of action. Unfortunately, introspective reports on what cues are used to control the selection and execution of actions of the type performed under the time stresses present in most sports may be misleading. Such reports often correlate more with prevailing coaching beliefs (e.g. 'I watch the ball all the way on to my bat') than they do with objective measures of actual information usage. Consequently, data derived from verbal reports on cue usage provide a suspect base upon which to develop training programs or instructional strategies.

Objective measures of information pick-up

More objective measures of the information pick-up of athletes of different skill levels have been derived from approaches in which the information available within the display is selectively manipulated, and its impact on the judgmental accuracy of experts and non-experts is measured. The manipulated displays have been primarily video simulations of the displays normally available to athletes during the performance of their sport (e.g. video simulations of the scene normally facing a tennis player returning an opponent's stroke). With improvements in technology it has become increasingly possible to conduct at least some examinations of information usage in game-like settings in which the required movement responses are identical to those in the natural task (e.g. in the tennis case, actually hitting the ball rather than just watching a video and reporting what stroke would be best).

5

A common approach is to occlude the visual displays shown to athletes at different time periods leading up to critical events (such as the racquet striking the ball in a tennis stroke) as a means of determining *when* successful information pick-up occurs for players of different skill levels. Consideration of the concurrent changes in the displays at these times allows inferences to be drawn as to what particular cues are informative for different players. For instance, by showing improvements in the prediction of the opponent's stroke direction in badminton in the period immediately preceding racquet–shuttle contact, and noting that the major motion during this period comes from the racquet, it is possible to infer information pick-up from the racquet.

More direct information on specific cue utilization has been provided in some studies through the use of techniques in which either visibility of specific cues is masked or, conversely, only vision of selected cues is provided. Prediction accuracies under these conditions are compared with control conditions with no occlusion to provide insight into the importance of the occluded cues for particular skill groups. For example, in cricket, the ability of players to predict in advance the type of ball being bowled when only vision of the bowling arm and hand is provided, plus the parallel loss of this anticipatory capability when vision of these cues is masked, suggests an important role for the arm and hand as anticipatory cues.

Displays in which only points of light are used to represent the position and motion of major joint centers within the opposing player's body, with normal display features such as pictorial cues for form, size, and orientation removed, are becoming increasingly popular as a means of ascertaining expert–novice differences in sensitivity to biomechanical information. Similarly, virtual, computer-generated images that make possible synthetic manipulation of biomechanical features in an opposing player's movement pattern are also increasingly in use as a possible tool to determine individual differences in cue usage. To date, the majority of research on expertise and information pick-up in sport has been related to studies of anticipation, but these approaches can also be applied to understanding the expert advantage in complex pattern recall and recognition situations of the type that exist in many team sports.

Expert–non-expert differences in cue usage

Although the available research indicates that the specific cues used by experts and non-experts for anticipation vary from sport to sport and situation to situation, there are nevertheless a number of generalizations that have emerged from this literature. The evidence suggests that the expert advantage exists on at least two fronts. First, experts appear capable of using all the cues that novices can use to extract information, but are able often to use these cues more effectively—as evidenced by faster or more accurate responses based on the same cues as used by the non-experts. Second, experts are also frequently shown to be able to pick up information from additional, unique cues that non-experts cannot use at all. In anticipation tasks these additional cues are generally ones that occur earlier in the opponent's movement sequence and therefore assist the experts with both earlier resolution of uncertainty about the opponent's action and, if needed, the making of an earlier start to initiating a movement response.

Point light studies support the view that the expert's advantage is linked to their superior pick-up of information from the biomechanics of the actions they are viewing and anticipating, suggesting that skilled athletes in many sports act rather like intuitive biomechanists in their understanding of the inherent relationships and predictabilities that exist within an opponent's movement pattern. The links (or functional mappings) between perception and action appear to change as skill is acquired, such that a particular cue or perceptual event may become progressively linked with initiation of earlier and earlier components of the athlete's movement response as the athlete becomes more expert. Relatively little is yet known about developmental trends in information pick-up (for example at what age the information pick-up skills characteristic of expert adults can be first acquired) or about important issues related to the pick-up (or avoidance) of movement deception (e.g. a 'fake' in basketball), yet such knowledge is important for informing practical tasks such as talent identification and tactical development.

The practice and developmental experiences of experts and non-experts differ

In contrast to the cross-sectional research comparing experts and individuals of lesser skill on particular tasks and skill sub-components, a growing number of studies now address the more longitudinal question of how expertise is acquired. These studies do so by examining, retrospectively, the backgrounds of groups of expert performers and searching for commonalities in their practice and developmental experiences that may help account for their acquisition of exceptional skill. Identifying some of the common background characteristics of experts as a group (i.e., addressing the question of 'who become experts?') as well as analyzing the scope and nature of their developmental experiences and practice histories (i.e., addressing the question of 'how experts became expert?') can provide important insight into the necessary and sufficient conditions that may need to exist for expertise to be acquired.

Relative age and expertise

Studies addressing the question of 'who become experts' have revealed that early experiences, and the conditions and context in which they occur, can have a remarkably enduring influence on the probability of expertise emerging. There is clear evidence that *when* one is born, or more importantly one's age relative to peers when first entering organized sport, can have a profound influence on the chance of ultimately becoming an adult expert. A large number of studies of this relative age phenomenon have demonstrated that both the chances of being labeled 'gifted or talented' and the chances of later becoming a world-class athlete are greatly increased if a person is older relative to their peers in their junior sport group or, indeed, in their class group. Athletes born in the first three months after the cut-off date for junior age group determination in a particular sport (e.g. those born in the months of January, February, and March for sports with groups determined on the basis of age at the start of the year) are disproportionately over-represented not only in junior representative teams but also in open-age representative teams in that particular sport. People born in the last three months before the cut-off date (birth-dates in October, November, and December for a January 1 cut-off date) are significantly under-represented. Although explanations of the cause of the relative age effect vary—from explanations based on the greater biological maturity of relatively older children to explanations based on the impact on self-confidence and practice opportunities arising from being relatively older—the pervasiveness of the effect makes it clear that

7

decisions made regarding the organization of junior sport should not be taken lightly. Experts in many sports apparently get a 'flying start' through being relatively older than their peers when they first take up the sport whereas many others, with the potential to become experts, are steered away from this pathway from early on by superficially innocuous factors, such as age grouping decisions. The provision of multiple developmental pathways for the emergence of expertise are described in detail in the chapter by Côté and Fraser-Thomas (Chapter 2).

The geography of expertise

Recent evidence also indicates that it is not only when one is born but also *where* one is born and raised that may influence who does and does not become an expert. In major team sports in North America and Australia, at least, people growing up in rural areas and smaller towns and cities have a much higher probability of becoming professional athletes than those growing up in larger cities, even though the latter may have access to superior sport facilities and more highly organized junior sport competitions. By way of example, more than fifty per cent of people in the USA are born in cities with a population in excess of half a million people, yet currently these larger cities produce less than twenty per cent of current National Football League (NFL), National Hockey League (NHL), Professional Golfers' Association (PGA), and Major League Baseball (MLB) players and less than thirty per cent of current National Basketball Association (NBA) players. This suggests that there is something about the experience or context of growing up in a less densely populated area that is favorable to the acquisition of expertise. Some insights into what these favorable aspects might be can be gleaned from the studies that have documented the practice histories of expert players and compared these (either directly or indirectly) with the normative developmental experiences of non-experts.

Quantity and type of practice

Developmental studies of experts from a whole range of different domains indicate, not surprisingly, that large volumes of practice are generally necessary for the attainment of expertise—indeed a rough guiding rule has been proposed that suggests some ten years or 10,000 hours of practice as the minimum amount necessary for becoming an expert (for a discussion of this see Baker and Cobley, Chapter 3). The developmental studies further suggest that it is not simply the sheer amount of practice but also the type of practice that is critical to whether or not expertise is acquired. Some evidence, both from sport and other domains, suggests that it is the amount of *deliberate practice*—practice requiring concentrated physical and/or cognitive effort undertaken with the specific goal of improving performance—that is most predictive of the attainment of expertise. Recent evidence from studies of team ball sports, such as basketball, hockey, netball, and Australian football, suggests that although deliberate practice may be critical, so too may be exposure, during the developing years, to many hours of unstructured (*deliberate play*) activities. Deliberate play consists of those activities, such as 'backyard/street matches', undertaken in situations that encourage improvisation and role-playing rather than pure repetition and where the principal emphasis is on fun rather than skill improvement (see Côté and Fraser-Thomas, Chapter 2, for greater detail). The most skilful team sport players have been found to differ reliably even from other team-mates playing at an elite level in terms of the amount of unstructured practice they have undertaken during their developing years. The expert players are also frequently characterized by having had a very broad-based experience of a range of different sports before specializing and having had early exposure to playing with or against adults. Rural environments and small-town environments are more conducive to creating these circumstances and this may, in part, help explain the advantage, noted earlier, that small population centers appear to hold in nurturing the development of sporting expertise.

RESEARCH INTO PRACTICE: USING EXPERTISE RESEARCH TO BENEFIT ATHLETES, COACHES, AND OFFICIALS

Although sport expertise as a field of study is still in its relative infancy, and there is far more left to learn than is already known, it is nevertheless possible to derive some important practical implications from what has already been revealed by the systematic, scientific study of sport experts. Implications can be drawn for the design of practice, for the design of junior sport systems, and for the design of talent identification programs that, interestingly, in many cases, suggest approaches that differ from those currently prevailing.

Implications for the design of practice

Training needs to address limiting factors to performance

A number of things in relation to the linkage between practice and expertise are apparent from the existing literature. There is little support for a pure talent-oriented view of exceptional sport skill—rather practice, and lots of it, is necessary to become an expert. Although large amounts of practice are essential for becoming an expert it is also apparent that not all practice is equally beneficial. Practice is most likely to be beneficial for the sustained improvement of sport performance if it is directed specifically at training one or more factors known to be limiting ones to performance. It makes more sense, in that context, for training efforts to be directed at the improvement of component skills known to differentiate reliably expert from non-expert performers than it does to direct practice to facets of performance on which non-experts are already indistinguishable from experts. Although training directed at factors such as general visual attributes (e.g. reaction time or visual acuity) or general motor skills (e.g. balance) can lead to improvements in these attributes, these improvements typically do not translate into improved sport performance simply because the factors being improved are not the ones limiting performance. In contrast, practice that can improve factors on which non-experts are systematically inferior to experts (such as pattern recognition, anticipation, and level of automaticity) has the obvious potential to help hasten the skill acquisition and performance of non-experts.

Perceptual training

A number of perceptual training methods have the potential to improve the pattern recall/ recognition, anticipation, and decision-making skills of athletes, although the efficacy of these

9

different approaches is only quite recently being examined experimentally. Approaches that have been suggested and/or tried include:

- video-based training to increase exposure to a large quantity and diversity of different sport-relevant patterns
- field-based training using occluding goggles to force increasing reliance on anticipatory cues
- color coding to highlight the location of critical information within the field of view
- video-based training in which only selected cues or types of information (e.g. only kinematic information) are made available
- presentations of the actual probabilities with which particular opponents choose different play options; and
- use of virtual environments.

The preliminary evidence is promising that at least some of the key perceptual attributes can be trained; however, a major challenge is that expertise in many aspects of performance appears to be largely acquired implicitly, without the direct conscious (or verbalizable) knowledge of the performer (see Masters, Chapter 7). As a consequence, traditional learning approaches that rely heavily on a combination of verbal instruction and concentrated explicit attention to key learning features may be contra-indicated, and alternative approaches may need to be developed. Implicit perceptual training approaches in which learning occurs without explicit attention being drawn to the essential cues (see Farrow and Raab, Chapter 10, for some specific examples) or training that makes greater use of guided discovery rather than explicit instruction (see Patterson and Lee, Chapter 9) may be more effective in the longer term for the acquisition of expert skill.

Training for automaticity

High levels of automaticity are also a hallmark of expert performance, yet relatively little evidence is yet available on how to effectively hasten the acquisition of expertise for sport tasks. For non-sport tasks, evidence is available that suggests that sustained improvements in the level of automatic control over a primary skill can be gained through lengthy periods of dual-task practice. In the absence of any evidence to the contrary, it would appear sensible for coaches also to consider routinely using a demanding secondary task (or even multiple secondary tasks) concurrently with the practice of primary sport skills as a means of stimulating the continuous automation of primary skills and the refinement of the essential multitasking skills of athletes (see Jackson and Beilock, Chapter 8, for some examples).

The importance of variety and diversity

For team sports, in which patterns of play are constantly varying and situations arise continuously that have not been specifically encountered previously, the evidence from a number of studies of developmental expertise suggests that exposure to a wide diversity of decision-making situations is critical. To this end it may be particularly important for coaches to design practice drills that make use of flexible rules and encourage novel solutions. The ability in practice to experiment, to make errors, and to find novel solutions without undue regard for the outcome of the movement may be particularly important for learning of innovative skills. If there is an excessive emphasis on movement outcome (in terms of success or failure), young players may be unlikely to experiment and consequently may become less likely to discover new play options or learn the boundaries for usefulness of traditional play options.[1] Actively encouraging children to become involved in a broad range of different sports during their developing years may also be advantageous, as some aspects of perceptual and decision-making skill may transfer between related sports and decrease the amount of deliberate practice (and associated time) needed to develop expertise in the sport of specialization.

Implications for the design of junior sport systems

Maximizing practice opportunities

A critical consideration in the design of junior sport should be to put in place systems that will maximize the frequency and likelihood of occurrence of the conditions known to favor the development of expertise. One obvious thing is to do whatever is possible to maximize the opportunity for young athletes to gain practice and play experience: common factors in the developmental backgrounds of many sport experts include essentially unlimited access to practice facilities and practice opportunities; the commitment of liberal parental time and resources to support practice; and the availability of siblings and friends with whom to practice. Ensuring the safety of places in which practice takes place and implementing a strategy of continually rotating player roles within each practice situation to ensure they all experience key roles within the game (such as the 'playmaking' roles like point guard in basketball) are examples of other proactive actions that can be taken to help remove impediments to gaining the sheer volume of practice necessary to become an expert.

Creating experiences that encourage the development of strategic skills

A related requirement in effective sport system design is obviously also to maximize the opportunity for young athletes to experience the specific types of practice known to be associated with the development of exceptional performers. This involves, as noted earlier, not only deliberate practice activities undertaken specifically to improve performance but also the provision of the conditions in the years prior to sport specialization that encourage sampling of a wide range of different sport tasks and the engagement in significant amounts of unstructured play activities. Evidence from studies of experts in a number of team sports indicates that many experts gain early exposure to competition with and against adults—something that is particularly pronounced among athletes coming from rural or small community backgrounds. Early exposure to adult competition may be advantageous because it ensures that players must develop strategic skills in order to succeed and limits the likelihood of young players succeeding simply on the basis of any physical advantages they may hold over peers of the same age. Early introduction to adult competition also provides an early start toward accrual of the experience that is necessary for the acquisition of the skills in the perception, recognition, and anticipation of adult movement patterns that are so central to adult expertise. Senior coaches and administrators should give serious consideration to providing regular opportunities for junior players routinely to train and play with adults in 'mock' competitions.

Specialization versus diversification

A major tension often exists within junior sports between the forces favoring early specialization and those favoring diversification of childhood sport experiences. Although there are currently a number of forces working in the direction of early sport specialization (such as the development of organized championship structures up to state and national level for increasingly young age groups; the extension of the duration of the playing and training seasons precluding involvement in other sports; aggressive campaigning by different sports to capture and retain 'talented athletes' into their sports; and government funding incentives to different sports based on participation levels), the evidence from recent studies of the developmental histories of expert team sport athletes would suggest a more cautious approach may be needed. These studies reveal that many successful athletes did not specialize in their chosen sport until aged at least 12–14 years and instead had a broad and diverse base of early sport experiences. Such a background not only enhances the chances of each player finding an activity to which they are suited (and which is of sufficient intrinsic interest to motivate sustained practice; see Young and Medic, Chapter 4) but also appears to be functionally beneficial for the eventual development of expertise in the specialist sport. For example, experience of a broad (rather than narrow) range of team sport environments may provide the basis for the later 'creativity' and 'innovation' that typifies the decision making of the team sport expert. Systems that seek to 'capture' talented athletes into a single sport from an early age may actually work against the development of creative, innovative athletes in their sport.

Dealing with relative age effects

In an earlier section we noted the powerful effect of relative age and the enduring and pervasive influence that seemingly arbitrary decisions regarding age bandings and cut-off dates for age group eligibilities can have upon the likelihood of any given child becoming an expert athlete. The principal concern for junior sport systems is that, if the relative age bias is not corrected, it may unnecessarily limit the experiences and success of those participants who are relatively young compared with their peers. This may not only hamper the development of such athletes but can also be sufficiently demotivating to cause them to drop out of the sport altogether and, through so doing, may unduly limit the talent base from which future experts may arise. It would seem prudent for those in charge of junior sport systems both to encourage actively rotation of pivotal decision-making roles in junior sport teams among all players and seriously to consider the use of seasonal variations in the cut-off dates used to determine age groupings. Moving the cut-off date from year to year, although administratively problematic, provides a means of ensuring that the relative age advantage is not persistently restricted to the same players.

Coaching philosophies for nurturing expertise

The effectiveness of a junior sport system in creating an environment that can facilitate the acquisition and nurturing of expertise is also clearly dependent on the extent to which the philosophies of coaching that are encouraged are consistent with the conditions known to be important for expertise to flourish. In keeping with the implications derived for practice it would appear important that coaching philosophies in junior sports avoid an undue outcome(win/loss)-focus, but rather encourage experimentation and routinely vary the practice environment to encourage creativity and the experience of as wide a variety of game-like decision-making situations as possible.

Implications for talent identification

Many countries, both now and in the past, have sought to develop systems to identify talented athletes at an early age and then direct them into sports that match their physical attributes (and 'talents'). Although there may be some scope to successfully identify future champions for sports in which the limiting factors are anthropometric and physiological parameters, such as body size, shape, and functional capacities (see Gulbin, Chapter 5), the evidence from the expertise literature is that such activities are probably fraught with difficulty for sports in which skill is a limiting factor. To date, the evidence is stronger that environmental factors such as the amount and type of practice are more powerful than any innate talents in predicting expertise in sports where refined motor skills are important. Even for those attributes in which clear expert–non-expert differences are known to exist, such as pattern recall, there is very little in the way of systematic evidence on the time course of the development of these attributes. Consequently, it is simply not possible, currently, to determine, with any certainty, the earliest time at which adult levels of performance on these key distinguishing attributes for experts can be accurately predicted. Even if such prediction eventually proves possible, the evidence on the developmental histories of current sport experts cautions against using early identification to promote early sport specialization. As discussed in the previous section, any benefits arising from early talent identification may well be lost if identification promotes singular practice in the selected sport to the exclusion of a broad, multiple-sport experience during the developing years.

CONCLUSION

Although there is an enormous amount yet to be discovered about expertise in sport, there is an impressive amount already known about experts that can have a positive impact on practical approaches to the development of elite performers. Both practitioners, by making better use of what is already known from sport expertise research, and researchers, by addressing some of the important practical questions in sport about which little is currently known, have key roles to play in realizing the benefits to sport that may arise from expertise research. The chapters that follow detail some of the many interrelationships between theory and practice in the development of exceptional performers. The chapters also highlight the broad applicability of the expertise model, not only to the understanding and improvement of athletes, but also to the understanding and improvement of coaches (see Horton and Deakin, Chapter 6) and officials (see McMahon and Plessner, Chapter 12).

KEY READING

Abernethy, B., Wann, J.P. and Parks, S.L (1998). 'Training perceptual-motor skills for sport'. In Elliott, B. (ed.) *Training in Sport: Applying Sport Science*. Chichester: John Wiley, 1–68

Côté, J., Baker, J. and Abernethy, B. (2007). 'Practice and play in the development of sport expertise'. In Tenenbaum, G. and Eklund, R.C. (eds) *Handbook of Sport Psychology*, 3rd edn. Hoboken, NJ: Wiley, 184–202.

Côté, J., MacDonald, D., Baker, J. and Abernethy, B. (2006). 'When "where" is more important than "when": Birthplace and birthdate effects on the achievement of sporting expertise'. *Journal of Sport Sciences*, (24): 1065–73.

Ericsson, K.A., Krampe, R.T. and Tesch-Römer, C. (1993). 'The role of deliberate practice in the acquisition of expert performance'. *Psychological Review*, (100): 363–406.

Farrow, D. and Abernethy, B. (2002). 'Can anticipatory skills be learned through implicit video-based perceptual training?'. *Journal of Sports Sciences*, (20): 471–85.

Helsen, W.F., Hodges, N.J., Van Winckel, J. and Starkes, J.L. (2000). 'The roles of talent, physical precocity and practice in the development of soccer expertise'. *Journal of Sport Sciences*, (18): 727–36.

Müller, S., Abernethy, B. and Farrow, D. (2006) 'How do world-class cricket batsmen anticipate a bowler's intention?'. *Quarterly Journal of Experimental Psychology*, (59), 2162–86.

Musch, J. and Grondin, S. (2001). 'Unequal competition as an impediment to personal development: A review of the relative age effect in sport'. *Developmental Review*, (21): 147–67.

Starkes, J.L., Deakin, J.M., Allard, F., Hodges, N.J. and Hayes, A. (1996). 'Deliberate practice in sports: What is it anyway?'. In Ericsson, K.A. (ed.) *The road to excellence: The acquisition of expert performance in the arts, sciences, sports and games*. Mahwah, N.J.: Erlbaum, 81–106.

Williams, A.M. and Hodges, N.J. (eds) (2004). *Skill acquisition in sport: research, theory and practice*. London: Routledge.

NOTE

1 Junior players who are relatively older than their teammates may be better positioned to experiment with different solutions without adversely affecting their task success and this may underpin (or reinforce) the powerful relative age effect.

Section 1

Developing elite athletes: from the backyard to the big stage

Chapter 2

Play, practice, and athlete development

Jean Côté and Jessica Fraser-Thomas

In coaching, play and practice are the variables that have the most influence on skill acquisition. However, there are many unanswered questions regarding how much and what type of play and practice activities are necessary at different stages of an athlete's development. Much of the experimental work on the relationship between learning and performance has been conducted using laboratory tasks in which changes in performance are recorded over a relatively small number of trials using novices as participants in the experiments; however, studying the development of expertise in sport is much more complex. From a coaching perspective it is often easy to focus on the factors that are most influential in the development of motor skills (i.e., specialized practice and training time), with little consideration for physical (i.e., injury, health) or psycho-social (i.e., enjoyment, drop-out, burn-out) costs; however, it is important also to consider the potential costs throughout development associated with a sole focus on practice and motor skill acquisition.

WHAT DOES THE RESEARCH TELL US?

The deliberate practice framework

The framework of deliberate practice developed by Ericsson and colleagues is based on the idea that expertise in any domain is tied explicitly to the amount and type of training or practice performed in that domain. Engagement in deliberate practice requires effort and attention, does not lead to immediate social or financial rewards, and is completed for the purpose of performance enhancement rather than enjoyment.

Studies in sports such as field hockey, soccer, figure skating, martial arts, middle distance running, and wrestling have shown that elite athletes can be consistently distinguished from non-elite athletes based on accumulated deliberate practice. Specifically, it has been suggested that ten years or 10,000 hours of deliberate practice are required to reach expert status in one's domain. As a result, it would be next to impossible for a late starter to overcome the early advantage provided to those who begin deliberate practice at a young age and maintain high numbers of deliberate practice hours over time. In sum, the deliberate practice framework suggests that a pathway to elite performance in sport requires early specialization and sport specific practice; this framework largely downplays the physical and psycho-social costs associated with this type of practice, especially in the early years of an athlete's involvement in sport.

Three testable tenets are at the foundation of the deliberate practice framework:

1. elite athletes specialize in their main sport at a younger age than sub-elite athletes
2. elite athletes start deliberate practice at a younger age than sub-elite athletes and
3. elite athletes accumulate more deliberate practice hours than sub-elite athletes throughout their career.

Tenet 1 suggests that elite athletes specialize in their main sport at a younger age than sub-elite athletes. This tenet has received support from studies of sports where peak performance is achieved before puberty (i.e., females' gymnastics and figure skating). However, this tenet is not supported by numerous interview studies with athletes who participated in a variety of sports as children and still reached an elite level of sport performance in adulthood.

Tenet 2 proposes that elite athletes start deliberate practice at a younger age than sub-elite athletes. This tenet is based on Ericsson *et al.*'s assumption that 'the higher the level of attained elite performance, the earlier the age of first exposure as well as the age of starting deliberate practice'. Again the only supporting evidence for this tenet is from studies of athletes involved in sports where peak performance is achieved before puberty. However, no studies in adult-peak sports (e.g. basketball, ice hockey, field hockey, triathlon) have supported this tenet. Studies of women's gymnastics and women's figure skating indicate differences in sport specific training between elite and less elite athletes as early as age seven. This appears to be the case because the window of time to accumulate the quantity of practice necessary for expert performance in early peak performance sports is smaller compared with later peak performance sports. Consequently, future experts in early peak performance age sports must devote all of their practice time to structured forms of training regardless of the potential negative physical and psycho-social consequences associated with this approach. For example, one recent study by Law *et al.* showed that, although expert rhythmic gymnasts specialized and engaged in deliberate practice earlier than less expert gymnasts, they also experienced more negative outcomes in the form of greater injuries and less enjoyment. Several other studies also suggest that the serious nature of early involvement in deliberate practice leads to less enjoyment, which in turn leads more young athletes to drop out or burn out of their sport. Furthermore, excessive forms of training during crucial periods of biological development can significantly increase the risk of overtraining injuries and can have negative effects on developing athletes' overall physical health.

Tenet 3 proposes that elite athletes accumulate more hours of training than sub-elite athletes throughout their careers. By and large, retrospective studies that compare elite and sub-elite athletes in various sports have shown support for this tenet; however, research indicates that differences between groups of elite and less elite athletes do not occur until later in development. For instance, comparisons of elite and non-elite athletes in soccer, field hockey, wrestling, and triathlon showed that training-based differences did not occur until 13, 15,

18, and 20 years of age, respectively. Prior to these ages the groups appeared quite similar with respect to sport-specific training exposure.

The Developmental Model of Sport Participation

Côté and colleagues' Developmental Model of Sport Participation (DMSP) highlights the importance of developmentally appropriate physical training patterns and psycho-social influences. The DMSP proposes a trajectory toward elite performance consisting of three distinct stages: the sampling years (childhood; age 6–12), the specializing years (early adolescence; age 13–15), and the investment years (late adolescence; age 16+). During the sampling years, athletes participate in a variety of sports with the focus being primarily on *deliberate play* activities. Deliberate play activities such as backyard soccer or street basketball are regulated by age-adapted rules and are set up and monitored by the children or adults involved in the activity. These activities are intrinsically motivating, provide immediate gratification, and are specifically designed to maximize enjoyment. The specializing years are seen as the transitional stage to the investment years. During the specializing years, youth engage in fewer sporting activities that are more competitive, which include both deliberate play and deliberate practice activities. During the investment years, youth usually commit to only one sport activity and engage primarily in deliberate practice.

Three testable tenets are at the foundation of the DMSP:

1. elite athletes sample various sports during childhood instead of specializing in one sport
2. elite athletes are involved in greater amounts of deliberate play than deliberate practice during childhood and
3. elite athletes are involved in more deliberate practice and less deliberate play during their teenage and adult years.

Tenet 1—that elite athletes sample various sports during childhood—has been supported by numerous qualitative and quantitative studies. Specifically, these studies suggest, contrary to the deliberate practice framework, diversified sport backgrounds can still lead to elite performance in sport. For instance, Baker and his colleagues found that athletes who had been involved in diversified sporting activities during childhood required less sport-specific training during adolescence and young adulthood to achieve elite status in their sport. From a skill acquisition perspective, Baker and colleagues suggest that a diversified (or generalized) approach to early athlete development leads to better sport specific performance because young athletes develop general capabilities applicable in a variety of sports. However, the researchers caution that, once general cognitive or physical adaptations have been made through involvement in various sport activities during childhood, training should become more specific (see Baker and Cobley, Chapter 3 for more on this issue).

One of the most important reasons that all children should be provided with sampling opportunities is motivation. Kirk suggests that quality early learning experiences through sampling and play during childhood develop not only physical capabilities, but also perceptions of competence, which in turn lead to motivation for continued participation. Motivation

19

theories suggest that children's perceptions of competence in late childhood (ages 8–12) are largely the result of comparisons with their peers. It is only at about the age of 12 or 13 that young adolescents are able to fully understand the differing effects that effort, practice, and ability have on their performances. For example, before the age of 12 or 13, children tend to judge their athletic ability in comparison with their peers (i.e., I run faster/slower than Joe) rather than in absolute terms (i.e., I can run 100 m in 14 s).

Tenet 2 of the DMSP suggests that elite athletes are involved in high amounts of deliberate play during childhood. Deliberate play allows children to experience sports in various contexts and further nurture the excitement associated with playing sport. From a skill development perspective, deliberate play activities allow children to experiment and be creative with the execution of their movements without worrying about adults (i.e., coaches and parents) telling them the *right way* to execute a skill. It has been shown that this implicit approach to skill development affords greater resistance to stress and that children are less likely to forget what they learned, as is often the case with more explicit approaches such as deliberate practice (see Masters, Chapter 7, for more on this issue). Still, the most important aspect of deliberate play resides in its inherent enjoyment and its potential contribution to stimulating children's motivation to invest in sport in their teenage years. A recent study found that high-level American baseball players who engaged in high amounts of baseball deliberate play from ages 6 to 12 were more likely to engage in baseball-specific training after the age of 13. This finding suggests that early deliberate play activities contribute to young athletes' motivation to pursue intense sport-specific training during adolescence.

Clearly, a healthy sport context that is in line with children's need to play and have fun during childhood should not be undermined. A recent study on the birthplace of over two thousand professional athletes provides further support for the importance of deliberate play during childhood. Côté and colleagues showed a birthplace bias toward smaller cities: professional athletes were over-represented in cities of fewer than 500,000 and under-represented in cities of more than 500,000. This finding could be attributed to the fact that children in smaller cities are more likely to engage in unorganized physical activities such as cycling, swimming, skating, and playing sports, without the structure and adult supervision required in urban settings, thus indicating that smaller cities present more opportunities for the types of developmental experience important during the sampling years. The effect of these enjoyable sporting activities during childhood probably has a lasting influence on children's motivation and determination to become high-level athletes. In contrast, the organized sport programs in bigger cities often reflect what adults think youth sport should be; they are often highly structured by parents, coaches, and other adults, they are more likely to focus on deliberate practice activities, and in turn, they may limit the time children spend actually playing sports.

Tenet 3 of the DMSP suggests that elite athletes increase the amount of time devoted to deliberate practice and decrease the amount of time devoted to deliberate play during their adolescent and adult years. One study that supports this tenet was conducted with professional ice hockey players. Soberlak and Côté showed that professional ice hockey players spent over 10,000 hours involved in sport from age 6 to 20. Approximately 3,500 of these hours were spent in play-like activities (i.e., deliberate play), and 2,300 hours were spent playing other sports. In addition, just over 3,000 hours were spent in organized hockey practice (i.e., deliberate practice), and just over 2,400 hours were spent playing organized hockey games. Of particular interest was that the greater part of the hours spent in deliberate play and participating in other sports occurred prior to the age of 15, whereas the majority of the hours spent in deliberate practice occurred after the age of 15.

THEORY INTO PRACTICE

Implication for coaches

Two general approaches of sport expertise development have been presented in this chapter. The deliberate practice framework emphasizes skill learning but gives little attention to the psycho-social context in which this learning occurs throughout development. On the other hand, the DMSP considers the physical and psycho-social costs associated with expertise development in sport.

Coaching within the deliberate practice framework

A coach whose only focus is to improve an athlete's current performance level will most often do so by maximizing deliberate practice time in training. Such a coach will focus on structured drills and activities with well-defined learning goals, provide regular feedback for skill improvement, and create ample opportunities for repetition. Within the deliberate practice framework, training activities are carefully monitored by coaches, and coaches' interventions are aimed at correcting errors and improving athletes' performance.

It is important to acknowledge the importance of deliberate practice and well-designed training sessions in the acquisition of sport skills; however, an over-emphasis on deliberate practice during childhood can lead to sport attrition, burn-out, injuries, decreased enjoyment and poor health. Coaches need to be aware that many children will not respond positively to a primary focus on skill acquisition, early selection of players for more competitive teams, year-round training in one sport, and a lack of opportunities to play and experiment with other sports. Coaching within this framework creates a sport context that constrains children's natural need for physical play and experimentation with various sports.

Sport is one of the rare activities of childhood that is inherently enjoyable while requiring concentration and effort. By encouraging early specialization and deliberate practice during childhood, coaches are imposing an adult model of sport on children; the enjoyment and experimentation associated with physical play and diverse sport participation are often neglected in order to increase training effectiveness and improve sport specific skills. In turn, children's perceptions of sport are altered, and young sport participants may be deterred from further involvement in sport at a recreational or elite level.

One could argue that participation in a large amount of deliberate practice at a young age could be done in concert with involvement in other sports and deliberate play. However, for a coach, this suggestion could be difficult to implement, considering the three tenets of the deliberate practice framework (i.e., that elite athletes specialize in their main sport earlier, start deliberate practice earlier, and accumulate more deliberate practice hours throughout their careers than non-elite athletes). These propositions leave little room for youth sport coaches to encourage their athletes to get involved in other sports and deliberate play activities.

Coaches of sports where early specialization and an emphasis on deliberate practice at a young age are the norm owing to an early peak performance age, such as women's figure skating and gymnastics, should take into consideration the possible costs of this type of training during childhood. Athletes who must engage in long hours of practice at younger ages in order to reach peak performance before puberty do not have opportunities to take part in other sports and deliberate play due to time and energy constraints. This type of environment creates high performance expectations from coaches, parents, and the athletes themselves. It is crucial that coaches of young elite-level athletes are sensitive to the psycho-social costs and health risks of high amounts of deliberate practice in childhood and implement appropriate support systems to minimize these costs.

Coaching within the developmental model of sport participation

In this chapter, we presented the DMSP as an alternative model of expertise development. The DMSP suggests various amounts of sampling, deliberate play, and deliberate practice at different stages of children's development. Specifically, the model suggests the importance of physical training and psycho-social resources being in line with the needs of children at various stages of development, so that children experience positive outcomes and stay involved in sport throughout development.

Contrary to Ericsson *et al.*'s suggestion that 10,000 hours of deliberate practice are necessary to achieve expertise in any domain, the DMSP suggests that expert performance in sports where peak performance generally occurs after the age of 20 can be achieved with 3,000–4,000 hours of sport-specific training (i.e., deliberate practice). The DMSP instead suggests that 10,000 hours of *total involvement in sport* (taking into account involvement throughout development in deliberate play, other sports, and organized competitions) is a better measure of expertise in sport.

Based on studies of expert athletes in sports where peak performance occurs during young adulthood (e.g. basketball, field hockey, ice hockey, and triathlon), it is possible to suggest general guidelines for percentages of time that athletes should spend in deliberate practice and deliberate play/other sporting activities during the sampling, specializing, and investment years. The data in Table 2.1 are based on an athlete who reaches peak performance during adulthood and thus would aim to accumulate approximately 10,000 hours of experience in deliberate practice, deliberate play, and other sporting activities by that age. Obviously, demands will vary between sports owing to differing peak performance ages and numerous other factors; however, the ratios suggested in Table 2.1 can serve as a general guideline for coaches wishing to develop athletes' skills while still being conscious of physical and psycho-social training costs.

Past research suggests that approximately fifty per cent of athletes' total time in sport be spent in deliberate practice activities, and the other fifty per cent be spent in deliberate play activities and other sporting activities. From a coaching perspective it is most important to see the progression from more hours of deliberate play during childhood to more hours of

Table 2.1 *Suggested percentage of time and number of sporting activities during the sampling, specializing, and investment years*

Stage of participation	Deliberate play/ other sport activities: % total involvement	Deliberate practice: % total involvement	Involvement in other sports: no. of sports
Sampling (age 6–12)	80	20	3–4
Specializing (age 13–15)	50	50	2–3
Investment (age 16–22)	20	80	1–2

deliberate practice during adolescence and young adulthood, and from involvement in two to four seasonal sports during childhood and early adolescence to investment in year-round training in one sport beginning late in adolescence. As previously mentioned, these figures vary according to sports. For example, Ironman triathletes will generally reach their peak performance level at an older age than ice hockey players and consequently, may spend more time doing other sports during childhood. As a result, it is difficult to suggest an average number of hours per week throughout development for involvement in deliberate practice, deliberate play, and other sports; however, as a general rule, the ratio of deliberate play/other sports to deliberate practice should be 80:20 during the sampling years, 50:50 during the specializing years, and 20:80 during the investment years. Table 2.1 serves primarily to highlight the importance of recognizing and respecting the different ratios of play to practice activities throughout the development of a committed athlete.

Coaching in the sampling years

Coaches should recognize that children's motivation to stay involved in sport either at a recreational or elite level is largely influenced by their experiences in the sampling years. The main goal of coaches during this period should be to focus their programs on intrinsically motivating behaviors (i.e., deliberate play and involvement in several sports) instead of externally controlled activities (i.e., deliberate practice). A supportive environment should be created to allow children to be involved in plenty of deliberate play and other sports. Because children don't understand competition and sport performances the same way adults do, coaches should not over-emphasize performance through deliberate practice or over-organize competition during the sampling years.

Coaches should avoid the tendency to 'over-coach' in the sampling years. One way to achieve this is by encouraging multisport involvement and avoiding an emphasis on year-round training in one sport. Specifically, the sampling years should focus on deliberate play activities without the pedagogical intervention of a coach or other adult (e.g. parent) that interrupts children's participation (e.g. providing instruction or correcting errors). The sampling years should also include a small number of deliberate practice activities that are not necessarily focused on only one sport. For example, a young athlete may be involved in baseball in the summer, soccer in the spring, and hockey in the winter, and receive deliberate practice training in these three sports during their different seasons. One objective of deliberate practice activities during the sampling years is for children to learn fundamental movement skills that can potentially be transferred across sports. However, the main focus of the sampling years should be to let children experiment with various ways of executing sport skills in various contexts through deliberate play and fun involvement in several sports.

The ultimate goal of coaches in the sampling years is to nurture children's intrinsic motivation for sport. Coaching techniques such as teaching games for understanding (see the book by Griffin and Butler in the reading list at the end of this chapter for more information) should be used with young children to create an environment of fun in organized sport. Furthermore, by encouraging deliberate play and the sampling of various sports, coaches can promote the development of self-regulation, decision-making skills, and feelings of competence and connectedness. These important skills and feelings are essential to the development of future self-determined expert and recreational athletes.

Coaching in the specializing years

Athletes in the specializing years make an informed decision about increasing their involvement in one sport and committing to train more seriously in this sport. During this transitional stage toward expertise, youth need to be nurtured and encouraged to get involved in sporting activities that may be perceived as less inherently enjoyable (i.e., deliberate practice) but are important in their development toward elite sport performance. A more equal balance of deliberate practice and deliberate play is suggested during the specializing years. It is important from a coaching perspective to ensure a balance between amounts of intrinsically motivating activities (i.e., deliberate play and other sporting activities) and performance-oriented sport-specific activities (i.e., deliberate practice) during the specializing years. This balance allows children to stay motivated while learning important sport-specific skills that move them toward the next level of elite sport performance.

Coaching in the investment years

During the investment years, athletes make a definite commitment to training and performance. Most hours of sport participation should be invested in sport-specific deliberate practice at this stage. Coaches should also try to make sure that athletes are involved in a small amount of deliberate play activities. The deliberate play activities during the investment years are to remind athletes of the intrinsic enjoyment that results from sport participation. Coaches could also encourage their athletes to participate in another sport in the off-season for relaxation or cross-training purposes. Although competition is not the most important activity to improve performance in all sports, competitive situations are critical for the development of perceptual and decision-making skills, skill execution, and physical fitness in many sports. Coaches in the investment years should promote competitive situations that are likely to have a direct effect on the athlete's progress toward elite performance.

One of the coach's primary goals during the investment years should be to provide physical and social resources to overcome the effort and motivational constraints associated with deliberate practice. The effectiveness of a coach during the investment years lies in his or her specific knowledge of the sport and the way he or she transmits that knowledge in training and in competition. Therefore, sport-specific knowledge and communication skills are important assets at this level of coaching. Further, a coach's commitment to establishing structured and competitive training sessions should be in line with athletes' levels of investment. By demonstrating enthusiasm in training and fostering a training environment that nurtures athletes' learning and motivation, coaches create a positive training environment, as illustrated in this quotation from an international-level rower:

> I think a coach that is willing to be in training at 5:30 in the morning and always be there is a big motivator for an athlete. It makes a big difference compared to a coach that sort of comes out maybe three or four times a week and doesn't really like coaching. . . I think if you see a coach that is willing to do everything that you are doing, it just makes that much more drive. I mean you have to be down at practice because there is someone waiting for you. . . It's nice to have a coach that's as fully motivated as you.

In sum, effective coaching during the investment years is dependent upon a coach's ability to set goals, to organize an optimal learning environment, and to relate personally to their athletes.

CONCLUSION

Although the deliberate practice framework provides the most evident model of expertise development, it does not consider physical and psycho-social costs to young athletes. In contrast, the DMSP provides a framework of elite performance and healthy development by looking beyond accumulated hours of deliberate practice. Although not all the outcomes of the DMSP have been directly tested, a growing body of literature supports its tenets. Concerted effort is required from coaches, physical education teachers, and parents to ensure that children follow healthy developmental sport paths, and stay involved in sport at either an elite or recreational level throughout development.

COACH'S CORNER

Eddie Jones

Coaching Consultant, Saracens Rugby Club

My experience of coaching rugby for the last 20 years or so has meant that I have seen many generations of players emerge. In my opinion, I think our current crop of players are generally not as skilled as previous generations. Obviously there are many reasons for this situation, including the amount of competition from other sports to secure the best talent. However, I think the lack of deliberate play, as the authors put it, is a key factor. Similarly, I think specializing too early is also limiting the skill development of our younger generation in team sports.

Thinking back to my own playing days, it was not uncommon for me and many others to play an organized cricket match where I would have my bat in the morning, then take off to play in a rugby trial game and then come back to field for my cricket team in the afternoon. As a result I was always thinking about the sports I was involved in. Whether I was aware of it or not I was probably transferring things I learnt from one sport to the other. When coaching I can clearly pick out those players who have played a variety of sports growing up relative to those that have predominantly specialized in rugby. A key difference is that those who have played lots of sports are usually more tactically astute.

How much play and practice?

I think it's critical that it's play before practice and not the other way around. As detailed in the chapter, if you play a sport for a period of time you start to develop a motivation to want to play it better, which then directs you down the path of more specific practice. This passion for self-improvement is not forced on you from the coach but is something developed by the player owing to their experiences. This process makes sense to me, rather than starting out with specific practice and perhaps never really developing a passion for the game.

I agree with what the authors propose regarding the progression from play to practice. Primary school children should be exposed to more play and less formal practice. Then as they get to secondary school at around 12–13 years of age, a format of two specific practice sessions and two play sessions could occur. Finally, as they hit 15–16 years of age they would then be training and playing competitive games regularly. The play element would still exist outside of the formal training and competition times owing to the internal motivation the players have developed to want to get better at their sport.

In Australia, our summer–winter program of sports provides an excellent framework to play a number of sports and strike a good balance between play and practice. For me, as I mentioned before, it was cricket and rugby. Summer meant playing cricket. Usually there would be lots of deliberate play after school with others in the neighborhood, and then there would be club or school training to attend and a game to play on the weekend. This would continue for four or five months. Then winter would arrive and rugby would commence, and we would play touch footy in school physical education and at every lunch break. In addition to the deliberate play we would attend club training and again play a weekend game. In thinking back, I think the fact that the seasons meant switching from one sport to another meant I never got bored with the one sport and was always happy to play and practice as much as possible.

The modern era

Contrast this to the modern generation. From what I'm told, many school children don't play any sports during recess or lunch breaks. On occasion even if the boys want to play sport, the schools, for policy (insurance) reasons, ban games such as touch rugby or *British Bulldogs* (a physical tag game).

Similarly, as the students get older and need to be exposed to more competitive play, the school calendar for organized competition is very brief. School rugby teams may play seven matches a school season. Hence they train, train, train, with only a little competition and deliberate play. Incidentally much of this training is based around winning the inter-school competition, meaning players are locked into playing positions and roles based on their current playing status (mainly decided by their physical stature). Although they may win the school 'A Grade' competition, this approach stifles their overall skill development, producing players with a limited set of skills.

Providing enough competitive play as players get to 16 years of age or older is still a problem we have in rugby in Australia. We need to have our players contextualize what it is they are learning in training into a game format. Unfortunately our players train more than they play. I see the benefits of playing more competitive games in other sports. Australian cricketers travel to England for the Australian winter to compete in the county cricket competition. Although the competition may not be as testing as the Australian equivalent, the sheer volume of competitive play allows the players to get valuable repetition in a game context.

Creativity is another area where I have seen a decline in modern-day players. I consider the lack of deliberate play to be one of the reasons for this decline. Play fosters inquisitiveness to learn and develop new skills. For instance, 'how can I bend this pass around that tree, or how can I dodge my mate from next door when playing one-on-one rugby in a narrow backyard?' A lack of creativity appears in all sorts of situations at the elite level. Rarely do players initiate their own warm-up with a ball. They have to be told by coaching staff to get underway. In past generations players would arrive early simply to throw the ball around before the formal training session began. A lack of creativity means we have fewer players with the decision-making skills required to win games of rugby.

A message to other coaches

I found this chapter to be particularly relevant to those coaching at the youth development level. At this level we seem to want to specialize our players too early, and the information in this chapter provides us with some good evidence not to specialize too soon. Importantly, we may have to create organized practice sessions simply to provide deliberate play opportunities to the players. This sounds illogical but until the players get back to discovering and playing the game for themselves, we need to make up this shortfall in school and club settings on their behalf.

KEY READING

Baker, J. and Côté, J. (2005). 'Shifting training requirements during athlete development: The relationship among deliberate practice, deliberate play and other sport involvement in the acquisition of sport expertise'. In Hackfort, D. and Tenenbaum, G. (eds) *Essential Processes for Attaining Peak Performance*. Germany: Meyer and Meyer.

Carlson, R.C. (1988). 'The socialization of elite tennis players in Sweden: An analysis of the players' backgrounds and development'. *Sociology of Sport Journal*, (5): 241–56.

Côté, J. and Fraser-Thomas, J. (2007). 'The health and developmental benefits of youth sport participation'. In Crocker, P. (ed.) *Sport Psychology: A Canadian Perspective*. Toronto: Pearson.

Côté, J., Baker, J. and Abernethy, B. (2007). 'Practice and play in the development of sport expertise'. In Eklund, R. and Tenenbaum, G. (eds) *Handbook of Sport Psychology*, 3rd edn. Hoboken, NJ: Wiley.

Durand-Bush, N. and Salmela, J.H. (2001). 'The development of talent in sport'. In Singer, R.N., Hausenblas, H.A. and Janelle, C.M. (eds) *Handbook of Sport Psychology*, 2nd edn. New York: John Wiley.

Ericsson, K.A. (2003). 'Development of elite performance and deliberate practice: An update from the perspective of the expert performance approach'. In Starkes, J.L. and Ericsson, K.A. (eds) *Expert Performance in Sports: Advances in Research on Sports Expertise*. Champaign, IL: Human Kinetics.

Griffin, L.L. and Butler, J.I. (eds) (2005). *Teaching Games for Understanding: Theory, Research, and Practice*. Champaign, IL: Human Kinetics.

Horn, T.S. and Harris, A. (2002). 'Perceived competence in young athletes: Research findings and recommendations for coaches and parents'. In Smoll, F.L. and Smith, R.E. (eds) *Children and Youth in Sport. A Biopsychosocial Perspective*, 2nd edn. Dubuque, IW: Kendall Hunt.

Kirk, D. (2005). 'Physical education, youth sport and lifelong participation: The importance of early learning experiences'. *European Physical Education Review*, (11): 239–55.

Law, M., Côté, J. and Ericsson, K.A. (2007). 'Characteristics of expert development in rhythmic gymnastics: A retrospective study'. *International Journal of Sport and Exercise Psychology*, (5): 82–103

Martindale, R.J.J., Collins, D. and Daubney, J. (2005). 'Talent development: A guide for practice and research within sport'. *Quest*, (57): 353–75.

Chapter 3

Does practice make perfect?
The role of training in developing the expert athlete

Joe Baker and Steve Cobley

I've always believed that if you put in the work, the results will come. I don't do things half-heartedly. Because I know if I do, then I can expect half-hearted results. That's why I approached practices the same way I approached games. You can't turn it on and off like a faucet. I couldn't dog it during practice and then, when I need that extra push late in the game, expect it to be there.

(Michael Jordan)

One of the most consistent relationships ever identified in science is the association between time spent practicing and improvements in performance. Although this conclusion may seem rather obvious and further examination a waste of research funds, it was not until recently that we began to understand how different amounts and types of practice affect skill development. Here is an example: while training for his record-breaking four minute mile, one of the most profound achievements in the history of sport, Roger Bannister limited his training to less than 30 minutes a day owing to his belief that the human body could not adequately handle a greater training load. Today top runners spend considerably greater amounts of time in daily training. What is more, researchers continue to make exciting developments in this area.

Like much sport-related research, the theoretical understanding of the relationship between training and performance originates elsewhere. In the late 1800s, one of the earliest studies of this relationship was conducted at Indiana University by William Lowe Bryan and his graduate student Noble Harter, who examined the development of telegraph skill—a worthwhile outcome considering the time period. Their research and other research examining the accumulated effects of prolonged practice and the rate of learning typically show that performance increased according to a power function, whereby rapid skill improvements during initial hours of practice are reduced and learners are required to invest progressively more hours to accrue progressively smaller improvements. This finding, better known as the power law of practice (Figure 3.1), has been demonstrated in numerous domains—everything from learning to roll cigars to learning how to read words printed upside down. Domains

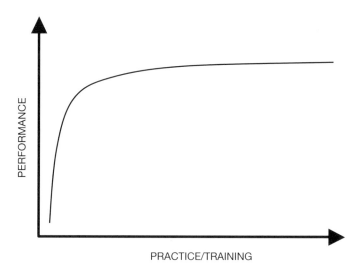

Figure 3.1 *Typical relationship between training and performance indicating rapid increases in performance at the onset of training and decreased improvements with additional training.*

outside psychology also noticed this phenomenon but called it different names such as the *law of diminished returns* or *ceiling effects*.

SIMON, CHASE, AND THE 10-YEAR RULE

In 1973, Herbert Simon and William Chase provided some of the first empirical support for the presumption that performance differences between individuals could be explained by time spent training. Their hypothesis was based on the perceptual–cognitive differences between grandmaster and lower level (i.e., master and novice) chess players. They found that differences between these skill levels were not attributable to a superior memory capacity but rather to the ability to organize information into meaningful *chunks* of information, much as skilled team sport athletes group players into offensive and defensive patterns (see Chapter 10 by Farrow and Raab for more on this concept). For Simon and Chase, this finding led them to consider whether the differences between their players were simply corollaries of a greater amount of time spent training and playing chess. In their examination, they concluded 'there appears not to be on record any case (including Bobby Fischer) where a person has reached grandmaster level with less than about a decade's intense preoccupation with the game'.

This statement, based on a simple investigation with three participants, has become the *10-year rule of necessary preparation*, a general criterion for expertise in domains ranging from running to tennis, from mathematics to music. In fact, there is some evidence to suggest that, in fields where the distinguishing characteristics between experts and non-experts involve the ability to process specific types of information (e.g. perceptual information), these differences are primarily the result of training rather than innate abilities.

ANDERS ERICSSON AND THE THEORY OF DELIBERATE PRACTICE

In cognitive science, the work of Simon and Chase prompted some researchers to adopt a nurture as opposed to nature perspective, to explain the acquisition of highly skilled performance. Currently, one of these is advocated by the psychologist Anders Ericsson and his colleagues. Over the past two decades, Ericsson has steadfastly defended his position that individual performance differences in any domain can be accounted for by the amount and type of practice performed. Likewise, he pronounced the role of genes in determining individual achievement as minimal and that this role could be circumvented by the performance of optimal amounts of quality practice. In a review of studies on skill acquisition and learning, Ericsson concluded that, with few exceptions, level of performance is determined by the amount of time spent performing a 'well defined task with an appropriate difficulty level for the particular individual, informative feedback, and opportunities for repetition and corrections of errors'.

Data from a series of studies by Ericsson and his contemporaries examining skilled musicians support the relationship between number of hours of practice and level of performance. They found that expert level musicians spent in excess of 25 hours per week engaged in specific practice activities (i.e., training alone), whereas less successful musicians spent considerably less time (e.g. amateurs < 2 hours per week) in such activities. These notable disparities in weekly volume of training accumulated to generate enormous differences after years of training. Expert musicians accumulated over 10,000 hours in such practices by age 20, whereas amateurs accumulated only 2,000 hours at the same age. These findings reflect the same positive relationship between training and improvement highlighted by Simon and Chase. However, what was unique about Ericsson's research is that it highlighted the importance of quality in practice, as emphasized through engagement in optimal types of training throughout skill development. Also, owing to continued optimization of training by expert musicians, they also maintained that the relationship between time spent in optimal practice and performance improvement was monotonic (i.e., linear), and not a power function. More simply, 1 hour of optimal practice has the same effect on performance, regardless of whether it is the first hour of training or the ten-thousandth hour.

Ericsson and his colleagues suggest it is not simply any type of training that differentiates individual skill levels, but the engagement in *deliberate practice*. Deliberate practice is the type of training athletes do that is not much fun, requires intense hard work and does not lead to instantaneous rewards—where the payoff is in the long run. For example, a swimmer can spend their time doing length after length of the pool (not deliberate practice), or they can attentively train the specific aspects of performance where they are weak—for example, focusing on stroke improvement, or doing intervals at near race pace (deliberate practice). Further, once a skill is well learned or a consistency in performance is established (i.e., the swimmer successfully adjusts stroke technique or consistently hits their interval times), then this type of training is no longer considered deliberate practice for this individual. Instead the swimmer now needs to move on to practices that require a renewed intense effort with the same high relevance for improving the current level of performance. According to deliberate practice theory, continually modifying the level of task difficulty so as to match current performance levels requires the learner continually to *reach*; perpetuating adaptations to higher amounts of training stress and simultaneously preventing performance plateaus.

31

Prior to Ericsson's research, general rules of learning had generally focused on the total quantity of exposure, such as the 10-year rule. The theory of deliberate practice brought the issue of training quality back to the forefront of learning and expertise research.

PERIODIZATION OF TRAINING STRESS AND DELIBERATE PRACTICE

Physiologists are aware of a similar concept brought to North America from Russia in the 1970s, known as periodization. The *Oxford Dictionary of Sports Science and Medicine* defines the term periodization as the 'organization of a training year into different periods to attain different objectives'. The purpose of designing training programs in this manner is to allow the athlete to attend to useful training objectives during early periods of the training year while maintaining an optimal level of readiness during the competitive season. Similar to the deliberate practice approach, the cornerstone of periodization is the optimal maintenance of training effort.

What we know about the human body's response to training stress comes from Han Selye's *General Adaptation Syndrome*. According to Selye, the body has a three-stage response to stress (in this case training stress). When the body is functioning normally and all systems are in balance, we are in *homeostasis* (Greek for *to remain the same*). Introducing a training stimulus promotes a stress response. The first phase of this response is *shock*, easily identified in sport by the acute muscle soreness, and performance decreases connected with the onset of a new or different training stimulus. During this phase, the body is moved out of normal functioning and must adapt to the new levels of stress. The second phase is *adaptation* and during this period the body adapts to the training stimuli and reattains homeostatic function. These adaptations can be positive, as when the body reorganizes its functional components to produce a superior, more capable operating system, or they can be negative, as when a physical injury or mental overload occurs. In the third phase, *staleness*, physiological adaptations are no longer being made and performance may again decrease unless training stimuli are modified. During this stage, the athlete has adapted to the previous level of physical or mental stress, and training at this level no longer disrupts homeostasis. The duration of the period from shock to staleness is determined primarily by the intensity of the training stress presented in phase one. High levels of stress require greater amounts of time to achieve adaptation.

Periodization of training is intended to prevent athletes from reaching or spending too much time in the third stage (staleness) by varying training schedules so that new training stimuli are presented at the end of the adaptation phase. If the time between when adaptation occurs and new training levels are introduced is too long, maximal training effects are compromised. On the other hand, if the time is too short, coaches and athletes run the risk of incurring injuries or overtraining syndrome. This notion of balance between training and recovery is at the very heart of Ericsson's theory of deliberate practice.

Despite being developed through work with musicians, researchers have also applied deliberate practice theory to sports, a wide variety of sports, in truth—ranging from karate to distance running, from figure skating to basketball. Although these studies have found good support for the notion that time spent in high-quality training was a good way to distinguish those at the top of their games from those at lower levels, they did encounter some problems applying Ericsson's original definition of deliberate practice. Most notably, athletes at all levels consistently report their practice activities as very enjoyable and intrinsically motivating, contrasting with a key component of the definition of deliberate practice activities.

Based on these difficulties there is some concern among sport scientists about exactly what forms of athletic training constitute deliberate practice. In Ericsson's original work, only practice alone was seen as meeting the requirements for deliberate practice. In studies of deliberate practice in sport, there are few, if any, training activities that meet the original criteria set out by Ericsson and his colleagues in 1993. Some researchers have argued that, given the unique requirements of sport performance, all relevant forms of training could be considered deliberate practice. The rationale for this is that even training that is lower in intensity may have a critical role in promoting positive performance adaptations. For instance, long slow distance runs would not be considered very effortful to an elite distance runner, yet this type of training is a staple of their program. This is also important in team sports where both individual and team practices are beneficial to improving various aspects of performance. Ericsson's position has also been criticized for not considering the specific needs of athletes at different levels of development (see Côté and Fraser-Thomas, Chapter 2, for more on this issue).

INCORPORATING DELIBERATE PRACTICE THEORY INTO ATHLETE TRAINING

The most salient message from Ericsson's research and other research in this area is that training quality matters. Although early investigations used simple measures of exposure such as total time spent practicing, more recent developments have solidified the conclusion that training content is also an important factor—some would argue the most important factor. This provides tangible information for coaches to use in their athlete development plans. Importantly, this research challenges the notion that athlete achievement can be solely attributed to biological unknowns such as genetic predisposition or innate talent, instead reinforcing the importance of practice. In the remainder of this chapter we consider the manner in which this information can be best used in day-to-day athlete training.

The qualities of elite and expert athlete training outlined above indicate that the foundation of successful athlete development involves performing enough (quantity) of the right type of training (quality) at the optimal time to maximize training adaptations (balance; see Figure 3.2). Most coaches and athletes are aware of the need to perform lots of high-quality training, but often the balance requirement is either neglected entirely or considered only superficially. There is considerable support from the field of psychology that stress, from any area of life (e.g. school, work, family), can have negative effects on an individual's ability to function. In order to understand the complexity of the balance requirement, coaches need to consider sources of stress from outside the sporting arena. For instance, physical issues such as having a chronic condition or low level of physical fitness will affect the athlete's response to the training stimulus designed by their coach. Similarly, psychological issues such as inadequate motivation, high trait anxiety and low self-efficacy, as well as social/environmental factors such as pressure from peers to engage in alternative activities, will affect the perspective an individual athlete brings to the training session (see Chapter 4 by Young and Medic for more

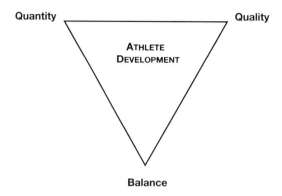

Figure 3.2 *The cornerstones of successful athlete development.*

on this). In order to maximize training for the developing athlete, coaches must attend to all of these factors.

A comprehensive plan for optimal athlete development should also recognize the diverse requirements of different levels of training. Below we consider how this three-factor approach can be applied to athlete development across a career, within a single year of training and within an individual training session.

Career plan

The balanced approach to managing training stress is essential for long-term athlete development programs. As outlined in Chapter 2, the DMSP developed by Jean Côté and his colleagues focuses on sport activities that are appropriate for athletes' specific needs at different levels of development (Figure 3.3). Early intense training is not appropriate because developing athletes are not typically capable of integrating this type of training stress, as evidenced by the decreased rates of enjoyment and increased rates of injury and drop-out associated with this training approach. Research suggests that the focus during early training should be on developing fundamental movement and cognitive skills, which lay the foundation for more specific and focused training in later stages of development. In the parlance of Côté's model, early sport experiences should focus on *sampling* a wide range of sports and physical activities, which will develop general physical and cognitive skills as well as psychological assets such as intrinsic motivation and self-efficacy. After this period of generalized involvement, athletes should begin

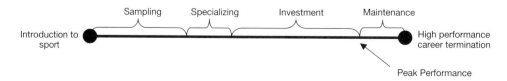

Figure 3.3 *Lifespan model for developing expertise (adapted from Bloom and Côté and colleagues).*

34

to focus their attention on specific skill development until it reaches the investment and maintenance stages where there is a solitary focus on sport-specific, deliberate types of practice.

The amount of time devoted to each stage (sampling, specializing, investment, maintenance) is dependent on several sport-specific contextual factors, including age of peak performance and the determinants of expert performance. Sports with earlier ages of peak performance will necessitate an earlier start to specialized training, whereas sports with later ages will allow for a more extensive period of generalization. Moreover, athletes in sports with aesthetic demands, such as gymnasts, often peak prior to biological maturation and, as a result, early training must be more specialized in order to amass the training required for performance adaptations. When developing training programs for athletes at a given stage of development, it becomes critical to balance the explicit requirements of the sport with the unique needs of the developing athlete.

Yearly plan

One method that good coaches use to manage training stress in their athletes involves dividing an athlete's training year into phases of training emphasis called *macrocycles*, with the length of each macrocycle varying relative to its proximity to upcoming competitions. For instance, recovery macrocycles (i.e., low-intensity cycles) usually occur immediately following the end of the competitive season (i.e., high intensity cycles) and are followed by a macrocycle focusing on physical preparation for the next year's competitive macrocycle.

Within each macrocycle are *mezocycles*, each made up of four weeks of training. The purpose of a mezocycle is to ensure that weeks of very high training intensity are followed by weeks of reduced intensity, thereby controlling training stress. The number of mezocycles in a macrocycle will vary relative to the length of the macrocycle. Each week of training makes up a *microcycle*. Training intensity in a microcycle is rotated in a manner similar to a mezocycle, where days of high training load are followed by days of reduced load. Figure 3.4 illustrates a hypothetical training program designed to balance training stress in manageable amounts across a year of training.

Daily plan

Research examining expert coaches (see Horton and Deakin, Chapter 6) typically shows that they spend a considerable amount of time planning individual practices. In order to optimize an athlete's training time it is critical to acknowledge the need for balance. At a very basic level, most practices begin and end with periods of reduced effort (warm up and cool down) to regulate the physical demands on the athlete; however, an optimized practice should have a plan for exposing athletes to the precise amount of training stress necessary for their continued adaptation. Optimized practice should also consider skill increments over time, as skill development is accompanied by improved movement efficiency, thereby reducing physical energy demands. Therefore, by necessity, optimal training and adaptation require regular evaluation of the rate of skill development, energy expenditure, as well as the overall fitness and well-being of all athletes.

35

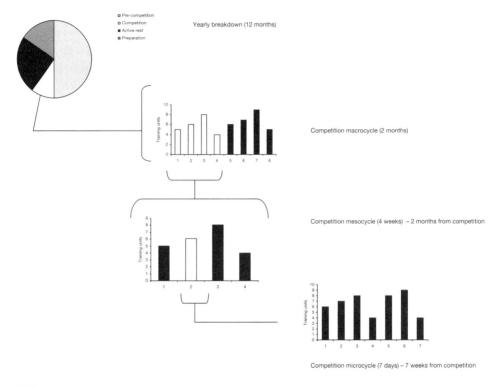

Figure 3.4 *Periodization model illustrating balance across different phases of training (adapted from Fry et al., 1992).*

Putting theory into action: dissecting your own training

In order to adequately assimilate the information in this chapter, it will be important for coaches and athletes to critically and objectively review their own training design habits. For example, they could consider a recent week of training with the following questions in mind:

1. What was the overall purpose of the week of training?
2. How did the individual training sessions fit together throughout the week?
3. What is the link between the current week and the preceding and following weeks?
4. How does this fit into the yearly plan for your athlete's development?
5. Based on the knowledge outlined in the preceding sections, how could this week of training be improved?

Once these questions have been considered for one week of training, coaches and athletes should consider other weeks to develop an understanding of the strengths and weaknesses of their training design practices relative to current empirical research. The challenge will be to identify consistently missed opportunities for improvement and modify behavior so they are not missed in the future.

Monitoring training effort

One of the most meaningful pieces of information that can be used by a coach relates to the actual measurement of the training stimulus an athlete receives. Recurrent, valid information about athlete training over time would provide invaluable data for designing the optimal training program. Ideally, actual training stimuli could be standardized to allow for an accurate evaluation of training stress from training session to training session. In reality, however, the physiological and psychological demands of different training activities make this quite difficult. Exceptions include sports where performance is largely determined by physiological parameters such as distance running and triathlon, which have similar performance and training requirements and allow overall training effort to be easily quantified by computing the training *load* associated with various forms and intensities of training.

To standardize different forms of training in triathletes, Hugh Morton and his colleagues developed a method where training time in each of the triathlon disciplines was converted into standardized training units (T_U) based on the duration and intensity of the activity performed. A T_U is made up of the product of the duration (time in minutes) and a weighting of intensity. Intensity is determined by the number of times the heart beats per minute (bpm), which can be measured using relatively inexpensive, commercially available heart rate monitors or by placing one's index finger on the carotid artery (or other artery) and counting the number of pulses per minute. The intensity weightings compare an athlete's heart rates during a training session with their maximal heart rate to attain a measure of how hard the athlete *worked* compared with how hard they *could have worked*. With this method, any form of aerobic training can be quantified using the equation in Figure 3.5, where D is duration of the activity, *HRex* is the heart rate during exercise, *HRrest* is the athlete's resting heart rate, and *HRmax* is the athlete's maximal heart rate. For instance, if an athlete's average heart rate during a 1-hour training session was 150 bpm, and their resting and maximal heart rates were 60 bpm and 200 bpm respectively, they would have performed 38.6 units of training.

The benefit of a standardized method of quantifying training is that it allows for the systematic and accurate profiling of athlete responses to varying training loads, which is particularly valuable for long-term development. However, this approach has many limitations. First, it is difficult (if not impossible) to quantify the cognitive/psychological demands of different types of training and, as a result, it only provides information about physiological training stress. Although this limits the formula's application in highly cognitive sports such as basketball, tennis, and cricket, coaches can still use the formula to monitor the stress associated with the physical aspects of training.

A simple way of monitoring all forms of training (and other) stress is through the use of practice logs that contain practice-to-practice information about training. Incorporating qualitative (such as a single question about whether practice was good, bad, or marginal) and

$$T_U = D * (HRex-HRrest)/(HRmax-HRrest)$$

Figure 3.5 Formula for standardizing physiological training stress in athletes.

quantitative (such as intensity measured via a heart rate monitor or the number of practice attempts at a given task) information into the log will allow measurement of the physical, cognitive, and emotional effectiveness of each training session. Although the specific design of the logs will vary from sport to sport and from coach to coach, they should provide information regarding training quantity (hours, minutes, attempts), quality (intensity), and balance (recovery from training stress, occurrence of other life stress). Moreover, the use of a similar log for coaches could provide additional useful information. Figure 3.6 provides an example of such a training log.

Generic Training Log (example)

[To be completed on the day following the training session]

Main training session target(s):   Microcycle number (1-4): _____

i) _____

ii) _____

Target total volume (hours & mins) of training in microcycle: _____

Target number of training sessions in microcycle: _____

Amount of time spent on targets during training session: _____

Number of attempts practicing targets (i.e. time/skill/technique or tactics):   _____

Accuracy in practice relative to target (i.e. time/skill/technique or tactics):   _____ %

Personal training session evaluation:

	Low									High
How physically effortful was the training session?	1	2	3	4	5	6	7	8	9	10
How much concentration and focus was required?	1	2	3	4	5	6	7	8	9	10
How relevant was training to performance improvement?	1	2	3	4	5	6	7	8	9	10
How much opportunity in the training session did you have to practice and rehearse skills, technique or tactics?	1	2	3	4	5	6	7	8	9	10
To what degree do you feel tired and muscle sore?	1	2	3	4	5	6	7	8	9	10
To what degree do you need more rest and recovery between training sessions right now?	1	2	3	4	5	6	7	8	9	10
How happy are you with training at the moment?	1	2	3	4	5	6	7	8	9	10
How happy are you with school/college/work right now?	1	2	3	4	5	6	7	8	9	10
How helpful/supportive are family, colleagues, and friends right now?	1	2	3	4	5	6	7	8	9	10
How good is your quality of sleep at the moment?	1	2	3	4	5	6	7	8	9	10
How fit and healthy do you feel overall?	1	2	3	4	5	6	7	8	9	10

Training units (T_U) monitoring for training session:

Duration of main practice (D in mins):	T_U target for session - T_U actual
Average heart rate in session (HRex):	T_U target for microcycle (MICRO)
Resting heart rate (HRrest):	T_U accumulated (Accum) in MICRO
Maximum heart rate (HRmax):	T_U MICRO – T_U Accum
T_U actual for session =	
T_U target for session =	T_U target for next training session

Figure 3.6 *An example of a generic training log.*

CONCLUSIONS AND GUIDELINES FOR COACHES AND ATHLETES

Our aim in this chapter was to provide an overview of recent findings from training and practice studies to facilitate the integration of this information into day-to-day athlete development. Below we summarize the most salient messages in a series of guidelines for coaches and athletes:

1. *When designing your long-term plan for athlete training, consider research applying Ericsson's theory of deliberate practice.* Is your practice designed to maximize the time spent with the athletes? Does it focus on quality or quantity? Do you extend the current skill repertoire of your athletes? How does each individual training session fit within a week of training? A month? A year? To be most effective, athlete development plans of all durations must be cohesively structured and interlinked.

2. *Be aware of the negative consequences of too much deliberate practice.* Deliberate practice, by definition, involves activities that are low in enjoyment, high in effort/intensity. As a result, an overemphasis on deliberate practice can easily lead to training plateaus and feelings of malaise associated with overtraining syndrome. If introducing this type of training to your group, experiment by exposing athletes to these conditions by degree. Try breaking up the periods of high physical and mental effort with intermittent breaks or changes in activity.

3. *Develop a strategic plan for athlete training and development specifically related to your level of competition and athlete ability.* Research has consistently and robustly indicated that athletes training at different levels of competition and with different levels of ability have dramatically different training requirements. It is critical that coaches and athletes design their training program with clear and relevant objectives in mind. Moreover, these objectives should be re-evaluated from time to time and adjusted as appropriate.

4. *Develop strategies to monitor exposure to training stress (and other forms of stress) in athletes to ensure balance and prevent staleness and other manifestations of ineffective training.* In this chapter, we discussed the use of standardized training units to monitor physical training stress. This is one option available to the progressive coach, but it should always be tempered with knowledge of psychological and cognitive stress. One simple way of monitoring all forms of training (and other) stress is through the use of daily practice logs that record information the coach can integrate into future training. These logs provide a useful tool for coaches and athletes.

Throughout this chapter, we have emphasized the relationship between training and environmental variables that promote or inhibit performance adaptations in athletes. Recent research provides exciting information for coaches to use to improve performance and development of their athletes. In particular, coaches and athletes should be mindful of striking the appropriate balance between meaningful, strenuous training and active or complete rest. This may be the coach's most important role. Careful attention to the balance between the quantity and quality of training within the context of the athlete's life may lead to the next level of sporting success.

COACH'S CORNER

Shannon Rollason

Head Coach, Australian Institute of Sport Swimming Program

Some background

My coaching experience started from the learn to swim area, juniors, then moved into the swim club juniors–seniors level. During the 1990s I had a 'licorice allsorts' approach within my squad that resulted in success as a club, but also with swimmers gaining national representation across all the strokes and distances. Since 2000, I have focused on the sprint events using a more deliberate practice approach. I believe this more deliberate approach to my training sessions has contributed to higher performance levels as a club and with athletes internationally. See Table 3.1 for a list of swimmers in my current squad.

Table 3.1 Shannon Rollason's AIS swimming squad (as of April 2007)

Swimmer	Stroke
Fran Adcock	100m and 200m backstroke
Angie Bainbridge	200m and 400m freestyle
Craig Calder	100m and 200m breaststroke
Sally Foster	100m and 200m breaststroke
	50m and 100m freestyle
Felicity Galvez	100m and 200m butterfly
Jodie Henry	50 and 100m freestyle: 2004 Olympic 100m Champion; World Record Holder 2004–06.
Belinda Hocking	100m and 200m backstroke
Alice Mills	50 and 100m freestyle: Commonwealth Record 50m, Freestyle and 200m Ind Medley
Reece Turner	200m freestyle
Tarnee White	50m and 100m breaststroke

Although I agree with the general concept of deliberate practice I don't know if my definition is exactly the same as the researchers (I'll let them decide that!). I always ask of my swimmers that if they are going to get into the pool to train then they must give 100 per cent and focus on what is required. All sessions are designed with the aim of making them race faster, although there are many ways to achieve this. Sometimes we can make this training fun, but often it is simply hard work. Certainly there is a minimum training load that needs to be completed, but quality is more important.

In my experience, I have definitely seen a relationship between the size of a swimmer's training history and their ability to adapt to training demands. The larger the volume of training completed, the quicker the swimmer adapts after a break or when something new is introduced into their program.

Macro level

I agree that we need continually to set challenges for the athlete to reach if we are going to get continued improvement. The way I do this is through planning. I look at four-year plans to coincide with the major competitive event in our calendar, which is of course the Olympic Games. Importantly, the training age of the athlete is critical in this planning. For instance I have a number of athletes entering their second Olympic cycle. I have developed a plan I feel will reduce staleness and get the best out of them in time for their second Olympics. The main change to their program is that I moved away from the training approaches that I thought were successful the last Olympic cycle. Hence, for the first two years of this new training cycle (2005 and 2006) I have tried new ways of training. In the third year (2007) I will gradually reintroduce what I thought were the best sessions or training approaches from the previous four-year block and integrate that with the new elements that have worked in the current four-year cycle. I have found this keeps the athlete mentally fresh and ready continually to try and surpass their previous best. Importantly, I am also invigorated by the changes to training and probably coach better as a result.

Micro level

Another critical aspect to training is reading the signs of your athletes in terms of their readiness to train. Body language, facial expressions, what they do and don't say all assist me to formulate the training plan for a week (see Table 3.2) or given session. I would like to think I am flexible enough to alter this when required. Hence, even though the theory of deliberate practice suggests you constantly need to up the ante, we have sessions where maintaining the current level of performance might be an achievement given the circumstances. Too much intensity without a break or too much high-volume, lower-intensity training can lead to burn-out, so it is critical to modify the training stress constantly.

Table 3.2 *A typical week for the AIS squad leading into the World Swimming Championships 2007*

Session	Description
Monday a.m.	Aerobic training with a progressive build-up in speed while maintaining efficiency. The focus of this session is on preparing the swimmers for the Monday p.m. session.
Monday p.m.	Quality high speed session: 8–15 second repeated efforts. If speed is good 30–40 seconds.
Tuesday a.m.	Gym and swimming in the pool with a focus on power. e.g. starts, turns, and pulling technique up to 8 seconds.
Tuesday p.m.	Endurance session: training sets depend on the athlete and event, but the working lactate range would be between 4mmol and 7–8mmol.

Table 3.2 Continued

Session	Description
Wednesday a.m.	Rest
Wednesday p.m.	Aerobic recovery: 4–6kms, heart rate kept under 60bpm. The exact number of kms depends on the athlete type.
Thursday a.m.	Skills session. Individualized approach based on athletes needs; e.g. focus on starts or turns etc.
Thursday p.m.	Quality backend speed: 30–40 second repeated efforts. Lactate range 12–16mmol.
Friday a.m.	Rest
Friday p.m.	Aerobic-threshold session: lactates 4–5mmol depending on the athlete and their event, and how they have coped with the training week.
Saturday a.m.	Gym and swimming session: aerobic over long distance at low intensity with a high expectation on skill execution.
Sunday	Rest

KEY READING

Baker, J., Côté, J. and Abernethy, B. (2003). 'Learning from the experts: Practice activities of expert decision-makers in sport'. *Research Quarterly for Exercise and Sport*, (74): 342–7.

Bloom, B.S. (1985). *Developing Talent in Young People*. New York: Ballantine.

Bompa, T.O. (1999). *Periodization: Theory and Methodology of Training*. Champaign, IL: Human Kinetics.

Ericsson, K.A. (ed.) (1996). *The Road to Excellence: The Acquisition of Expert Performance in the Arts and Sciences, Sports and Games*. Mahwah, NJ: Erlbaum.

Ericsson, K.A., Krampe, R.T. and Tesch-Römer, C. (1993). 'The role of deliberate practice in the acquisition of expert performance'. *Psychological Review*, (100): 363–406.

Fry, R.W., Morton, A.R. and Keast, D. (1992). 'Periodisation of training stress: A review'. *Canadian Journal of Sports Science*, (17): 234–40.

Hackfort, D. and Tanenbaum, G. (2006). *Essential Processes for Attaining Peak Performance*. Germany: Meyer and Meyer.

Morton, R.H. (1991). 'The quantitative periodization of athletic training: A model study'. *Sports Medicine, Training and Rehabilitation*, (3): 19–28.

Rushall, B.S. (1990). 'A tool for measuring stress tolerance in elite athletes'. *Journal of Applied Sport Psychology*, (2): 51–66.

Starkes, J.L. and Ericsson, K.A. (eds) (2003). *Expert Performance in Sports: Advances in Research on Sport Expertise*. Champaign, IL: Human Kinetics.

Chapter 4

The motivation to become an expert athlete
How coaches can promote long-term commitment

Bradley W. Young and Nikola Medic

Research on sport expertise has emphasized the large amounts of deliberate practice that must be amassed for aspiring athletes to become experts (see Côté and Fraser-Thomas, Chapter 2, and Baker and Cobley, Chapter 3). It is generally accepted that athletes need to engage in many years of continuous and focused training in sport before they may excel on an international stage. Talented performance is also the product of the environment in which an athlete interacts (i.e., training contexts) and the people with whom an athlete interacts in relation to their sport (e.g. peers, parents, and coaches). Developing athletes need to be motivated to practice on a near-daily basis over an extended period of time in order to attain expert levels of performance.

This chapter discusses the *motivation to practice* in individuals aspiring to become expert athletes. Although this has been identified as a ripe area for investigation, very little research has directly investigated it. Information pertaining to the topic is largely derived from international-level athletes recalling the conditions that motivated them in their childhood and teenage years. We present relevant information from these interviews complemented (where possible) with insights obtained from research in other achievement domains such as music and academia. The road to expertise clearly demands that a developing athlete have an intense and enduring persistence to their sport. Therefore, we also present information from other relevant motivation theories that have examined youth and non-expert populations. In these latter cases, we discuss factors that have motivated non-experts to persist or persevere. Generalizations are made to experts under the assumption that experts are ultimately the greatest *perseverers* over many years of training.

This chapter will discuss three themes that should help coaches understand the various factors and conditions that enhance and sustain the motivation of athletes through development from the *backyard to the big show*. Although we recognize the extraordinary influence that parental, familial, and peer influence have on developing athletes, it is our intent to focus our discussion of motivation on aspects that relate to coaches. Thus, with respect to each of the three themes, we offer applied guidelines or strategies that coaches might consider in their interactions with developing athletes.

THEME 1: THE QUEST FOR COMPETENCE AND MASTERY ENCOURAGES PERSISTENCE

Perceived competence refers to an individual's judgments about their ability in a particular sport. High levels are important because they facilitate positive expectations for success and behaviors such as persistence, the choice of challenging tasks, and high effort—these are all important for enhancing practice conditions. According to one model of motivation (Achievement Goal Theory), an athlete's motivation is also based on the types of goal they set for themselves (see Table 4.1). For instance, when an athlete is *task-oriented*, their perceptions of success are based on mastery criteria (i.e., whether they have made progress relative to their own previous standards, whether they have experienced improvement in specific sport skills) and self-referenced criteria, such as whether they exerted high levels of effort. On the other hand, when an athlete is *ego-oriented*, their perceptions of success are based on normative standards, such as outperforming or defeating others, and on achieving more with less effort.

Research with sub-elite and youth populations has shown that a high task-orientation is closely associated with many positive outcomes, even in athletes low in perceived ability. For example, athletes who have task goals perform better and spend more time practicing than those who have ego goals. Alternatively, high ego-orientation is associated with positive outcomes, but only when an athlete feels very competent in their capabilities. When an athlete who predominantly holds ego goals has fragile beliefs in their competence, their motivation is more likely to wane. One implication of these findings is that *coaches should find ways to*

Table 4.1 *Examples of task and ego goal statements made by young athletes when they feel competent during sport training*

Task goal statement	Ego goal statement
I worked really hard at nailing my landing on that vault maneuver.	I did the vault maneuver as well as all the others gymnasts without having to work hard at it at all in practice.
Because I can notice myself getting more accurate with my throws, I want to go and practice more.	I have the best scores for throwing accuracy compared with all the other players on our team.
When I learn a new skill, it makes me want to practice more.	I am the only one on our team who can do that drill right.
I pick up new skills in training by focusing on what I am doing and trying really hard.	The rest of the players in the group can't do as well as me.
Although others finish the workout intervals ahead of me, I have improved my personal interval times by almost two seconds, and this makes me want to train more.	I beat all the others in the intervals in workout. I'm the best.
When I practiced my start from the blocks and it became smoother and more powerful, it felt right.	
In practice, it is important for me to do my very best.	

enhance athletes' perceptions of competence. This seems increasingly important in children's competitive sport, which has many inherent features that are ego-involving (e.g. evaluations of the public performance, win–loss records, competition), and where winning is never guaranteed. As a result, developing athletes are often placed in situations during competition where their competence may be threatened. At least in the training environment, the role of the coach should be to emphasize task-enhancing conditions more often than ego-involving conditions. Coaches should try to find ways to structure the training environment so that it more frequently encourages athletes to adopt task rather than ego goals.

What factors contribute to an athlete's higher sense of competence?

Psychologist Alberta Bandura has an approach for enhancing an athlete's motivation that concentrates on the most significant sources of competence information. There are several sources, but the ones that appear easiest for a coach to convey directly in the practice environment are previous successful experiences, information derived from modelling (social comparison), and verbal persuasion. Most importantly, research has shown that the most successful athletes were typically provided with many opportunities to experience success during their developmental years. In younger athletes, opportunities for success are assured when complex skills are simplified or segmented properly, when instructions for drills or game rules are modified, or equipment is modified to reflect the needs and capabilities of athletes at this stage of development. For basketball players younger than 11 years of age, for example, it may be beneficial to practice shots at an 8-foot basket rather than a standard basket, allowing athletes to experience early success, which will probably result in higher perceptions of competence. Research has also shown that successful athletes more frequently evaluate their performance on aspects of mastery, enjoyment, and effort, rather than performance outcomes alone. Finally, successful athletes had coaches who more frequently emphasized instructions that were athlete-centred and focused on mastery, rather than on competitive outcomes alone. It appears that successful athletes learned how to evaluate their sport performance from a mastery perspective as a result of their interactions with their coach.

Research has also shown that athletic performance and persistence can be increased when athletes observe successful performances by someone else (i.e., a model). For example, if a young gymnast is uncertain about her capability to execute a novel and complex vault maneuver, she will gain perceived competency from first watching a similarly aged and similarly experienced peer perform it safely and with relative success. Without any prior experience on the vault task, and owing to the uncertainty that she has in her own ability, the gain in competency beliefs that she gets from watching a peer model becomes even greater. In addition to social modelling, athletes can use self-observation (e.g. watching their successful performances on video) to enhance perceptions of competence. This type of self-observation should complement more traditional strategies where coaches provide evaluative feedback for athletes' unsuccessful performances in order to work with them to identify discrepancies between what was done and what was intended, eventually helping them to correct and minimize mistakes.

Finally, research has shown that athletic performance and persistence can be improved by verbal persuasion. Coaches can be persuasive especially if they are perceived to be trustworthy and credible, or to possess expertise. In order to enhance persistence to practice, coaches should work with athletes to help them develop personal mastery goals.

How can coaches craft the motivational climate in training to encourage persistence?

In addition to focusing on the individual athlete, an emphasis on specific aspects of the training environment that is created by coaches (motivational climate) can positively influence an individual's goal orientations. Research has shown that, when coaches structure the training environment such that it emphasizes interpersonal competition and rivalry, and when coaches provide mainly normatively referenced feedback to athletes, an athlete is likely to adopt an ego-orientation. When coaches craft an environment that focuses on the learning *process* rather than *outcome*, the mastering of the skills, personal improvement, co-operation, and effortful involvement, an athlete is likely to adopt a task-orientation. If coaches can organize the practice environment so that athletes more frequently interpret their behaviors relative to task goals rather than ego goals, this will help to promote motivation to practice and persist. Because young athletes begin to judge their capabilities relative to others (i.e., normatively) around 12 years of age, coach strategies used to promote a task-oriented climate are especially valuable in late childhood and early adolescence.

In particular, one acronym, TARGET, has proven useful for enhancing young athletes' task goal orientations, intrinsic motivation, effort, and persistence. TARGET relates to structural features of the practice environment: *Task design*, *Autonomy*, *Recognition*, *Grouping*, *Evaluation*, and *Timing*. These practice design guidelines have been shown to enhance the task motivational climate because of their emphasis on individual challenge, short-term goals, individual skill improvement, and self-referenced criteria for interpreting success:

*   *Task design*: Drills entailing variety and diversity are most likely to facilitate learning, persistence, and task involvement. Athletes should engage in different tasks and have different assignments that allow them to develop a sense of their own competency without having to compare their performance with others'.
*   *Autonomy*: When possible, coaches should involve athletes in the learning process by giving them choices and distributing authority and responsibility. Players should occasionally be given the opportunity to choose the tasks they want to learn, be expected to set up equipment and drills, and monitor their own progress during testing sessions. It is important that athletes perceive these choices as meaningful as this will ensure that their interests guide their choices.
*   *Recognition*: Coaches can recognize good practice habits by giving rewards to athletes. It is important, however, that rewards be understood correctly by athletes. Rewards should not be perceived as bribes or controlling, but should convey positive information and positive feedback regarding an individual's skill acquisition. Rewards that are often public invite ego-enhancing comparisons between athletes. When recognition for accomplishment or progress is private between the coach and athlete, feelings of competence are less likely to derive from doing better than others and more likely to derive from perceptions of mastery.

- *Grouping*: The categorization of young athletes (e.g. into first team versus second team) during practice sessions should be avoided because of potentially high variability in maturity levels. The resulting motivational climate could promote low perceptions of ability in many group members and afford few opportunities to experience success for athletes who are late-maturers, relatively younger, or less experienced. This could eventually result in a greater likelihood of young athletes with elite potential dropping out of the sport. During practice, coaches should often include individual drills and, when these are impractical, they should consider small group co-operative tasks.
- *Evaluation*: Coaches should teach athletes to use self-referenced ways of assessing their performance during practice. Developing athletes should not only be recognized for their achievement outcomes, but also for their efforts and attempts to learn and master new skills. Evaluation should involve multiple self-tests, and self-tests should frequently be private in nature. When coaches offer evaluative feedback, it should be given directly to the athlete and not broadcast publicly.
- *Timing*: The *time* that coaches allocate for the completion of a practice task should be flexible and relevant to each individual athlete. Such flexibility demonstrates a coach's awareness of individual differences in their athletes' learning.

In sum, it is critical that coaches use the training environment to foster a strong task goal orientation and feelings of mastery and competence. This is not to deny that ego goals are important; in certain circumstances they stoke the fire that athletes need during competition. Coaches might even consider the discretionary use of ego-enhancing strategies in the practice environment (e.g. during game simulation drills or time trials, or privately with athletes who have strong ego-oriented dispositions). However, in light of the fact that youth sport is already laden with ego-enhancing features, and that the purpose of training is foremost skill development, our recommendation is that coaches should consciously construct their practice environment to emphasize task goals whenever possible, as this is most associated with the persistent motivation needed on the *road to expertise*. Deliberate attempts by the coach to structure the practice environment to promote a mastery focus should prove effective. Coaches might also consider doing formal goal setting exercises with their athletes with an emphasis on mastery goals that are both short-term and long-term in nature. Goal setting exercises will draw the attention of young athletes to sources of information that will enhance their sense of competence and positively influence their performance in training.

THEME 2: LONG-TERM MOTIVATION DEPENDS ON A TRANSITION TO SELF-REGULATION

In order for young athletes to develop long-term motivation, practice efforts in the early years of sport training must be positively reinforced in a variety of ways. Positive reinforcement is when rewarding conditions or materials are bestowed on an individual following desirable behavior, with the aim to increase the probability that those behaviors will occur in the future. Behavioral theorists argue that successful teaching and coaching occur through the effective arrangement of reinforcing conditions under which students learn. Effective reinforcers help speed up learning and performance levels that would otherwise be acquired slowly, by trial

47

and error, or not at all. Educational psychologist Benjamin Bloom (1985) conducted retrospective interviews with high-level performers in tennis, swimming, and music to uncover the conditions and activities that these individuals recalled as being important to their development. In our reappraisal of the rich information described in this research, we were able to identify many instances during the early years of sport involvement where experts' motivation to practice was reinforced by various agents—parents, the first coach, and indirectly by the local community.

Parental reinforcement

Parents were shown to be most influential in socializing children into sport. They introduced their child to the field and found their first instructor. Parents also played a critical role in helping to establish early practice routines. They instilled a value for sport in their child, and had high expectations. During this time, parents used a variety of positive reinforcers such as praise and material rewards and, on some occasions, used sanctions to discourage improper practice behaviors from emerging.

Effective reinforcement by instructors during the earliest years of development

Based on Bloom's interview research, we discovered four commonalities regarding how coaches reinforced an expert's early motivation to practice. First, the initial coaches took a *special interest in the child*. The instructors designated the child as a *fast learner* relative to their peers, and this attribution guided the amount of time that they spent with the child. Experts recalled that special attention (e.g. extra practice time with the coach) reinforced a feeling of uniqueness in them and provided motivation to work hard in practice in order to continue getting this attention. Second, the coaches offered *praise and approval* to make early drill work more interesting. In tennis practices, for example, coaches offered praise and positive feedback for displaying mastery. Initially, coaches praised players 'just for getting the ball in' and freely gave positive feedback for successful approximations of skills. Some players recounted that their first coach was quite liberal with positive feedback, offering it 'anytime they did anything right'. Third, coaches offered tangible *rewards and prizes* as motivational incentives during drills and tests in practice. For example, tennis coaches rewarded children with soft drinks, candy, and sometimes money, for successfully hitting targets set up on the other side of the net. Finally, initial coaches *monitored and tracked progress* by closely observing and keeping records of the child's improvements and learning. Coaches then used these records to prove to the child that they were progressing and that, if they kept at it, they would make further advancements.

Clearly, the initial coaches used a multitude of reinforcers to motivate experts when they were child athletes. Instructors rewarded effort, performance improvements, and enthusiasm during practice. Experts reported that their first instructors almost exclusively used positive instead of negative reinforcement, and never mentioned instances of punishment by their first coach. It appears that the emphatically positive nature of coach reinforcement is important, a notion that is confirmed by other youth sport research. For example, the sport psychologists

Smith, Smoll, and Curtis (1979) demonstrated how deliberate attempts by coaches to use regular positively oriented feedback results in athletes who enjoy the sport experience more, like their coaches and team-mates to a greater degree, and, most importantly, are more likely to return to play for the following season. Positive coach reinforcement is related to persistence in sport, at least for young athletes. The behavioral coaching literature also suggests several ways in which the reinforcement strategies used by coaches should change over time. Whereas instructors should initially reinforce mastery instances quite liberally, and rather immediately, this reinforcement should be presented more intermittently and in a delayed fashion as athletes develop and age.

Coaches provided opportunities to experience success through early competitions

Coaches entered children in local contests and competitions in the early years, indirectly affording broader opportunities for social reinforcement. Coaches emphasized the need to enter competition early where children could demonstrate their skills, test themselves, and be rewarded for their past practice efforts. Competition enabled developing athletes to discover reasons to work further. Opportunities to display competence, either by winning or doing well in an event, became incentives to do more intensive practice. World-class tennis players recalled that, as a younger player, losses to older opponents by progressively less each time in early rounds of tournaments were incentives to keep working hard in practice. Eventual Olympic swimmers were not necessarily record-breakers from the start, but they did well enough that their successes reinforced their practice efforts and further motivated them to increase their involvement, to swim more often, and to swim against better competition. In the first year or two, the practice routine of experts was adhered to in large part because teacher and parent approval was reward for their progress. However, as athletes progressed in age and development, their sources of perceived competence changed from coach and parental approval to the reinforcement and recognition of their development and accomplishments by the local sport community or by media coverage. The opportunities for such reinforcement were indirectly related to coaching decisions regarding a child athlete's entry into competitions and tournaments. Recognizing that the sense of competence derived from public recognition of sport accomplishments is very much ego-oriented, it is imperative that the coach continues deliberately to structure the motivational climate in daily training so that it accentuates a mastery goal focus.

The transition to self-regulation

In Bloom's research, positive reinforcement by the coach was reported as an important source of motivation in the first two or three years of athletes' sport training, for athletes whose starting ages ranged from 7 to 11 years. It should be noted that this information pertains to two sports, namely tennis and swimming, where athletes generally train close to 10–15 years before reaching international levels. In the early years of development, the coach has various means of reinforcement to regulate the actions of athletes with respect to training and is, in many respects, responsible for their early motivation to practice. In certain sports, coach

49

reinforcement is effective in the first few years as much of the training that an athlete does is prescribed and closely monitored by the coach. However, as athletes develop, there should be less emphasis on reinforcement by the coach, and increasingly greater emphasis on teaching the athlete how to self-reinforce. Ultimately, at the highest levels of development, the athlete should regulate their own motivational incentives. This is particularly the case in sports where an athlete must engage in increasing amounts of deliberate practice without a coach. For example, it is not uncommon for elite 17-year-old athletes in sports such as distance running, cycling, or triathlon to spend more than seventy per cent of the training time outside the supervision of a coach. In the later developmental years, athletes must take on greater responsibility for effectively self-controlling, or *self-regulating*, their practice routines. At expert levels, the responsibility for generating and maintaining motives for practicing rests with the athlete themselves, rather than with others such as the coach.

Self-regulating athletes demonstrate responsibility for planning, monitoring, and evaluating aspects of their daily practice routines as they relate to an overriding long-term goal. Self-regulating athletes demonstrate proactive efforts to learn how to effectively to control the intensity and duration of their behaviors across a multitude of potential training activities, while negotiating variables such as fatigue and injury, and while considering how the chosen training activities serve their preparation for upcoming competitions. Expert athletes engage in this self-regulatory process across weeks, months, and years of training in order to optimize training conditions and continually to maximize their development.

Drawing upon research with acclaimed writers and academics, Barry Zimmerman (1998) described pertinent psychological processes that underscore self-regulated learning and proposed that a self-regulatory cycle was important for exceptional development in various domains, including sport. The psychological processes of *goal setting, self-monitoring, self-evaluation*, and *self-reaction* were extremely important. Self-regulated learners always set goals for daily productivity and made lists of things to accomplish prior to practice sessions. They systematically self-monitored by observing and tracking their own efforts, performance, and event outcomes during training. By self-monitoring, they were further encouraged to self-evaluate the outcomes of their behavior during practice sessions, and to evaluate skill-based progress. Self-reaction was a natural extension of self-evaluation for self-regulated learners. If they observed their own outcomes favorably, they often rewarded themselves. For example, if they were satisfied with their level of effort/productivity in a just-completed practice session, they would give themselves leisure time in front of the television. Conversely, if they were dissatisfied, they would deny themselves such a luxury and would instead 'punish' themselves by doing chores or housework. In this manner, self-regulated learners were skilled at self-reinforcing practice behaviors that they acknowledged as beneficial for their development, and at discouraging themselves from actions that they judged to be ineffective during training.

By self-monitoring and self-evaluating after each practice session, self-regulated learners gain information about learning processes that can be used to change subsequent training goals, strategies/activities, or practice efforts. Zimmerman suggested a four-step self-regulated learning (practice) cycle (see Figure 4.1):

- *Step one*: An athlete sets goals for how they want to perform in practice. The athlete should identify performance aspects and technical elements that they need to work on to improve their current skill level. They should strategically plan how to address those needs in training (e.g. which types of drill should be done? what activities should be prescribed?).

- *Step two*: An athlete makes himself or herself aware of whether they have chosen the correct means of addressing their weaknesses in practice—this can be done by constantly monitoring how training activities are executed.
- *Step three*: By monitoring his/her event outcomes (e.g. interval times, heart rate, shooting percentage, accuracy scores, etc.) after each practice, and cumulatively over weeks of practice, the athlete can become aware of whether the chosen practice strategies are improving his/her performance.
- *Step four*: The athlete evaluates whether the practice strategies have resulted in the desired improvements. If they have not improved adequately, the athlete might consider modifying their initial practice activities/strategies, or perhaps revisit their original practice goals. If the athlete decides that they have made sufficient improvements, they will reinforce their current training behaviors and might consider other goals that they need to work on in training.

Coaching strategies for encouraging self-regulated practice habits in athletes

After a practice session is completed, the physiological training benefits may not be fully realized for several weeks. Moreover, performance outcomes are achieved only after months

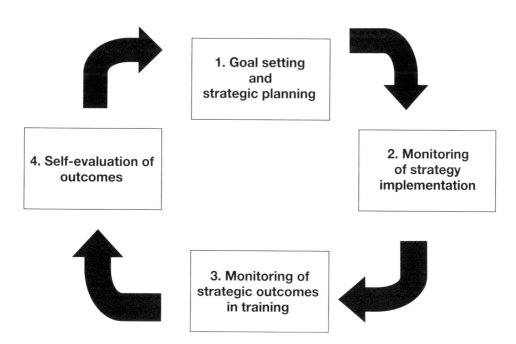

Figure 4.1 *The four steps in a cyclical model of self-regulated learning for sport training (adapted from Zimmerman 1998: 83).*

of accumulated practice bouts. It is sometimes difficult for athletes to remain motivated with such delayed outcomes. By encouraging athletes to keep track of their daily self-regulatory thoughts in a personal journal, coaches can help athletes become aware of relationships between their prior practice strategies and eventual performance outcomes. A *personal training log* of information about prior practice bouts (with documentation about strategies, activities, efforts, and productivity) is extremely important because it allows athletes the opportunity to reflect upon successful links between training and outcomes. By studying such cause–effect links, an athlete is able to shepherd their motivation across long periods of training with the faith that what they are doing in training now will manifest itself at later points in time.

A personal training log is a medium within which athletes can self-monitor, self-evaluate, and self-generate feedback about their goal-oriented training behaviors. If done regularly so that it becomes habitual, training log use encourages the self-regulatory mechanisms that underpin the motivation to practice over extended periods of time. Elite athletes testify to the value of personal training journals, and our own recent field research demonstrates the value of regular log use. An intercollegiate swim team who used take-home training logs for one month showed significantly better compliance with their coaches' in-pool training prescriptions, and reported greater intention to be at all practices on time. After developing a routine with training logs, swimmers felt that they were more confident in regulating their lives away from the pool in order to arrive punctually for all practices.

Coaches should introduce personal training logs to athletes in early adolescence. Initially, coaches will need to educate young athletes on the value of such logs from both a motivational and an informational perspective. Coaches can instruct the athletes on what type of information is typically maintained in a training log. This information should be sport-specific and, early on, generic in nature. For example, athletes could be instructed to record information about a just-completed training bout (e.g. number of sets, repetitions, pace times, and recovery intervals) immediately after practice while still on-site. When the athletes are young, the amount of information to be monitored should be limited. Periods at the end of practice should be scheduled to allow athletes to use their logs and to interact with the coach as they would for any other practice activity. During such interactions, coaches might teach athletes how to recognize progression and evidence of mastery by encouraging athletes to compare their effort, performance times, and/or strategies on successive workouts.

The coach should direct training log use until they sense that the athletes are developing a personal accountability to their logs. As this becomes apparent, coaches might schedule on-site training log completion sessions more intermittently, instead encouraging athletes to record and reflect in their logs at home. Coaches might selectively reinforce the on-site use of logs after certain practices, for example, after standard *barometer* workouts that repeat several times over the course of the annual training cycle. In this manner, monitoring becomes necessarily tied to the athlete's personal search for improvement and mastery, thereby encouraging self-evaluation. Coaches might inform athletes that their personal logs can be more than just archives of quantitative measures, but also forums for journaling and commenting on how they felt about their workouts. If the athletes *buy into* self-monitoring and self-evaluation, they should naturally begin to self-reward in their logs as well. As older athletes make a habit of using their take-home logs, both athletes and coaches can begin to view the log and its information as conversation pieces to discuss:

(a) what has been (or has not been) working in practice, and
(b) levels of preparedness for future competitions.

The information that is contained within personal logs will evolve depending on the personal needs of each athlete and their level of development. For example, logs might begin to accommodate more than just information specific to training prescriptions, such as aspects related to recovery (e.g. hours and quality of sleep, resting heart rate), fatigue, and muscle soreness.

THEME 3: EXPERT MOTIVATION INVOLVES A PROGRESSIVE COMMITMENT TO ONE SPORT

The tremendous investment of time and effort by athletes who eventually become experts is the result of an intense and enduring commitment. Tara Scanlan and her colleagues (1993) conceived the Sport Commitment Model (SCM), a framework that outlines several factors that help to explain the nature of commitment. The SCM outlines five factors that influence a developing athlete's resolve and desire to continue in a sport. Four factors—sport enjoyment, involvement opportunities, personal investments, and social constraints—are positively related to increased commitment. The remaining factor— attractive alternatives—is negatively related to commitment. The SCM is valuable for understanding the long-term motivation of experts because it takes a holistic perspective to examine why an athlete chooses to commit (or not commit) to one sport among a host of other potential activities in their life.

Sport enjoyment refers to the fun, pleasure, and positive feelings that athletes derive from their experience in sport. Such feelings can be perceived in training and competitive contexts, as well as broader aspects of the sport experience. In the sport training setting, in particular, athletes might perceive enjoyment when they engage in deliberate play or free play activities (see Côté and Fraser-Thomas, Chapter 2, for more on this concept), when they experience discovery and the inherently pleasant sensations accompanying movement. Athletes also gain pleasure from instances of mastery during training. Sources of enjoyment in the competitive setting are often outcome-related and might relate to whether one is satisfied with winning, or achieving certain levels of performance. Athletes also derive enjoyment when their achievements gain them tangible rewards or social recognition. With respect to broader aspects of sport, athletes enjoy the new friends they meet, and the new places and the life events that they experience through sport travel. Enjoyment has consistently emerged as the strongest predictor of sport commitment in studies of youth athletes from a variety of sports. Research by Scanlan and colleagues revealed that adult international-level rugby players also unanimously identified enjoyment as a salient influence on their enduring commitment.

Involvement opportunities refer to enjoyable conditions that an athlete anticipates as part of their sporting experience at some point in the future. Developing athletes who perceive increasing opportunities associated with their sport involvement become progressively more

53

committed to their sport. Elite adult athletes are motivated by the anticipation of factors such as commerce, friendships, touring/traveling, or being selected to play in World Cup or international matches. Some evidence also suggests that opportunities for social recognition are more strongly related to commitment for elite youth athletes than opportunities for social affiliation.

Personal investments relate to the personal resources such as time, energy, and money that individuals have already put into their sport and that cannot be recovered if they quit. In theory, it is hypothesized that the more that has been devoted to the sport, the greater one's commitment to the talent field. Some research with youth athletes has demonstrated low to moderate support for this hypothesis; however, research with older adolescents and international elites shows that the relationship between personal investments and commitment is perhaps weaker.

Social constraints refer to perceived pressure from parents or coaches that instils a sense of obligation to continue involvement. Hypothetically, the more obligated an athlete feels to satisfy the desires or expectations of significant adults, the greater their commitment will be. Feelings of obligation are not necessarily healthy, intrinsic forms of motivation and therefore may lead to negative feelings if they are a primary motive for extended periods of time. Research findings pertaining to social constraints in the SCM have not been consistent. One interesting finding, however, was a positive relationship between coach obligation and sport commitment. Adolescent athletes reported greater commitment under conditions where they perceived pressure from the coach to keep playing their sport and that their coach would be upset and disappointed in them if they quit playing. Bloom's retrospective interviews with experts also uncovered information pertaining to obligation, which appeared in the earliest years of sport involvement. Many experts recalled beginning their sport because they wanted to please their parents or because they felt a sense of responsibility to meet the expectations of their first coach. Obligation as a form of motivation appeared very early in the developmental trajectory; however, as developing individuals became more self-motivated in their approach to practice, it faded as a prominent motive. For example, in a sample of New Zealand All Blacks rugby players, obligation was non-existent as a motive for sport commitment.

Attractive alternatives refer to the appeal of other activities that compete with continued participation in the main sport. An athlete will elect to participate in an activity other than sport if the perceived benefits of that experience outweigh the perceived benefits of sport involvement. An athlete's commitment reflects decisions that they make to maximize positive and minimize negative experiences. If valuable opportunities and enjoyment are no longer found in sport to the same extent as they could be found elsewhere, the athlete will probably withdraw from sport. The SCM presents a perspective in which the sport commitment of a developing athlete arises from the continual appraisal of costs and benefits associated with different types of activity.

The developmental path toward an exclusive sport focus

Most retrospective research on experts shows that as children they are as diverse in their extracurricular activity interests as less-skilled athletes (see Chapter 2 for more on this concept). Although there are exceptions for multidisciplinary sports (e.g. triathlon) and sports where performance is constrained by age of maturation (e.g. gymnastics), the developmental path of expert athletes generally shows a progressively exclusive focus on one sport across the adolescent years. In light of this trend, a consideration of attractive alternatives, particularly with respect to how they compare with enjoyment and valuable opportunities through sport, is important at different stages of development. In childhood, the benefits afforded to one sport should not enormously outweigh benefits from additional sports or non-sporting activities so that a *sampling* of activities can be maintained. Children should be exposed to benefits from a range of activities and should be afforded opportunities to enjoy various interests. Sampling protects the child from an overemphasis on one sport activity, which researchers have shown to be associated with later costs, such as lack of enjoyment, injury, and burn-out, that terminate sport involvement. Coaches should respect the need for young people to have well-rounded participation in various activities and refrain from demanding their all-or-none dedication to one sport in the early years. With regard to schedules, coaches should constrain the length of their sport season and respect the *off-season* as a time for young people to do other things. Within the sport experience, coaches should afford many opportunities for fun—play is particularly important.

From ages 13 to 15, when potentially expert athletes begin to *specialize* (see Chapter 2), the attractive benefits (real and anticipated) of involvement in one or two sports should be advertised and reinforced compared with benefits from alternative activities. The secondary sport of interest should ideally serve a cross-training function to complement the athlete's primary sport activity. With respect to the primary sport, costs will rise as developing athletes spend significantly greater amounts of time in structured practice. Coaches therefore should use strategies to emphasize the benefits of sport involvement for the athlete, to offset these costs. For example, coaches can schedule travel tournaments, team social outings, and other occasions that afford enjoyment. Within the sport arena, aspects of play should be maintained, and a mastery-oriented climate should be nurtured around structured practice activities. Coaches should also consider strategies to avoid committing athletes to more than two sports in a calendar year. If a developing athlete judges their involvement in three or more sports throughout the year to be attractive, then the athlete might develop a 'Jack-of-all-trades' mentality and will likely not have the proper commitment to realize their optimal development. By late adolescence, it appears that an almost exclusive commitment and *motivation to train* for one sport on a year-round basis is necessary to reach the international stage. Although costs of involvement in this one sport will certainly have mounted, it is imperative that supportive adults (including coaches) use strategies to highlight the overwhelmingly positive benefits of continued investment. Coaches might also clarify the large costs (i.e., the sacrifice of other competing interests) at the highest levels of development so that the athlete will make informed decisions regarding their commitment to the sport. Based on the SCM, adult experts should be understood as individuals who are exclusively committed to their sport because they perceive the positive opportunities associated with the experience still to outweigh the tremendous costs of time, effort, and money that could be invested elsewhere. Sport is still the most attractive activity in their life, giving them the greatest opportunities for enjoyment.

CONCLUSION

The intent of this chapter was to review themes associated with a *motivation to practice* that might explain aspects of long-term development of expert athletes. Generally, motivation to practice must endure over a tremendous amount of time if an athlete is to accumulate the requisite amount of deliberate practice to become an expert sportsperson. We have presented evidence that the motives for practicing on the *road to expertise* are varied. First, aspiring athletes must be engaged in a structured training environment that provides opportunities for success, that emphasizes a mastery-orientation, and that is rich with information indicating that they are becoming increasingly competent. Second, over the course of talent development, there must be a transition from coach and parental reinforcement (based on behavioral principles) in the early years to self-reinforcement and self-regulation by the athlete later in development. An aspiring athlete will not persist in the sport unless this change in the agency of motivation takes place in the middle years of development. To practice like an expert, an athlete must have refined self-regulatory skills and be responsible for his/her own motives for practicing. Third, it is important to consider the motivation of experts from a long-term and holistic perspective. As an athlete develops through the teenage years, there should be a gradual increase in commitment to the ultimate sport domain, at the expense of other interests. For a competitive athlete to persevere with their sport in late adolescence and beyond, the enjoyment and involvement opportunities associated with one sport must outweigh the attractiveness of all alternative activities.

Another goal of this chapter was to frame the motivational themes for consideration from the perspective of a coach. Thus, we have offered strategies and recommendations in light of each of our motivational themes that will hopefully inform how coaches choose and design training activities, how coaches structure their practice environment, and how coaches encourage their athletes to appraise their own training efforts.

COACH'S CORNER

Greg McFadden

Head Coach, AIS/Australian Women's Water Polo Team

Motivation can be influenced at an organizational and individual level

Establishing a coaching and learning environment that motivates athletes to develop their skills is a critical aspect of expertise development. My recent coaching experiences have provided me with some clear insights into the factors that influence the maintenance of motivation. Before my current coaching appointment as Head Coach of the National women's team I was the AIS men's coach. This program was set up specifically to develop our junior sub-elite male players (aged between 16 and 18 years of age), providing a pathway from junior competition into the open ranks.

A number of decisions we made at both the sport organization level and at the individual athlete level had pronounced effects on the players' motivation. At the organizational level, Australian Water Polo (our governing body) agreed to allow the AIS team to compete in the National League competition. Essentially, this meant talented 16–18-year-old boys were competing against men, including many of our Open National team members. We felt any risks, primarily to their ego, were far outweighed by the advantages of being allowed to compete on a weekly basis against physically bigger, more skilful and smarter players. Basically, we felt such an approach would fast-track the boys' skill levels. And it did.

A common question was 'how did you manage the group when they were getting beaten 20 goals to 3 each game?' This is where the importance of setting short- and long-term goals was highlighted. When playing against the top teams, we would set goals such as attempting to score 4 goals ourselves or restricting the opposition to 20. It was never about winning or losing. These goals would change against one of the lesser teams, where our goals may have meant we were going for the win. Evaluation of the players' performances in terms of their ability to execute the skills and tactics we had practiced was also an important aspect that helped us focus on process rather than outcome.

Interestingly, (at the time of writing) the World Governing Body (FINA) has decided to cease having an Under 20 (years of age) World Championship and instead wishes to introduce an Under 18 event in its place. From an Australian perspective, this is a negative, with the reasons directly linked to player motivation. It is unusual for a 17-year-old to force their way into the Open National team. Hence, after competing in the proposed Under 18 World Championships, these players don't have any International competitions as a carrot to motivate them to continue in the sport and aim their sights on making the Open team. As a result we are concerned many players may simply drop out or lose the desire to make that extra effort required to make it to the next level of expertise.

Both the above examples illustrate the powerful influence the sport organisation and its governing body can have on the potential motivation of the athletes. These issues are exemplified in sports such as water polo in Australia, where we don't have as many players in the sport to begin with relative to some of the other sports.

When looking at the motivation of athletes at an individual level, the chapter's description of athletes having a task- or ego-orientation toward goal setting is very much what I have experienced as a coach. Interestingly, I have found that those athletes that are on the periphery of a team and are the less-skilled players tend to have the ego-orientation. A good example is when they are dropped from a team. They often ask 'why me?' and say they feel they are more skilful than player X who I have kept in the squad. In contrast, the better players when dropped ask what they need to do to get better and see being reselected as a challenge.

When designing the training environment, athlete motivation is obviously critical. I tend to break down a skill or tactical situation to the level that the athlete can cope with so that they experience some degree of success. For instance, coaching shooting skill may start with a focus on using the legs, then we would progress to the lower body movement, and then finally the upper body contribution. Similarly, with tactics I may break the situation down to three attackers versus two defenders so that the attackers have the necessary time and space to work the move required. As success is experienced I will then add another defender, close down the space, etc.

Transition to self-regulation

My experience in coaching our senior women's team compared with the men's junior team (previously discussed) highlights how the development of self-regulation occurs as you become more experienced. The first thing you notice is that players take less of an interest in feedback from friends and family, who in most instances don't really understand the game anyway and just tend to give positive reinforcement. Rather, the players look for critical scrutiny: 'how can I get better?'. I often talk to the women about the importance of their being able to evaluate their own game. They should know whether they played well or not. I see my role as drawing their attention to whether or not they executed the more critical aspects of the team's game plan. It is up to them then to evaluate their own performance within that framework.

Coupled to self-regulation is the maintenance of motivation. We are always talking about how our team aim is to be the best team in the world, as illustrated by the team that won the 2000 Olympic gold medal. At a personal level this means the players' aim is to become the best player in the world in their playing position. As a coach this has established some great motivation as we now have a situation where there are multiple players competing for the same position in the team. I can constantly select different teams from one competition to the next, so that none of the players feels overly secure and they keep pushing themselves to become better than their current performance level. Importantly, the players have been educated about this selection process in advance, and so it isn't perceived as a negative but rather simply the way it is if you want to be the best.

Progressive commitment to one sport

I read with interest the section on the pathway to developing expertise. In the past, water polo had two pathways. You either were a swimmer and switched to playing water polo or you followed a seasonal approach where you played a team sport such as rugby league in the winter and water polo in the summer. Then, aged 16, you tended to commit to playing water polo. Generally, the players that played other team sports were more successful than those from a swimming background because they had an understanding of how to create space, when and where to pass, etc. Unfortunately I am a little concerned with the current situation where players are tending to specialize in water polo from much younger ages, i.e., between 12 and 14 years of age, because our playing seasons go for nine months of the year rather than just six months. This leads to players who become one-dimensional in their skill set and game understanding. Throwing a pass in water polo to a heavily guarded team-mate usually means your team-mate gets forced underwater, and the opposition steals the ball and swims off. Nothing much is said as the game simply continues on down the other end of the pool. If the same situation occurred in rugby league, the player having to catch the poor pass would get physically smashed by the opposition, and your team-mates would certainly let you know that the pass wasn't good enough. This understanding of when to pass and when to hold on to the ball is certainly transferred from one sport to the other, yet if the player has only played water polo the message may take longer to be learned purely because of the culture and nature of the sport.

KEY READING

Bloom, B.S. (1985). *Developing Talent in Young People*. New York: Ballantine.

Duda, J.L. and Ntoumanis, N. (2005). 'After-school sport for children: Implications of a task-involving motivational climate'. In Mahoney, J.L., Larson, R.W. and Eccles, J.S. (eds) *Organized Activities as Contexts of Development: Extracurricular Activities, After-School and Community Programs*. Mahwah, NJ: LEA.

Ericsson, K.A. (ed.) (1996). *The Road to Excellence: The Acquisition of Expert Performance in The Arts and Sciences, Sports and Games*. Mahwah, NJ: LEA.

Martin, G.L. and Lumsden, J.A. (1987). *Coaching: An Effective Behavioral Approach*. St. Louis: Times Mirror/Mosby.

Roberts, G.C. (ed.) (2000). *Advances in Motivation in Sport and Exercise*. Champaign, IL: Human Kinetics.

Scanlan, T.K., Carpenter, P.J., Schmidt, G.W., Simons, J.P. and Keeler, B. (1993). 'An introduction to the Sport Commitment Model'. *Journal of Sport and Exercise Psychology*, (15): 1–15.

Scanlan, T.K., Russell, D.G., Beals, K.P. and Scanlan, L.A. (2003). 'Project on elite athlete commitment (PEAK): II. A direct test and expansion of the Sport Commitment Model with elite amateur sportsmen'. *Journal of Sport and Exercise Psychology*, (25): 377–401.

Smith, R.E., Smoll, F.L. and Curtis, B. (1979). 'Coach effectiveness training: A cognitive-behavioral approach to enhancing relationship skills in youth sport coaches'. *Journal of Sport Psychology*, (1): 59–75.

Treasure, D.C. and Roberts, G. (1995). 'Applications of goal theory to physical education: Implications for enhancing motivation'. *Quest*, (47): 475–89.

Zimmerman, B.J. (1998). 'Academic studying and the development of personal skill: A self-regulatory perspective'. *Educational Psychologist*, 33(2/3): 73–86.

Chapter 5

Identifying and developing sporting experts

Jason Gulbin

Indeed, it is not difficult to imagine that some unsuspecting individuals will pass their lives unaware they possessed extraordinary talents in events such as luge or fencing or steeplechase.

(Thomas Rowland, 1998)

Tom Rowland's observations about unfulfilled sporting greatness are believable. For instance, the summer and winter Olympic Games provide the opportunity to compete in approximately thirty-five sports with almost four hundred separate events or chances to become an Olympic champion. Furthermore, with the inclusion of the non-Olympic sports, there are literally hundreds of unique sporting niches that may be perfectly matched to an individual's make-up. However, the reality is that individuals are likely to be exposed to only a handful of sports, with the short list typically influenced by a myriad of socio-cultural factors such as parents, peers, siblings, teachers, coaches, equipment, facilities, finances, time and transportation.

Although the aforementioned factors may affect the number and type of sports ultimately selected for specialisation, distilling potential into expertise requires a rare blend of genetics, environment, good planning and luck. Top class sporting potential is exhibited by many, but attaining sporting expertise and, better still, sustaining it (e.g. sports mastery) are the domain of the few. An expert athlete is characterised by moving within a defined space, in a defined way, within a defined time frame with the aim of producing a defined level of performance. Therefore, predicting years in advance how an athlete might jump, balance, learn, evade, react, spin, stroke, stop or start in a competitive environment is an incredible expectation! Predicting the next generation of sporting masters such as Lance Armstrong, David Beckham, Michael Jordan or Ian Thorpe is highly improbable, particularly when the evidence regarding the constitution of sports mastery has yet to be catalogued. That said, both the art and science of talent identification can increase the probability of identifying and developing individuals with the potential to become sporting experts.

ADOPTING A REALISTIC POSITION ABOUT THE ORIGINS OF TALENT

Currently, there is a major disconnect between sport expertise theory and the conduct of applied programmes in high performance sport. A number of published works have been abundant on philosophy but scarce on hypothesis testing and application. Based on the often cited retrospective observations of expert musicians, cigar rollers and chess players, sport expertise theory has not extrapolated well to athletes. This is highlighted by psychologist Anders Ericsson's extreme pro-environmental position in relation to the acquisition of sporting expertise (see Baker and Cobley, Chapter 3). Ericsson *et al.* (1993) maintain the belief that everyone is capable of becoming an expert provided they engage in high-quality practice and begin their specialisation as early as possible. This would translate to a talent identification programme that would be inclusive of absolutely everyone and ideally aimed at very young children. As noted by sport scientist Joe Baker (2003), such an approach should be discouraged given the pitfalls of early specialisation for later specialising sports.

Without putting too fine a point on it, theories such as these have yet to be supported by a single prospective study. For example, research would be required to demonstrate that physiologically unremarkable individuals, as evidenced by average maximal oxygen uptake, can achieve sporting expertise in endurance events such as middle distance running or time trial cycling.

Similarly, other untested academic theories in talent identification have also failed prospectively to develop sporting experts from theoretical philosophies. For example, one researcher, Angela Abbott, has provided a perspective that, because psychological skills may discriminate between experts and non-experts, it must automatically follow that psychological attributes must become the fundamental factor on which to base selections of future talent (Abbott and Collins, 2004). Yet, in practice, it would be difficult to find a coach or talent spotter willing to select a world-class cyclist, for example, based on psychological skills alone. The evidence is clear: world-class cycling performances are achieved by those who have inherited and developed outstanding physiology. When physiology is more or less matched within a homogeneous pool of world-class cyclists, only then do psychological and tactical discriminators become highly important.

Thus it would seem that the balanced view of genetics and environment both contributing to the origins of talent is a more realistic position. Rather than debate whether nature or nurture is responsible, established research suggests that the relative contribution of both is the only point of difference. In practice, Australian swimming physiologist David Pyne has noted that swimming success can be achieved by both the genetically gifted 'thoroughbreds' and the 'workhorses' who are characterised by less natural ability but greater work ethic and dedication to their training.

One philosophical model that seems to have got it right is that proposed by Françoys Gagné (2003). As illustrated in Figure 5.1, Gagné sensibly integrates the contribution and order of nature and nurture to the evolution of natural gifts and the subsequent and systematic development of outstanding talents. Basically this model asserts that the origins of talent begin with innate natural gifts or abilities that are transformed into expert performances via learning and practising throughout development. The rate of this skill acquisition phase is

61

ultimately influenced by three significant catalysts: chance events (e.g. good and bad luck, chance of being born into the 'right' family), intrapersonal factors (e.g. motivation, perseverance) and environmental factors (e.g. coaching, access to resources). The conceptual model provides a clear framework that is inclusive of both the biological and social sciences and, importantly, resonates with what actually happens in talent identification practice throughout many elite sport agencies.

THE TALENT IDENTIFICATION PERFORMANCE CURVE

The odds ratio of forecasting sporting experts from a novice or sub-elite level can be improved greatly by an evidence-based approach. Enhancing the probability of identifying and developing a talent pool with the potential to become sporting experts would ideally follow the sequence below:

1. establish a clear strategy or objective for the programme
2. orchestrate a quality talent development environment
3. undertake an evidence-based identification phase.

It should be noted that at first glance the sequence may appear out of order, with some expecting points 2 and 3 to be reversed. Unfortunately, this approach would reflect a poor example of a talent identification programme with the development phase addressed as an afterthought. It is relatively easy to screen, measure and identify athletes, but it is far more difficult to create an environment that allows the gifted or talented athlete an opportunity to thrive. By having a carefully planned talent development environment preceding the recruitment phase, the opportunity for athlete and programme disappointment can be minimised.

Figure 5.2 attempts to illustrate these main sequential elements associated with the aims, selection and delivery of a high-performance talent identification programme. In summary, the notable features depicted on the graph include recognition of key benchmarks, three distinct zones of variable width denoted by sub-elite, elite and mastery levels, and a representative performance time curve revealing a rapid period of early development followed by a slower performance progression over time.

The goal of the talent identification programme should begin with a gap analysis of the current talent pool in relation to the desired benchmark undertaken. Assessing the size of the gap is an important beginning as this will initially help with the talent identification strategy or its priority. In this case, the benchmark of interest is a world-level performance, and the relative difference between current national performances has been indicated. A small gap between the relative benchmarks might indicate that the current national talent pool is realistically capable of achieving world results and that resources might be preferentially deployed to support the current elite talent within the sport. On the other hand, a large gap between world and current senior national performances may highlight the weakness in performance depth and may require an injection of new talent. In the quest for medal success, the predicted separation between the entry point and the benchmarks of interest are an important consideration when time and resources are limited.

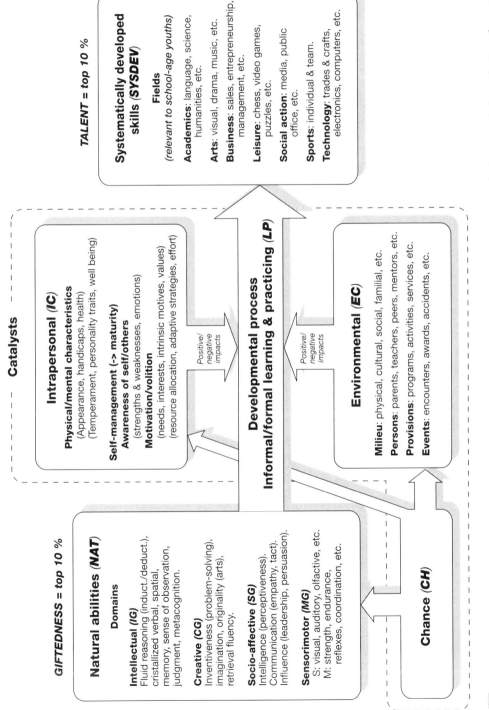

Figure 5.1 Gagné's Differentiated Model of Giftedness and Talent (2003). Systematically developed talents result from the transformation of innate gifts that are subjected to a learning and practicing developmental process. This process is affected by the three key catalysts of chance, intrapersonal and environmental factors.

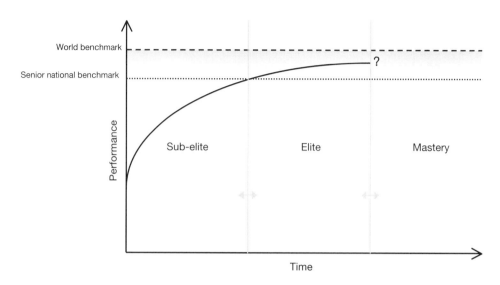

Figure 5.2 *Generalised time course for talent identification. The representative curve has been designed to illustrate the concepts of the talent identification process. Multidisciplinary research has an important role in modifying the shape and length of the performance curve.*

Injecting fresh talent into the elite competition level could occur through accessing talent from outside the sport (i.e., talent detection) or promoting existing sub-elite talent from within the sport (i.e., talent selection). Either approach is likely to help raise the level of the senior national performances in one of two ways. The first results from the higher-quality talent eventually surpassing the existing and inferior quality talent, and the second occurs as a result of 'upward-pressure' on existing athletes. This phenomenon occurs when the new talent creates a healthy competitive environment within the elite squad and forces the original talent pool upwards by challenging them to refocus on raising their own level of performance.

Exactly where the performance curve begins (that is, the entry point for the talent) will depend on the age and quality of the athlete, the relative benchmark of interest, and the type of sport. Younger and novice athletes will typically be further away from expert benchmarks, whereas older and experienced athletes are capable of commencing much closer to them. Sports where the depth of competition is shallow and the demands of the sport are more easily quantifiable have a higher possible entry point. For example an experienced sprint athlete can progress rapidly from novice to elite bobsleigh competition, whereas the separation between sub-elite and elite level performance in golf could be substantial. In the case of the sprinter switching to bobsleigh, the sub-elite entry point could be very close to the national benchmark level followed with a short transition time period and steep rate of development as the athlete moves from sub-elite to elite level competition. Conversely, an inexperienced (or novice) golfer would typically enter at a much lower entry point and probably experience a more modest rate of development over a reasonably longer time period before reaching the first benchmark. This is in part owing to the fact that the sport of golf is extremely popular and accessible to many people, and golfing performance is arguably less reliant on rare inherited physical and physiological traits.

Promoting higher entry points for the talent identification performance time curve will be affected by the quality of the selection process. The fundamental principle of talent identification is to understand as fully as possible the demands of elite performance in order to select these qualities in emerging athletes. Scientific research is critical to maximising our understanding of what it takes to make it to the top in sport. Of course there will always be exceptions to any rule or typical data set, but the observed anthropometric, biomechanical and physiological demands that have been well quantified in many sports are a key beginning.

Although many sport performance data have been collected in laboratories, there are an increasing number of studies that are collecting excellent information from real-time field and competition trials. This has the capacity to greatly assist our understanding of the requirements for success. For example, it is well known that world-class road cyclists have impressive aerobic power that enables them to maintain high power outputs for extended time periods. However, AIS scientist David Martin has demonstrated, using data collected directly from instrumented cranks at international competition, that there is much more to the story than having a big aerobic engine. For example, Martin discovered that, in comparison with non-top-twenty female road cycling competitors, the top twenty riders spend more time in high intensity output bands (>7.5 W.kg), and less time in the very lowest power bands (<0.75 W.kg). Thus, the data reveal that, in addition to traditional aerobic cycling tests, the talent identification of potential elite women cyclists must also include tests that measure the athlete's capacity repeatedly to produce energy anaerobically. When future studies quantify the skill and tactical capabilities of the elite rider, then talent identification cycling programmes will attempt to find and replicate these traits in the physiologically talented.

A major goal of the talent identification programme is to facilitate rapid skill acquisition and to launch the talent into senior national level competition. The shape and length of the performance curve will be influenced by Gagné's catalysts of chance and intrapersonal and environmental factors, with the quality of athlete and coach being a significant modifier. As depicted by the graph, the talent identification process has performed its function when the sub-elite talent crosses the threshold into elite or senior level competition. Whether that athlete remains at this level or progresses to mastery levels is beyond the predictive capacity of the talent identification process. The certainty in predicting absolute winners or long careers within elite sport is extremely low.

MODIFYING THE TALENT IDENTIFICATION PERFORMANCE CURVE

The discipline of skill acquisition has an enormous role to play in helping coaches and athletes modify the shape and length of the development curve. The goal of any intervention should be an increase in the amplitude of the curve (e.g. achieve world best), reduction in the time spent within the sub-elite zone (i.e., increased rates of development), and then an increase in the length of the curve beyond the sub-elite zone to achieve long, injury-free careers potentially leading to sport mastery. The science of skill acquisition has a number of opportunities to modify all aspects of the talent identification performance curve, but has the potential to be especially influential at the pre-entry and entry levels, and in the sub-elite zone.

65

Pre-entry level

Social research data are indicating that there is a decline in physical activity levels in children and a decrease in the quality and volume of physical education. Thus it would seem that long term, the apparent decline in fitness, activity and health has the potential to significantly compromise the entry level of talent into high-performance sport.

The talent flow diagram (Figure 5.3) illustrates the importance of the undifferentiated talent that forms the origin of the talent flow. Basic fundamental movement skills are acquired through play, school and clubs in this important sampling period. Emerging from this population of early movers are two major talent pools. According to Gagné, the *gifted* are considered to be the top 10 per cent of the population that spontaneously demonstrate their abilities with little formal and systematic training. In contrast, *talented* athletes represent the top 10 per cent of those who express their skills and abilities following a systematic development phase. In other words, a gifted athlete could high jump a bar set at 2 m with minimal practice, whereas a well-coached and practised high-jump talent could achieve the same benchmark with a far more polished and refined technique. These two differentiated pools ultimately converge to produce sub-elite and elite athletes. As noted in the illustration, the talent can flow between these talent pools.

Although it is not unusual for gifted academics and musicians to be exposed to accelerated learning environments, it is rare that the motorically gifted are provided with the equivalent opportunity. These individuals are characterised by demonstrating outstanding physical skills and co-ordination that would outrank approximately 90 per cent of their peers. Those with poor innate sensorimotor abilities are often provided with remedial support, but few programmes, especially within the school curriculum, target the gifted mover.

An interesting approach recently implemented by the Swiss Olympic Association (SOA) has been to support gifted movers through their 'Talent Eye' pilot programme. As a key stakeholder in the end process of the athlete development pathway, the SOA has elected to

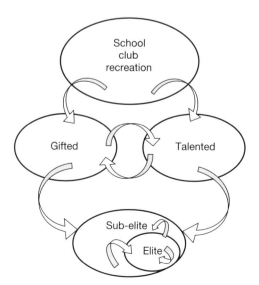

Figure 5.3
Talent flow in high-performance sport. The flow of athletic talent begins with the undifferentiated talent at the flow's spring, to the cascading and recirculating talent within and between the gifted, talented, sub-elite and elite talent pools.

be proactive in providing extension opportunities for the motorically gifted, rather than passively accept what talent ultimately presents to them. The regional scheme involves bringing together the best 6–8-year-olds who are demonstrated standouts in physical education classes. One afternoon per week, in a central location, the students engage in specialised movement classes and then try multiple sports via introductory lessons one other morning per week. Thus, the students are exposed to advanced instruction and challenge and a broad movement base. Other useful aspects include the child's experience of playing and competing with other gifted children in the region rather than just dominating a single class or year level within the school. Additionally, children are presented with a 'smorgasbord' of sports to try, which is especially convenient for parents wanting to present sporting options to their children.

This model provides an interesting approach that attempts to develop a rich repertoire of movement skills at a critical age period that may ultimately lead to higher residual levels of gifts or talent. This in turn may lead to higher entry points into the sport-specific talent development pathways and the opportunity to favourably modify the talent identification curve. At this point, intervention programmes at the headwaters of the talent flow remain speculative, and longitudinal case/control studies evaluating the effectiveness of these programmes are required.

Entry level

Improving the probability of identifying which intake of gifted and talented athletes are capable of advancing towards the benchmarks of interest requires a clearer picture of what constitutes an elite performer. Multidisciplinary scientific approaches are required to develop richer data sets that can help to deconstruct the qualities of elite athletes. This would require longitudinal and intervention studies from the sociological, psychological, molecular biological, physiological, biomechanical and technological sciences to advance our knowledge and understanding of the phenomenon of sporting expertise. The pay-off will be a greater conversion from entry level to elite.

For some sports higher entry points are possible to avhieve. As indicated in Figure 5.3, the talent flow diagram illustrates the capacity for talent to recirculate and to allow sport switching or talent transfer opportunities. That is, a sub-elite athlete in one sport may become an elite athlete in another, or vice versa. This is the case of Rowland's unsuspecting steeplechaser spending their precious but limited development years in a sport where the development curve simply may not lead to expertise. However, equal interchange between sports is not possible. Some sports such as gymnastics and athletics have a broad appeal to a number of sports, and tend to be a donor to a number of recipient sports capable of accommodating these skills.

There are three levels of talent transfer that allow an athlete to redistribute their skills or physiology to potentially influence their entry level. Level 1 occurs when the donor sport closely matches the demands of the recipient sport. In this instance, the sports are similar and require similar skills and physiology (e.g. indoor volleyball to beach volleyball, sprinting to bobsleigh, BMX cycling to track cycling). Level 2 transfer occurs when athletes bridge the gap between quite different sports, although the physiology and skills between the donor and recipient sports are similar (e.g. gymnastics to diving, cycling to speed skating, weightlifting to shot-put). Level 3 is the domain of the gifted and versatile athlete who can transfer between

67

sports that are quite dissimilar and require very different skills and physiology (e.g. swimming to boxing, canoeing to judo, rowing to high jump).

There have been a number of documented instances where athletes have been able to transfer their skills and switch sports in even the highest echelons of competition. To illustrate this point, Table 5.1 provides a summary of those athletes who achieved expertise in different events at the Olympic Games through a talent transfer approach.

Sub-elite zone

Structurally, replicating environments where junior athletes in particular are exposed to top-class coaching and support structures in sport science and sport medicine and are optimally challenged in fun and competitive environments will accelerate sub-elite development. In numerous talent identification programmes implemented by the Australian Sports Commission, talent-identified athletes receiving highly skilled coaching and immersed within a cohort of equally competitive peers have achieved strong national and international competition results. Comparatively, injecting gifted and talented athletes into routine club environments, which can have inferior coaching, competition and sport science and medicine support, can lead to

Table 5.1 *Talent transfer examples of athletes who have achieved sporting expertise in summer and winter Olympic Games*

Type of transfer	Athlete	Donor sport and performance	Recipient sport and performance
Level 3	Eddie Eagan (USA)	boxing, light heavyweight 1920 — Gold	bobsleigh, 4 man 1932 — Gold
Level 3	Jacob Tullin Thams (NOR)	ski jumping, large hill 1924 — Gold	yachting, 8 meter 1936 — Silver
Level 2	Christa Luding-Rothensburger (DDR)	speed skating, long track 1984 and 1988 — 2 Gold, Silver	cycling, 1000m 1988 — Silver
Level 1	Willie Davenport (USA)	athletics, 110m hurdles 1964–76 — Gold, Bronze	bobsleigh, 4 man 1980 — Gold
Level 2	Chris Witty (USA)	speed skating 1998 — Silver, Bronze	cycling, 500m 2000 — 5th place
Level 2	Clara Hughes (CAN)	cycling, road race and time trial 1996 — 2 Bronze	speed skating, long track 2002 and 2006 — Gold, Silver, Bronze
Level 3	Hayley Wickenheiser (CAN)	ice hockey 1998–2006 — 2 Gold, Silver	softball 2000 — 8th place
Level 3	Igor Boraska (CRO)	rowing, eights 2000 and 2004 — Bronze	bobsleigh, 4 man 2002 — 26th place

* Donor refers to the original sport while the recipient sport receives the talent from the donor sport.

drop-out or poor performances. Although limited resources are usually prioritised for senior athletes, the potential to increase the sophistication of the learning and practising environment within a sub-elite framework, particularly at club level, is desperately needed.

The ideal balance between the quantity and quality of practice remains elusive, yet this has the capacity to drastically shape the direction in which the curve transitions to elite level competition. With respect to training volume, it is unequivocal that skill repetition will lead to an increase in skill execution. However, what might be the minimum volume of skill repetition needed to generate the same outcome? Would this be contingent upon the quality of the coach and athlete? Conversely, what additional learning experiences might be incorporated to supplement the training and maximise the rate of development? How can coaches maximise the inclusion of technology such as eye tracking devices, three-dimensional global positioning systems, virtual reality simulators, miniature cameras and integrated data recorders? Can advances in molecular biological techniques truly allow a coach to individualise a training plan so as to be certain of eliciting a response to any given stimulus? Can sophisticated non-linear modelling techniques provide more accurate measures of predicted versus actual development pathways?

Answers to unresolved questions such as these will emerge from much needed multi-disciplinary, evidence-based research. Teams of coaches, athletes and scientists focused upon fine tuning the shape of talent identification curves will significantly advance our understanding of how experts are identified and optimally developed.

COACH'S CORNER

Terry Holland

AIS and National Head Coach, Australian Women's Skeleton Program

On the perspective of innate natural abilities

How many piano concertos have you heard 'interpreted' by a computer that can approach that extra something that is provided by the emotional interpretation brought by a 'naturally gifted' classical pianist. You or I could take piano lessons every day for the rest of our lives and still possibly never attain the level of success that is realized by the 'naturally gifted' artist. The same applies for athletes. I am convinced that your success in any given sport is well predicted by the gene pool within which you swam. I need only look in the mirror to be reminded that I am almost exactly the same height and weight as my father and my paternal grandfather. Despite every possible natural approach to increasing muscle mass and speed, my performance output has remained within a certain range during my entire athletic career.

The feel-good psychology of 'if-you-want-it-hard-enough-you-can-achieve-it' is unsupported by actual fact and has resulted in far too many athletic hopefuls fruitlessly pursuing sport success for which they are actually unsuited (other than the fact that they possess irrational belief that the power of will can overcome their genetic disqualifications for success in a particular sport).

I am absolutely convinced that although you can teach a certain amount of skeleton driving skill to most people, there are definitely some individuals that will never have the cognitive ability and reaction capabilities to become effective drivers on a skeleton sled. For example, I have coached a number of athletes who clearly possess an innate ability to sense lateral movement without any visible input, whereas others have no idea whatsoever that they are skidding significantly. Some people have the temporal sense to know, at discrete moments in time, that they are moving fractions of a second faster or slower on one run compared with an immediately previous run.

On the pursuit of an evidence-based approach to athlete identification and development

One of the reasons that the research component of the AIS approach to skeleton has been fruitful is the fact that there has been good co-ordination between the researchers and the coach. The willingness of the AIS to understand that they knew the limitations of their scope in skeleton was one of the keys to the research success. Rather than impose preconceived, research-oriented convictions on how to approach finding answers for skeleton, the AIS group worked carefully in conjunction with the coach first to explore which of their research ideas might be fruitful when vetted by practical sliding experience. This common-sense, non-egocentric approach to things worked well in maximizing the quality of research results by avoiding unnecessary dead-ends that might otherwise have resulted in an intellectually isolated approach to research choices. The projects we took on were mutually agreed upon, and although some of the results were more applicable than others, there were no results that were a waste of anybody's time. Sometimes the simple knowledge of which path should not be pursued is almost as valuable as discovering which path warrants further investigation.

On the role of skill acquisition to future performances in the sport of skeleton

My research preference for skeleton is very heavily biased by the fact that skeleton is such an extremely venue-oriented sport. Because of the fact that actual experience on a particular track can so heavily outweigh any other combination of skeleton performance aspects (aerodynamics, runner/ice interaction, push times, etc.) the ability to gain experience on a track that is analogous to actual time on the specific track in question is the most important aspect of improvement in the sport, particularly for countries without domestic sliding facilities.

The development of virtual experience capabilities, in my mind, is far and away the premier task facing the development of medal-capable performance with the Australian skeleton project. Although there have been some prior attempts at a variety of computer-simulated sport experiences in the past, I think that the state of virtual reality technology development has advanced rapidly enough in the last several years to allow the opportunity for another attempt at applying the technology to skeleton. Just a simple look around at the state of the art in interactive video gaming technology should give reason to consider such an approach. The introduction of such game systems as the Nintendo Wii, with its real-time, interactive, spatially oriented controllers is just one example of the dawning of a new era of cost-effective interactive technology being applied to real-world movement and task-specific activity. I am convinced that there exists the as yet unco-ordinated presence of technical and software components in the current marketplace that could be assembled (by application-specific experts) into an affordable skeleton simulator that could allow unfettered virtual access to every track in the world. This would allow unprecedented preparation for competition at any level on any track, under any 'ice condition', and provide the biggest single advancement in the sport since the introduction of the helmet.

The other most significant research development that offers, in my opinion, the next greatest chance for valuable improvement is the application of rapidly evolving nano-technology. There have been significant developments in the nanotechnology field that I suspect have direct and beneficial application to skeleton, primarily in surface pattern on runner and skeleton pod use. The successful application of such technology could result in margins of improvement that would allow, with all other aspects being equal, the difference between podium finishes and almost-podium finishes. I think that the use of the correct developments in this technology will be as significant as the use of the 'hydrodynamic riblet' technology in the world of sailing ten or fifteen years ago.

On the importance of research complementing coaching

My recommendation to other coaches is simple. Put the development of your sport and your athletes first and foremost. By orienting your efforts toward another aspect of understanding your sport you may learn that you possess untapped knowledge about your sport that opens new possibilities that you had previously never enjoyed the chance to explore. The successful application of your knowledge will result in the successful track of your athlete's advancement to a faster and higher level of achievement in a shorter period of time. If you start each day questioning what you know and exploring the possibilities of what you don't know, then even simple trial and error will assist you in either reaffirming your convictions or discovering the existence of small areas of your sport that warrant re-examination. Push your technical support resources. Challenge them to expand their own perspective and challenge their own understanding of sport, and together both the coach and the researchers can co-ordinate the best possible approach to merging the value of experience with the possibilities of scientific research.

Figure 5.4 *AIS Skeleton athlete in action with a simulated sled push at the Australian Institute of Sport.*

KEY READING

Abbott, A. and Collins, D. (2004). 'Eliminating the dichotomy between theory and practice in talent identification and development: considering the role of psychology'. *Journal of Sports Sciences*, 22(5): 395–408.

Baker, J. (2003). 'Early specialization in youth sport: a requirement for adult expertise?'. *High Ability Studies*, 14(1): 85–94.

Ericsson, K.A., Krampe, R.T. and Tesch-Römer, C. (1993). 'The role of deliberate practice in the acquisition of expert performance'. *Psychological Review*, 100(3): 363–406.

Gagné, F. (2003). 'Transforming gifts into talents: the DMGT as a developmental theory'. In Colangelo, N. and David, G.A. (eds) *Handbook of gifted education*, 3rd edn. Boston: Allyn and Bacon, 60–74.

Gulbin, J.P. and Ackland, T.R. (in press). 'Talent Identification and Profiling'. In *Applied Anatomy and Biomechanics in Sport*. Champaign, IL: Human Kinetics.

Martin, D.T., McLean, B., Trewin, C., Lee, H., Victor, J. and Hahn, A.G. (2001). 'Physiological characteristics of nationally competitive female road cyclists and demands of competition'. *Sports Medicine*, 31(7): 469–77.

Pyne, D. (1996). 'Designing an endurance training program'. *Proceedings of the National Coaching and Officiating Conference*, Australian Coaching Council Inc., Brisbane, Bruce, ACT, Nov–Dec 1996.

Rankinen, T., Bray, M.S., Hagberg, J.M., Perusse, L., Roth, S.M., Wolfarth, B. and Bouchard, C. (2006). 'The human gene map for performance and health-related fitness phenotypes: the 2005 update'. *Medicine and Science in Sports and Exercise*, 38(11): 1863–88.

Rowland, T. (1998). 'Predicting athletic brilliancy, or the futility of training 'til the salchow's come home'. *Paediatric Exercise Science*, (10): 197–201.

Schumacher, Y.O., Mroz, R., Mueller, P., Schmid, A. and Ruecker, G. (2006). 'Success in elite cycling: a prospective and retrospective analysis of race results'. *Journal of Sports Sciences*, 24(11): 1149–56.

Section 2

Designing practice to make athletes think (but not too much!)

Chapter 6

Expert coaches in action

Sean Horton and Janice M. Deakin

A discussion of expert coaches never proceeds too far before the name of John Wooden is mentioned. The 'Wizard of Westwood' coached the UCLA Bruins men's basketball team for 27 years, compiling a .808 winning percentage along with a record ten National Collegiate Athletic Association (NCAA) titles, seven of those occurring in a row. Wooden was also an accomplished player in his day, and is the only person to ever be inducted into the National Basketball Hall of Fame as both a player and a coach.

Wooden's accomplishments have inspired numerous books and academic articles, along with endless speculation as to the secrets of his success. Critics note that he was blessed with phenomenal athletes during his tenure, such as Kareem Abdul Jabbar and Bill Walton, both of whom went on to spectacular professional careers. Wooden, however, also won championships with teams considered far less talented that were never expected to win.

Most would agree that Wooden's incredible success at UCLA establishes him as an expert coach. There is less agreement on what, specifically, constitutes that expertise. Is it his ability to produce wins and championships, or is it his ability to teach the game? Is it his ability to motivate his players, or his technical and/or tactical knowledge? Perhaps it is a combination of all of these things. Identifying and quantifying expertise in coaching remains a hotly debated and challenging task.

WHAT DOES THE RESEARCH TELL US?

Defining expertise in coaching

Trying to determine what defines an expert coach is problematic, for few objective standards exist by which to judge coaches. There is no international ranking of coaches, and no competition where coaches can test their skills against one another. By comparison, identifying expertise in athletes is a much easier task, as there are usually clear benchmarks for determining experts. Performance times, world rankings, or placement in major international competitions all provide clear-cut and reasonably objective measures of where an athlete ranks.

Coaches, on the other hand, are normally judged by the performance of their athletes. Compiling a high winning percentage, or developing a number of world champions is considered a sign of coaching expertise. Thus a coach's reputation depends as much on the success of their athletes as it does on their actual coaching methods. Such narrow definitions of expertise are problematic for coaches working with athletes at the sub-elite level, as they may also be expert coaches.

Coaches in many countries, if they want to coach at an international level, are required to ascend though a multilevel certification system. This in itself, however, is generally not enough to guarantee expertise. Although it may guarantee a certain level of knowledge and technical ability, most coaches would agree that certification in and of itself is insufficient and needs to be combined with other sources of experience and development.

Despite the difficulties in measuring coaching expertise, researchers have attempted to identify and examine the knowledge structures of great coaches. This has generally fallen within two lines of questioning:

1. what do expert coaches see that other coaches might miss?
2. do expert coaches organize training sessions that are more efficient and effective than those of non-expert coaches?

What expert coaches see and do

Research with swimming coaches shows that experts do indeed have deeper and more developed knowledge structures specific to swimming technique. In one particular experiment, coaches observed underwater video recordings of four swimmers of different skill levels and were then asked to analyze the strokes and to provide instruction. Whereas novice coaches were somewhat superficial and vague in their analysis, expert coaches were very precise in their assessment and specific in their recommendations for improvement. Expert coaches had the ability to extract more from the information presented and were able to provide fundamentally better solutions to the problems the swimmers were facing. Not surprisingly, expert coaches appear to 'see' more and offer better feedback to their athletes. This phenomenon is not unique to sport and has been reported among expert chess players, medical practitioners, and physicists. In all instances, experts are able to quickly and efficiently identify higher-order concepts—they see the big picture. As a result, they are able to intervene with solutions or suggestions that have greater relevance for improving problem solving or skill production. For the expert coach, this generally results in feedback and error correction that have an immediate and large impact on skill development.

The second question revolves around the design of practice sessions, and whether expert coaches do this more effectively than non-experts. We've learned a lot about the type of training that is required to become an expert. Although the contribution of innate talent or genetic gifts to achieving excellence is still debated, it is clear that, irrespective of talent, an extraordinary amount of 'deliberate practice' is required to achieve expertise in virtually any athletic endeavor. This term, coined by Anders Ericsson *et al.* (1993) from their study of musicians, theorized that the key determinant of improvement is the number of hours engaged in specific types of practice, which they defined as effortful, highly relevant to performance and not inherently enjoyable. Of interest is the fact that, for musicians, the only component of practice that met the definition of deliberate practice, and differentiated between the three skill levels of musicians (expert, master teacher, and conservatory students), was the amount of time they spent practicing alone. Expert musicians had logged thousands more hours of solo practice than master-level teachers who in turn had spent considerably more time in this very specific activity than music students (see also Baker and Cobley, Chapter 3).

Although researchers in the sporting world have debated the precise definition of deliberate practice and its usefulness as it applies to athletes, there has been considerable support for much of what Ericsson and his colleagues found with musicians. A clear relationship exists between level of performance achieved and time spent in specific practice activities in sports. In both music and sports, the activities most related to performance achievement (i.e., solo practicing the violin, on-court training in real time) and the activities done with a mentor (violin lessons, work with a coach) are the most highly rated practice activities on the dimensions of relevance, concentration, and effort.

The job of the coach, then, is to design practices that meet these requirements and will lead to maximal improvement in their athletes. Understanding what expert coaches do, and how they structure practice, becomes valuable information for athletes and coaches alike.

In 1975 two education researchers, Roland Tharp and Ron Gallimore, conducted one of the first studies that attempted to systematically analyze a coach's behaviors. The authors developed the Coaching Behaviors Recording Form (CBRF) to observe John Wooden during his final season at UCLA. They found that seventy-five per cent of Wooden's coaching behaviors consisted of some form of instruction. These instructions were normally quick, pointed and delivered in rapid-fire succession as the play swirled around him. Wooden had the ability to dissect what was happening on the floor and convey instructions quickly to players, providing immediate feedback and correction.

Since that initial study, a number of other researchers have conducted systematic observations of coaches' training sessions in the attempt to understand the nature of the interactions with athletes. One noteworthy study looked at Jerry Tarkanian, another highly regarded collegiate basketball coach. The researchers divided the general category of 'instruction' into three sub-categories, technical, tactical, and general instruction. Technical instruction generally consists of working on specific individual skills, such as footwork, or the technical aspects of shooting a basketball free throw. Tactical instruction normally consists of spatial and movement aspects of play that are designed to outsmart opponents and to gain the upper hand in a game situation (see McPherson, Chapter 11, for a discussion of tactics). General instruction revolves around the organization of drills, player substitutions, and other aspects of instruction not related to tactics or technique. The researchers found that Tarkanian spent approximately double the amount of time on tactical components as he did providing instruction on technique, and they hypothesized that extensive tactical knowledge is a hallmark of an expert coach working with skilled athletes.

A recent study that we conducted at Queen's University involved five Canadian National teams in the sports of basketball, soccer, and wheelchair basketball. Our approach included both systematic observation of practices as well as interviews with coaches and players. National teams in Canada operate under specific constraints, as most teams have the opportunity to centralize for only a few weeks per year. These pre-competition training camps often consist of player selection along with tournament preparation. This necessarily impacts on a coach's instructional strategies, particularly the time that they can devote to developing technical skills.

We measured how often behaviors occurred (behavior frequency) and for how long these behaviors occurred (behavior duration, see Table 6.1). Measuring the length of time that coaches were engaged with the athletes in addition to the simple frequency count illustrated the importance of instruction in the practice setting, particularly tactical instruction. This one category constituted almost half the time that coaches were speaking to athletes. Although this emphasis on tactics may be in part due to the time constraints imposed on Canadian coaches and the need to get systems in place quickly for an upcoming competition, the interviews with the coaches supported the notion that tactical instruction plays a crucial role in coaching at the elite level, and heavily influenced how they designed their practice sessions. Overall, our analyses of practice sessions across sports found that coaches spent the majority of practice (sixty per cent) observing in silence. When they were speaking to their players, however, it was overwhelmingly of an instructional nature (thirty-two per cent, see Figure 6.1).

Practice design

A coach, particularly in team sports, is often responsible for constructing virtually 100 per cent of an athlete's practice time. Even in individual sports in which athletes habitually have more personal control over their training sessions, coaches are typically highly involved in

Table 6.1 *The number of recorded behaviors and the corresponding percentage values as measured by frequency and duration (Canadian national team coaches)*

Category	Frequency, absolute value	Frequency, %	Duration, %
General instruction	2425	27.9	24.9
Praise/encouragement	2266	26.1	6.9
Tactical instruction	2160	24.8	46.5
Other	486	5.6	10.4
Technical instructions	425	4.9	3.9
Hustles	273	3.1	0.8
Humor	235	2.7	1.3
Modeling	149	1.8	3.5
Nonverbal reward	105	1.2	0.2
Uncodable	63	0.7	0.1
Scolds	59	0.7	0.3
Criticism/reinstruction	36	0.4	1.1
Nonverbal punishment	2	0.02	0.00
Total	8684	99.9	99.9

Table from Horton *et al.* (2005). Reprinted with the permission of Edizioni Luigi Pozzi (Italy), publisher of the *International Journal of Sport Psychology*

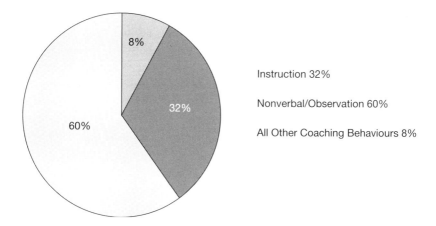

Instruction 32%

Nonverbal/Observation 60%

All Other Coaching Behaviours 8%

Figure 6.1 *Average amount of time Canadian national team coaches spent observing, instructing, and engaged in other coaching behaviors during practice sessions.*

helping athletes construct a training regimen that fulfills the tenets of deliberate practice, that is, practice that requires a high degree of concentration and effort, and is directly relevant to performance. This seems to correspond with Wooden's philosophy of an optimal practice environment: 'In every facet of basketball, we work on pressure. The opponent provides that during the game. I tried to provide it in practice with drills that re-created game conditions'.

Earlier work conducted at our institution involved videotaping the practices of an expert collegiate volleyball coach, and these practices displayed this same emphasis on pressure, intensity, and relevance to performance situations. The drills she utilized with her players closely simulated game conditions and were geared specifically to upcoming opponents, and the intensity level was virtually equivalent to what players faced in matches.

In interviews we conducted with national team coaches in Canada, similar themes around pressure and game simulation emerged. Each of the coaches emphasized the importance of creating a game-like atmosphere in the practice sessions. One coach noted:

> That's what you need to do, as a coach. . .you have to create game-like situations, whatever it may be. Constantly making adjustments, making drills increasingly complex and more game-like, so that guys see the situations in practice that they're going to see in a game.

In a similar vein, another coach stated:

> Get them to that place mentally, so that they feel that same type of pressure and energy and excitement. And if they can compete and finish it then yeah, if they can close out in practice against the top player on their team, then chances are they're going to be able to close out and defend the top player on the other team in a game.

Time use

Intimately connected to practice design is the manner in which time is used during practice. Considering the vast number of hours required to obtain expertise in any endeavor, efficient use of time is of paramount importance. Anders Ericsson found that expert musicians spent upwards of 50 hours per week on music-related activities. Only 27 of those hours, however, were spent in deliberate practice, or practice that was most beneficial to improvement. Ericsson speculated that this amount of deliberate practice represented the upper limit of what musicians were capable of each week; trying to practice more could result in injury and/or burn-out. Considering that we all have the same number of hours in the day, it would seem that maximizing the time spent practicing becomes a crucial variable in any success achieved (see Chapter 2 by Côté and Fraser-Thomas for considerations in youth sport). And, not surprisingly, the research suggests that experts seem to use their time more productively than non-experts.

Individual sports such as figure skating are similar to music in that the coach/teacher provides instruction and helps to establish training objectives, but much of the athlete's actual practice time is unsupervised by the coach. In addition, our research shows that skaters (like musicians) identify the key components of practice as those that are consistent with the notions of deliberate practice and mirror the demands of competition.

A time–motion analysis of skaters' solo practice sessions (i.e., without their coach) revealed some discrepancies between what athletes report as being most important and how they actually spent their time in practice. Although skaters saw the acquisition and mastery of new jumps as critical for performance success, the bulk of practice time was spent on jumps that were already well established in their repertoire. It appeared that skaters practiced what they 'knew' rather than what was 'new'.

Even more fascinating was the fact that skaters' intentions for their practice sessions were in stark contrast to what they actually did on the ice. Elite skaters, immediately prior to their training sessions, estimated that they would attempt seven double jumps and twenty triple jumps in the session. In actuality, once out on the ice the elite skaters attempted an average of thirty doubles and six triples. Intermediate and novice skaters were equally inaccurate in their prediction of how they would structure their time in practice. Elite-level skaters did make better use of their time on the ice (active eighty-five per cent of the time, as compared with fifty per cent for less accomplished skaters) but even with elite skaters not all time in practice could be considered 'deliberate', highlighting the important role a coach can play at this level of performance.

Practices in team sports, even under the constant supervision of a coach, often suffer from the same under-utilization of time. One study that used time–motion analysis to examine the practices of high-level junior ice-hockey players found that, on average, the players were inactive forty-eight per cent of the time. Contrast this with an expert volleyball coach who we videotaped. We employed time–motion analysis similar to that used with the figure skaters and found that her athletes were active in practice ninety-three per cent of practice time. The seven per cent of time that was 'inactive' generally consisted of organized rest breaks, and coaching instruction normally took place during these breaks. Thus the time that was inactive was actually highly structured.

Stoppage of drills for instruction was minimal in an effort to keep the action as continuous as possible. Drills that were not accomplishing the coach's objectives were quickly altered or adapted, almost on the fly. Facilitating this kind of smooth transition from drill to drill, thereby maximizing athletes' practice time, requires considerable thought and advance preparation on the part of the coach. Precise planning prior to practice, as well as a thorough evaluation after each practice, meant that this coach was able to get the very most out of the somewhat limited time on court. Practices themselves were relatively short (average of 86 minutes) owing to the fact that this was a university team operating under space and time constraints, yet the extent to which the coach planned, prepared, and evaluated practice sessions allowed her to make use of virtually every minute her athletes were on the floor.

Coach Wooden noted that he often spent as much time planning a practice as conducting it, and meticulously planned each detail so that players were always active, either engaged in drills or shooting free throws. No one was permitted to stand around watching. Wooden wrote highly detailed cue cards for every single practice session and kept all of these for future reference. He often returned to these cards to compare the progress of his current team with teams from past years. His record-keeping was such that he 'could tell you what we did every minute of every practice in my twenty-seven years at UCLA'.

Communicating with athletes

In addition to the knowledge that coaches need to impart to their athletes, there is the issue of how best to communicate this knowledge. Sport, particularly at its highest levels, takes place in an ultra-competitive environment where there is pressure on athletes to perform and pressure on coaches to win. A losing record often results in a coach losing his or her job. How can a coach get the most from players, given the pressure to produce? A professional soccer coach in England noted the delicate balance such an environment presents, commenting that the psyches of even the highest-level athletes can be fragile: 'Most of them are insecure, and most of them are frightened to death five minutes before they go out for a game. . .whether you're a professional football player or a young kid, you need plenty of encouragement'.

As a result, this coach is relentlessly positive with his players, continually trying to build their confidence. And although players need a 'kick in the behind' from time to time, this was normally done privately, away from the rest of the team. Berating a player for his poor performance in front of the whole group was seen as totally unproductive. Research on youth coaching has emphasized the importance of support and praise in working with young athletes in order to encourage continuing participation in the sport. Our findings suggest its importance at the highest levels as well.

One note of caution: although praise is clearly an effective tool, its mindless overuse is potentially problematic. Indeed, the research shows a great disparity in how often coaches compliment their athletes. Studies examining coaches at a variety of levels, from youth programs to national teams, have shown praise–scold ratios as high as 35–1, whereas other studies have shown much lower praise–scold ratios. Of interest is the fact that Coach Wooden seemed to scold just as much as he praised his athletes. Wooden was known for his rather stern manner during practice sessions. Of note, however, is the fact that he never used physical punishment, such as running laps, with the players. Furthermore, his on-court, drill-sergeant demeanor was balanced by a grandfatherly image off the court. Wooden didn't swear, nor smoke nor drink, and he was known for caring deeply about his players. In spite of the relatively low amount he praised athletes during practice sessions, Wooden considered his emphasis on teaching and instruction to constitute a positive approach: 'I believe that is the positive approach. I believe in the positive approach. Always have'.

THEORY INTO PRACTICE

Coaching as teaching

Great coaches tend to be great teachers. Wooden always considered himself a teacher first and foremost, and a quote from one of Canada's national team coaches displays similar sentiments: 'I think that good coaching is really just good teaching. Everything I am doing is designed to teach, teach, teach'.

The research supports this notion; good coaches spend the majority of their time in practice sessions instructing. The higher the level of the athlete, the more this instruction seems to take on a tactical component. This probably occurs for two reasons:

1. Athletes at an elite level are already proficient at a technical level, and changes are more in the way of small refinements rather than major alterations in technique.
2. Generally very little differentiates athletes technically at the elite level, thus tactical or strategic advantages may be the deciding factor in competition, hence a coach's emphasis on developing strategies to use against opponents.

This is reflected in the drills that make up practice sessions.

Effective utilization of practice time

Overall, the research shows that high-level performers, both athletes and coaches, tend to do more with the time that they have. Both the ice hockey and the figure skating examples we outlined clearly show that time on the ice is not necessarily reflective of time spent in deliberate practice. It would seem that a large amount of practice time is wasted, or spent in less than optimal activities. Coaches attempting to maximize their athletes' potential should first seek fully to exploit the time they have before looking for more practice hours. The expert volleyball coach we studied was extremely adept at squeezing every minute from practice sessions that were, in her view, shorter than she would have liked. Although the length of practice sessions was beyond her control, she was able to control the pace, intensity, and quality of the time she did spend with her athletes.

Making the most of practice time is not necessarily synonymous with working harder within a particular practice session. Coaches need to be mindful of appropriate work-to-rest ratios that allow athletes to recover between elements within a practice session as well as between practice sessions. The notion of training cycles has as much impact within sessions as it does between sessions and seasons. For example, figure skaters who are attempting to add new jump elements to their repertoire need to be guided through practice in a way that optimizes their strength, endurance, and information-processing skills such as error detection and correction. In order to maximize the relationship between these variables, the number of actual jump attempts made within a single practice session should be controlled and monitored. In general, an inverse relationship exists between the difficulty or 'effortfulness' of the element and the number of times it can be attempted within a single practice.

Optimizing practice time involves getting the most from each individual session and also structuring the season to ensure continuing improvement and prevent loss of valuable time due to overuse injuries, staleness or burn-out. Our national team coaches spoke of how the emphasis, demands, and focus of practice would change depending on where they were in their season. Pre-season practices were often vastly different from those near the end of the season or during play-offs. Videotaping practices at different times during the year and using time–motion analysis to assess the sessions can provide valuable feedback. The opportunity to see exactly how practice time is utilized, and how that changes as the season progresses can be a helpful self-monitoring tool for coaches.

Game simulation

Developing drills that simulate game scenarios is something that is common to all great coaches. Often this is a gradual process, slowly building the speed and complexity of a drill until it is at game speed. But ultimately athletes need to practice the way that they play. Drills should match the physical demands that players will face in games, as well as the psychological demands they will encounter. Coaches often simulate specific scenarios they are likely to encounter in match situations. This can range from plays designed to score points in the dying seconds of a game, to bringing in fans to heckle their players in preparation for playing in an opposing team's arena (see Jackson and Beilock, Chapter 8). The more realistic and game-like the drill, the more likely players will be able to execute in a match situation. Wooden's practices seemed to go one step further, often exceeding the demands the players would face in games. His players have commented on the fact that games appeared to take place in slow motion because the pace in practices was so high. This was reiterated by one of Canada's national team coaches:

> My players often said that we went into games so well prepared, in part because games weren't as tough as practice. You can really put them in stressful situations, and I believe in making practice tougher than any game they'll play.

The practice environment

Research from education suggests that the ideal learning environment is one that combines 'high standards and emotional warmth', and the research from sports suggests the same. Our study of Canadian national team coaches revealed that they were highly demanding of their players in their expectations of effort and intensity, but the practice environment was rich in praise and encouragement. Being highly demanding of athletes is generally a very good thing. The coaches with whom we spoke all brought a very high level of intensity and passion to their sport, and they expected the same from their athletes. Coupling that intensity and passion with a supportive environment that involves the appropriate amount of praise is a formula that has worked for many successful coaches.

Pressure and performance

How do you get athletes to perform at their highest level, particularly when the pressure is at its greatest? The English soccer coach noted the extent to which his athletes were 'scared to death' prior to matches, and illustrates the pressure and anxiety even highly paid professional athletes face on a regular basis. The spotlight in high-profile sports, where every move is dissected and critiqued by potentially hostile media and fans, can be unnerving for even the most confident of athletes.

Helping players deal with such pressures is an important aspect of coaching success. It is interesting to note that one of the most successful coaches of all time, Coach Wooden, rarely talked about winning with his athletes. Jammal Wilkes, one of Wooden's former players, noted that he played on teams that won seventy-three games in a row, and yet never did Wooden talk about winning: 'All he ever asked is that we leave the floor at the end of the game with our head up'. In stark contrast to the Hollywood pre-game pep talk that involves lots of shouting and exhortations from the coach, Wooden exuded calm and composure prior to games, as this is how he wanted his athletes to be when they hit the floor—calm and composed (see Jackson and Beilock, Chapter 8, for more information on choking and dealing with pressure).

Often thoughts of winning or losing a game or match are disruptive and harm performance. As Wooden demonstrated in his pre-game talks with his players, focusing on the process, rather than the end result, can be an effective way of reducing anxiety and helps players perform to the best of their abilities in pressure situations. There are a number of ways in which coaches can help athletes perform under pressure. Closely simulating game conditions is one primary method, as it allows athletes to adjust to both the physiological components and the psychological aspects of competition. Knowing what to expect, and learning how one's body and mind will react to pressure situations, are crucial skills for an athlete to have before experiencing it in competition. One of the most valuable lessons an athlete can learn is where their 'arousal' or energy level should be for them to perform optimally. This will necessarily vary from athlete to athlete, but managing their arousal level is a skill that must be learned and developed. Simulation can be an effective tool for helping athletes deal with the nerves and excitement that are an inevitable component of high-level competitive sport.

CONCLUSION

John Wooden coached the UCLA Bruins for 27 years, winning ten NCAA titles in that time, yet that first national title did not come until his fifteenth season as their coach. All ten titles came in his last 12 years, the last in 1975, after which he promptly retired. One has to wonder how many more titles might have come UCLA's way had Wooden stayed on a few more years.

Wooden believes he improved as a coach every season: 'I hope I was learning the very last year I coached. I don't think I learned as much the last year as I did my first year but I hope I learned a little bit each and every year'.

Each off-season Wooden set out to research one particular aspect of the game he felt he could learn more about, such as the intricacies of rebounding or shooting free throws. These research projects involved library searching and reading, along with discussions with other coaches and players he considered knowledgeable. In this way he kept improving his coaching knowledge and abilities year after year. Wooden's remarkable success in the last phase of his career does not appear to be accidental, but instead the result of years of hard work and concentrated effort. This attribution for his success perhaps shows how the theory of deliberate practice can affect the development of expertise in coaching:

> When you improve a little each day, eventually big things occur . . . . not tomorrow, not the next day, but eventually a big gain is made. Don't look for the big, quick improvement. Seek the small improvement one day at a time.

COACH'S CORNER

Patrick Hunt

AIS and Basketball Australia
Head Coach, National Intensive Training Centre Program (NITCP),
Manager, National Player & Coach Development

I thoroughly enjoyed the chapter presented and only regret that it was one chapter as there is so much more that needs to be considered in developing coaching expertise. Based on my experiences as a coach and coach mentor I have found that coaches develop their skills in a variety of ways. The list below summarizes most of these:

How do coaches develop?

- playing experience
- formal coach education courses (level 0, 1, 2, and 3 coaching diplomas, degrees)
- informal coach development experiences
- trial-and-error practice experiences
- competition experiences
- program planning and implementation experiences
- critical evaluation of coaching experiences in both practice sessions and games
- life experiences.

Obviously all these experiences add up to make you the coach you are. I would stress that, although coach education courses are vital, they are only one small part of the coach development process, but are often considered all that is needed. I think coach education courses need more content that focuses on the real world of coaching, which I like to term 'Practically applied coaching competencies'. These competencies include the following:

- coaching in detail—the ability to analyse a skill and break it down into its key components
- reinforcing the detail—based on being able to break the skill down, be able to coach the skill without over-instructing
- coaching on the run—the ability to summarize a key skill in one key phrase or term that players instantly understand and change their behavior as a result; this process means being able to develop meaningful cue words (action words) that capture the essence of the skill
- the 'coachable' moment—the ability to recognize the time to intervene in a practice session to highlight a key behavior that has occurred
- reducing empty feedback and using action terms, in other words being prescriptive not descriptive.

The above competencies can be illustrated using the basketball defensive stance when defending a player with the ball. Through coaching in detail the stance can be broken down into five key components:

- feet shoulder-width apart, parallel
- nose behind the toes
- one hand on the ball, 'spear hand', the other hand up defending the pass, 'deflection hand'
- knees bent
- head in middle of stance.

Then, through the process of reinforcing the detail at practice over a period of time, coaches are able to coach on the run by using the term 'stance' to summarize all of the above components of the skill. Obviously this process takes time but is an effective way of changing a player's behavior quickly in a practice or competition setting.

It might sound like a cliché, but the best coaches learn from every experience they have. A significant proportion of coach development time can emerge from the practical experiences a coach accrues. If coaches can take advantage of this as a learning experience through specific evaluation of their performance, their coaching expertise will continue to develop. A message to the researchers: we need more research that examines what is the best method of evaluating coaching performance. We need a method/system for this evaluation that is non-threatening to the coach and provides practical feedback that a coach can then go away and work on.

Over time we have found the development activities listed below to be particularly beneficial for our coaches:

- Interstate Coaching Experience (ICE) program
- Australian development camps
- NITCP camps

- coaching clinics
- coaching clinics sessions, which occur during practice sessions
- coach evaluation/feedback sessions
- NITCP international study tours
- interaction with visiting international coaches.

All of these experiences involve coaches interacting with other coaches. Informal and formal mentoring opportunities develop from such programs, and attendees are exposed to different ways of preparing a player, in particular, methods to develop a player both in terms of their individual skills but also being able to integrate these skills into the team dynamic.

Stages of a basketball coach's development

If I was to attach a timeline to a coaching lifecycle as it evolves from a first-time beginner coach through to an advanced coach I would describe the process as shown in Table 6.2. As you can see, there is a basic progression from the mechanics of coaching, such as developing a good database of drills and strategies, to the more personalized aspects of coaching, which are all about developing effective relationships with players and other staff.

Table 6.2 Stages of a coach's career

Stage of career	Coaching need	Description
Beginning	'yearning for drills'	looking for textbook drills
	'yearning for plays'	looking for textbook plays
Intermediate	reinforcing detail	developing acceptable standards of skill execution at practice
	game coaching techniques	when to call a time out, player match-ups, strategic changes
	coaching on the run	using succinct coaching terms
	changing behavior techniques	using different coaching methods as required
	anecdotes	use as another means of getting a message across
Advanced	detailed information	imparting necessary but large amounts of information pitched to an individual's skill level
	implementation information	does practice transfer to the game?
	'the art of coaching'	knowing how to change behavior at an individual and group level and integrate
	the 'coachable moment'	recognition of when it occurs
	personal examples	use personal coaching and playing experiences

Those coaches that reach the advanced stage of coaching usually find they need to spend more time developing what I refer to as the non-technical areas of coaching. These include:

- conflict resolution
- negotiation skills
- IT user-friendly skills
- management techniques/planning evaluation
- group dynamics
- stress management
- managing relationships: other coaches; support staff; athletes.

Summary

The development of coaching expertise is a continual process of formal and informal experiences that, if evaluated, can improve one's coaching skills. I don't think coaching expertise can be categorized as something that one reaches after 10 years or 10,000 hours, as most expert coaches continually refer to how much they are still learning. I think this was a key message illustrated by John Wooden in the chapter.

KEY READING

Bloom, B.S. (ed.) (1985). *Developing Talent in Young People.* New York: Ballentine.

Bloom, G.A., Crumpton, R. and Anderson, J.E. (1999). 'A systematic observation study of the teaching behaviors of an expert basketball coach'. *The Sports Psychologist*, (13): 157–70.

Deakin, J. and Cobley, S. (2003). 'An examination of the practice environments in figure skating and volleyball: A search for deliberate practice'. In Starkes, J.L. and Ericsson, K.A. (eds) *Expert Performance in Sports*. Windsor: Human Kinetics, 115–36.

Ericsson, K.A., Krampe, R. and Tesch-Romer, C. (1993). 'The role of deliberate practice in the acquisition of expert performance'. *Psychological Review*, (100): 363–406.

Gallimore, R. and Tharp, R. (2004). 'What a coach can teach a teacher, 1975–2004: Reflections and reanalysis of John Wooden's teaching practices'. *The Sport Psychologist*, (18): 119–37.

Horton, S., Baker, J. and Deakin, J. (2005). 'Experts in action: A systematic observation of 5 national team coaches'. *International Journal of Sport Psychology*, (36): 299–319.

Potrac, P., Jones, R. and Armour, K. (2002). 'It's all about getting respect: The coaching behaviors of an expert English soccer coach'. *Sport, Education and Society*, (7): 183–202.

Starkes, J.L. (2000). 'The road to expertise: Is practice the only determinant?'. *International Journal of Sport Psychology*, (31): 431–51.

Tharp, R. and Gallimore, R. (1976). 'What a coach can teach a teacher'. *Psychology Today*, (January): 75–9.

Wooden, J. (1988). *They Call Me Coach*. Chicago, IL: Contemporary Books Inc.

Chapter 7

Skill learning the implicit way—say no more!

Rich Masters

History records that Harry Vardon won six Open golf championships and that he missed a *very* short putt to win a seventh championship in 1902. Legend recounts that a gentleman watcher was so amused by this easy miss that Vardon was provoked to challenge him to a small wager that he could not make the same putt himself. Good sport that he was, Vardon even passed on a variety of verbal instructions on how best to make the putt, and suggested that a week should be long enough to put these into practice. One week later, an expectant crowd gathered around the green to watch Vardon collect on his wager.

INTRODUCTION

For most of us, the acquisition of sport-specific motor repertoires begins as a child at play in a yard, on a field or by a court—perhaps emulating a favorite sporting superstar. At some point, some of us stop *playing* and begin seriously to consider the idea that we too can be a superstar. Suddenly, the pressure is on to get skilled and win. Coaches, administrators, parents and grandparents, and even well-meaning friends (often with an inflated recollection that they were *handy* at school) get involved, providing advice and tips on how best to execute the shots or make the moves.

Skill learning for the weekend warrior and the would-be superstar is very different. For the weekend warrior, acquisition of sport-related skills is about leisure, pleasure, and health. For the would-be superstar, acquisition of sport-related skills is about records, fame, income, and medals. These very different motivational states shape the way in which movements and skills are learned, modifying the type of knowledge that is built up to support movement output (see Young and Medic, Chapter 4). For the would-be superstar, skill learning becomes an active pursuit, followed in earnest. Fun is set aside, or lost, and for many years skill learning is dominated by the testing of hypotheses in order to establish the best way to move to achieve the desired level of performance. Correct hypotheses (e.g. flexed knees = more power) are stored as rules for future reference (explicit knowledge), whereas incorrect hypotheses are discarded or ignored.

The consequence of this aggressive search for effective skills is that, over time, the performer accumulates a deep pool of explicit rules and knowledge. With practice the skills become expert and automatic, but they are inescapably linked to an explicit, highly verbal mode of control. At inopportune moments (e.g. match point down in the fifth set) or when too much time is available in which to construct the necessary movements (e.g. a gently lofted catch to the outfield), verbal modes of control can regress the normally fluent skills of the expert to the erratic and error-prone ways of the beginner. In essence, conditions such as over-eagerness to perform well or too much time to think can result in *reinvestment*: the tendency to direct conscious attention to the mechanical details of how the skill should be performed. Most athletes have, at some point in their career, faced this problem.

SOME EVIDENCE, A QUESTIONNAIRE, AND A QUOTE

There is now evidence that shows that the larger the pool of explicit knowledge that a performer has accumulated about the mechanics of his or her skills, the greater the chances that reinvestment will occur—especially under pressure (see Jackson and Beilock, Chapter 8, where they discuss paralysis by analysis). Additionally, different performers have different propensities to reinvest. Every club or team has at least one member who incessantly rehearses their technique, and we all secretly admire (or envy) performers who are so 'chilled out' that they never seem to think about what they are doing or how they are doing it. This propensity to direct attention to the mechanics of one's skills can be measured using a questionnaire called the Movement Specific Reinvestment Scale (MSRS). The scale also assesses the propensity to be self-conscious about one's movements. Although these two facets of the human personality are related to each other, there is evidence available from the study of populations with movement disorders, such as Parkinson's disease and stroke, that shows that a strong predisposition to think about the mechanics of one's movements (i.e., a high score on the MSRS) is associated with greater functional impairment of the movements. Additionally, anxiety to move effectively, which is a natural emotion in those who move awkwardly, can cause patients consciously to monitor the mechanics of their actions even more than they normally would, in an attempt to reduce the awkwardness of the movements. Similarities exist in the sporting world, where athletes can become so conscious of flaws in their technique that they reinvest to such an extent that they develop their own pseudo-clinical skill disorders, such as the 'yips' in golf or 'dartitis' in darts.

The MSRS consists of a series of questions, as presented in Table 7.1. Normally, the questions are presented in a random order, and the performer is asked to rate the strength of their feelings on a six-point Likert scale that ranges from *strongly disagree* (1 point) through *moderately disagree* (2 points), *weakly disagree* (3 points), *weakly agree* (4 points), *moderately agree* (5 points) and *strongly agree* (6 points). The minimum score for each personality trait is thus 5 points, and the maximum score is 30 points.

Although it is probably not easy to modify the predisposition for reinvestment, which may (or may not) be an integral part of an athlete's personality, it is certainly possible to reduce another component of reinvestment—the degree to which explicit knowledge is accumulated during learning. This is not an easy task for the coach, however. Modern coaches are subject to considerable pressure to nurture the skills of the learner to an expert level in the shortest possible period of time. These pressures emanate from sport administrators and associations,

Table 7.1 *The Movement Specific Reinvestment Scale**

Conscious motor processing

I reflect about my movement a lot.

I'm always trying to figure out why my actions failed.

I'm always trying to think about my movements when I carry them out.

I'm aware of the way my mind and body works when I am carrying out a movement.

I rarely forget the times when my movements have failed me, however slight the failure.

Movement self-consciousness

I'm concerned about my style of moving.

I'm self conscious about the way I look when I am moving.

I'm concerned about what people think about me when I am moving.

If I see my reflection in a shop window, I will examine my movements.

I sometimes have the feeling that I'm watching myself move.

* The scale is used to assess the propensity that individual performers have for conscious motor processing (i.e., to turn their attention inward to the process of movement in order to control the mechanics of their movements) and for movement self-consciousness (i.e., to worry about their style of movement and about making a good impression when they move).

who are fiscally restrained to meet the costs associated with producing top performers—the sooner the performer is on the circuit the better the budget looks. Parents have their own budgets to consider, and the performers themselves are often in a hurry too—time is short when you want to be a superstar, and most sports propagate the adage that 'if you haven't *made it* by the time you are 16 or 17, you never will'. In short, the coach comes under significant pressure to accelerate the learning process. In order to do this, the coach will set about persuading the learner to adopt certain fundamental methods and techniques that are *in vogue* or that anecdotal experience or history have shown to be the most effective. The coach will provide this information in a number of ways, that, in about seventy per cent of cases, involve explicit, verbal instructions. Although there are some indications that such information can promote more rapid learning, it becomes almost impossible for the performer to carry out the skill without at some point exerting conscious control over it. As we have seen, this conscious control is what may lead to skill breakdown. This is particularly the case when the performer becomes highly motivated to perform well, which is not surprising given the huge cost and many long hours of work that are invested in becoming an expert. As all performers know, and the Zen Bhuddist teacher Diasetz Suzuki beautifully articulates, best execution of skills in such cases occurs when there is no interference from consciousness:

Thinking is useful in many ways, but there are some occasions when thinking interferes with the work, and you have to leave it behind. . . It is for this reason that the sword moves where it ought to move and makes the contest end victoriously.

(D.T. Suzuki, 1959)

91

MORE EVIDENCE, A RULE, AND A BIT ABOUT THE HISTORY OF IMPLICIT *MOTOR* LEARNING

Considerable evidence now exists in the scientific literature to show that excessive conscious control of one's skills (reinvestment) is avoidable if the skills are learned implicitly, without recourse to hypothesis testing (e.g. bent knees = more power) or accumulation of explicit knowledge. After all, if the athlete does not have access to explicit, conscious knowledge of how to move, how then can they use such knowledge to control the skills? Dramatic support for this claim is evident in the well-documented case of the patient who suffered from severe wastage of his left frontal and temporal lobes and left hippocampus—the areas of the brain that are heavily involved in verbal aspects of motor control. The patient exhibited very poor social skills; however, he showed no reduction in the ability to follow the (complex) rules that are so much a part of the traditions of golf. For example, Rule 12-1 of the Rules of Golf stipulated by the Royal and Ancient Golf Club of St Andrews, states that:

> In searching for his ball anywhere on the *course*, the player may touch or bend long grass, rushes, bushes, whins, heather or the like, but only to the extent necessary to find and identify it, provided that this does not improve the lie of the ball, the area of his intended *stance* or swing or his *line of play*. . . [and] a player is not necessarily entitled to see his ball when making a *stroke*. . .

This ability to *abide* by the rules and etiquette of the game was retained despite a complete inability explicitly to *define* the specific rules and etiquette. More importantly, from the perspective of the implicit motor learner, the patient's golf skills improved substantially after the verbal control areas of his left hemisphere were damaged—reduced interference from explicit verbal knowledge lowered his handicap.

Other evidence supports this conclusion. For example, electro-encephalographic (EEG) studies have shown that patterns of brain activation in experts are different from patterns of activation in novices, with expert performers showing low *coherence* or communication between the verbal–analytical (T3) region of the left hemisphere and the motor planning frontal region (Fz) of the right hemisphere.

Communication between the two regions has also been shown to increase under high-anxiety conditions. This finding provides good evidence for the theory of reinvestment, implying that directing attention inward to the mechanics of one's skills (especially under pressure) increases the involvement of the verbal–analytical left temporal regions of the brain, which then interfere with the motor planning frontal regions of the brain that control the actual skill performance.

My first efforts to cause implicit *motor* learning, in 1992, used a dual-task approach (requiring the learner to complete two tasks at once) to prevent learners from testing hypotheses about the motor movements that they were making. Novice learners were asked to generate letters from the alphabet in a random order while they were learning to golf putt. The task is harder than it may seem because the learner must constantly monitor each letter to ensure that it has not been repeated previously or placed in a sequence of letters that makes up a real name or word. This early work showed that people who carried out a second task at the same time, while learning to golf putt, accumulated little or no conscious, explicit knowledge of their putting skill when compared with people who learned by self-discovery or who were provided with explicit coaching instructions. Importantly, the performance of the implicit learners was found to remain stable under conditions of psychological pressure that normally are enough to cause the skills of an athlete to fail as a consequence of reinvestment. In the laboratory, these psychological pressures are usually caused by the presence of an audience or by peer pressure or financial enticements.

In the intervening decade since this work was carried out, a variety of implicit skill-learning approaches or paradigms have been proposed and validated. Much of the work has been carried out by myself, Jon Maxwell, and colleagues and has included paradigms that encourage implicit learning in an environment in which performance mistakes seldom occur (we sometimes call this errorless learning), where visual feedback about the success of the skills is not provided, by presentation of instructions in the form of analogies and even by presenting feedback about the success of the skills that falls below the normal threshold for conscious awareness.

From an applied point of view some of these techniques are difficult to maintain over the extended periods of practice necessary for expertise to develop (see Section 1 of this book for a discussion on the development of expertise). With the exception of analogy learning, which will be discussed shortly, these techniques also cause skill learning, in the early stages at least, to be slower than normal. This can undermine a performer's perceptions of his or her competence or ability, which tends to reduce the motivation to continue practicing (see Young and Medic, Chapter 4). As all coaches know, but do not always practice, anything that undermines the sense of self-competence (confidence) of an athlete should be avoided. Despite the significant challenges to the coach in overcoming these difficulties, the advantages associated with learning skills implicitly are significant. Recent work has suggested that skills that are learned implicitly are performed better in front of an audience, create less interference when the performer has a complex decision to make, and even appear to be resistant to physiological fatigue. Beginners who learned to perform a rugby pass implicitly maintained their passing accuracy when significantly fatigued at an anaerobic or aerobic level, whereas those who learned explicitly did not. Furthermore, one year later, passing performance remained robust under physiological fatigue, despite the complete absence of passing practice during the year.

AN APOCRYPHAL STORY

If coaches are to exploit the advantages of teaching skills implicitly, they will need to rise to the challenge of adapting the laboratory-developed implicit learning paradigms for the field. For some coaches this will require a pedagogical about-turn and perhaps even the sacrifice of a cow, as Luis Suarez, the manager of Ecuador, told his players prior to the 2006 Soccer World Cup. Suarez recounted to his players the apocryphal story of a master and his servant who came upon a shack and a cow during their travels. The inhabitants invited them in and treated them to a wonderful meal and an excellent night of sleep. The master asked how

93

such a poor family could provide such wonderful hospitality, to which they replied that their cow provided all that they needed through its milk, and the beef and hides from its calves. Upon leaving, the master instructed his servant to return to the shack to kill the cow. The servant did so, but with great guilt. Many years later he returned to the shack to find out what became of the poor family. The shack was gone and in its place stood a beautiful mansion, surrounded by magnificent gardens. When the servant knocked on the door to ask what became of the family he was amazed to find that it was they who lived in the mansion. How can this be, he asked, to which they replied that many years earlier they had lived in poverty with only a single cow to provide for their needs. As luck would have it, the cow had died in mysterious circumstances, compelling them to take a new path in their lives—a path that led to fame and fortune. At the end of this story, Luis Suarez said to his players: 'Gentlemen, we are going to play in the World Cup. It is time to kill your cows'. Ecuador went further in the 2006 tournament than ever before in their history.

The coach who goes to the lengths needed to provide an environment rich in implicit skill learning will reap the benefits of producing performers who can 'step up to the plate' when it matters, but the coach who argues that he or she is paid to provide people explicitly with knowledge of what they are doing wrong, may not. What follows is a discussion of some of the ways in which implicit learning techniques can be adapted for use in the field. The intention is not to provide a comprehensive list of implicit learning paradigms as alternatives to explicit practices, but rather to stimulate thoughts on how to create a unique environment for performers in which they learn their skills implicitly.

METAPHORICALLY SPEAKING. . .

Analogies can be used to present the key coaching points of a to-be-learned skill as a simple biomechanical metaphor that can be reproduced by the learner without reference to, or manipulation of, large amounts of explicit knowledge. This allows the coach to instruct the performer implicitly without resorting to presentation of verbal instructions. Most coaches have resorted to the use of analogy at some point when instructing an athlete (e.g. swing like a pendulum when putting, punch the ball when volleying or put your hand in the cookie jar when taking a shot at basketball).

There is empirical evidence available to show that in tennis (and table tennis) a right-angled triangle analogy can be employed to teach beginners a topspin forehand shot implicitly. The learner is simply instructed to strike the ball by bringing the racquet (or bat) squarely up the hypotenuse portion of the right-angled triangle. Not only do analogy learners seem quickly to identify and mimic the biomechanical constraints of the skill that they are trying to produce, but they do so without acquiring explicit knowledge of how they are producing the skill. Typically, the learner will automatically take a semi-western style grip of the racquet, accompanied by a stance well suited to the generation of high racquet speed when brushing up the back of the ball and so on. The learner is unlikely to be explicitly aware that he or she is using any of these underlying rules for a topspin forehand and, moreover, should exhibit the advantages that are characteristic of an implicitly learned skill.

The extent to which analogies are effective is perhaps best illustrated by the success of those who use them. American Dr Tom Amberry became the world record holder for basketball free throws in 1993. Remarkably, he was 71 years old at the time, which makes a mockery of the adage that 'you must *make it* before you are 16 or 17 or you never will'. Amberry made 2,750 throws consecutively without missing, over a 12-hour period, and is said to have only stopped because the gymnasium was booked for a college game. Amberry advises that his routine for free throwing is to bounce the ball three times, with the inflation hole up and then to imagine that his arm is 15 feet long and simply drops the ball through the basket. When combined with 'putting your hand in the cookie jar' (see Figure 7.1) this is likely to be a powerful analogy.

Currently, there is no sport in which a comprehensive directory of analogies exists for each movement or technique, and nor is there likely to be, given the multitude and complexity of ways in which each of us as individuals can manipulate our bodies. Coaches must, therefore, develop their own repertoire of analogies. Care should be taken in this, for it is not uncommon for coaches to defeat the purpose of the analogy by following it up with an explicit diatribe on just what effect the analogy has on the performer's technique.

Recent work has also shown that there are cultural differences in responsiveness to analogies. For example, the right-angled triangle analogy has been shown to be an ineffective method for teaching a topspin forehand implicitly to Hong Kong Chinese learners, who understand the physical principles of a right-angled triangle, but appear unable to map these principles to their movements. It is likely that the analogy conveys an inappropriate abstraction to Hong Kong Chinese learners that makes it difficult to translate the conceptual image into movement. In response to this problem an alternative, culturally relevant, analogy has been

Figure 7.1
An analogy for basketball shooting: putting your hand in the cookie jar.

developed and validated (i.e., 'move the bat as though it is travelling up the side of a mountain'). The new analogy, while appearing to encapsulate the same fundamental geometric attributes of the right-angled triangle analogy, is perhaps more culturally decipherable.

An additional advantage of analogy learning is that it appears to allow many *bits* of information about a skill (i.e., rules or instructions) to be presented to the learner in one manageable *chunk*. This contrasts with traditional coaching methods, which involve the explicit presentation of many individual *bits* of information about how to move. Considerable practice is required before the learner can integrate these many bits of information into a manageable chunk, as is clear when one considers the length of time that it takes for most tennis beginners to learn how to make a ball toss with the left hand, scratch the back with the racquet in the right hand, bring the back foot through alongside the front foot, flex the knees, snap the wrist and strike the ball.

An advantage of 'chunking' in analogy learning is that considerably more information than normal can be presented to the learner in a short period of time. Presumably, analogy learning should therefore provide a faster route to expertise, although to date no empirical evidence exists to support such a claim. The implications for elite performance development, however, would be significant and might have potential to take years off the *10-year rule of necessary preparation* that is typically provided as a yardstick of the time it takes to become an expert (see Baker and Cobley, Chapter 3). The duration of financial support required from sport governing bodies would be reduced, parents would come under less pressure to remortgage the house, drop-out rates from demotivation would be lower and failures under pressure reduced.

ERRORS OF THE PAST

It is probably true to say that most professional athletes have spent most of their career testing hypotheses and accumulating knowledge about their sport, in search of better control of their skills. The goals that performers set for themselves are therefore important. Specific, challenging goals have been shown, beyond doubt, to be more effective than non-specific or easily achieved goals. Challenging goals, however, are likely to encourage performers actively to test motor hypotheses in order to achieve them. For example, a cricketer for whom a long throw to the stumps is extremely challenging is likely actively to try to figure out the best way to make that throw. In so doing, the cricketer will learn the skill explicitly, so it may be preferable to set goals that are just easy enough to be achieved without recourse to hypothesis testing. For example, the cricketer might be better first to set a goal to make a long throw to the side of a barn. Once that specific goal is achieved, the cricketer might progress to the more challenging goal of hitting the stumps.

It is not uncommon to see even a great performer lose confidence and, perhaps as a consequence of unrealistic or over-challenging goals, make changes to what has for years been an effective way to move. During one low point in his career, Seve Ballesteros, a winner of five major championships in golf, famously used forty technical rules (swing thoughts) to think about when he played a shot. Alternatively, it is not uncommon, even at the local driving range, to see performers begin to test hypotheses about their swing simply as a means to overcome boredom with the practice regime or to make the swing *even* better. This seems to be common in professional golf, for example, where many players seem to tinker constantly with their swing as they search for perfection.

This raises an interesting question: is it possible to relearn implicitly a skill that has been developed over many years and that is supported by a substantial pool of explicit knowledge? Implicit skills can arise in two ways, either because the performer has never had conscious access to explicit knowledge of how to execute the skill, or because the performer has gradually lost conscious access to the knowledge, through forgetting.

For an athlete who wishes to relearn implicitly, the answer may be to carry out many trials using an implicit technique, such as errorless learning, until access to explicit knowledge components of performance has been submerged by implicit processes. John Wooden, one of America's great basketball coaches (see Horton and Deakin, Chapter 6), is said to have once stated that winners are simply those who have made more errors. But all those errors become learned—and so must be unlearned. Errorless learning results in skills that are implicit because the absence of (motor) mistakes means that the performer doesn't need to test hypotheses about the best way to move. This causes a passive state of accumulating knowledge when performing. For example, a golfer who thinks too much when standing over short pressure putts should be encouraged to carry out many trials in which performance is error free (e.g. perhaps from a few centimeters or from gradually increasing distances). An accompanying benefit of such a course of errorless learning is that this makes it possible for the performer to build a history of successful experiences, which helps to recover lost confidence—after all, to complete many trials without a mistake is bound to increase confidence in one's abilities.

A potential criticism that may be directed at this form of errorless learning is that it tends to limit variability during the learning process, which is normally seen as a disadvantage by those who advocate development of skills that are flexible and adaptable (see Patterson and Lee, Chapter 9). The jury is out on this one. Errorless learners may, in fact, have flexibility to be variable in the way that they complete the skill from trial to trial because the task is so easy—that is, they can succeed in many different ways without making an error. Alternatively, coaches might consider employing errorless paradigms that create variability from trial to trial without sacrificing errorlessness. For example, in learning to shoot in basketball, the performer might complete different learning sessions from very close to the basket, from a greater distance but to a very large-diameter basket or with a beginner's ball. Alternatively, the place-kick in rugby union or rugby league might be learned first from directly in front without a crossbar, then from an acute angle without goal posts, then from a great distance with the crossbar present at a very low height and so on. Once again, it is for the coach, with his or her specific expertise in a particular sport, to find effective ways in which to articulate these principles in the field.

SEE NO EVIL, HEAR NO EVIL

An alternative way to learn or relearn skills implicitly might be to provide the performer with no visual feedback for a long period of time. In the same way that errorless learning makes hypothesis testing pointless because the movement is always successful, this form of learning renders hypothesis testing impossible because the performer *sees* no information with which to test hypotheses. There is a story of a little-known Norwegian biathlon competitor who was so poor at the shooting discipline that he could not sleep for thinking about it. His vastly experienced coach advised him to shoot into the sky whenever and wherever he could, so he took to carrying his gun with him wherever he went, and whenever the urge took him he would take pot-shots into the sky. He eventually won gold at the Winter Olympics. Although this story may (or may not) be an urban sport legend, there are examples of legendary performers, renowned for their stability under pressure, who, somewhere in their skill-learning past, have trained without feedback or practiced without error. Jonny Wilkinson, for example, kicked the winning goal for England in the final of the 2003 Rugby World Cup and is said to have practiced his kicking into a net for hours on end. Such practice would provide little or no feedback with which he could test hypotheses about his skills—nor would errors be apparent. Similarly, Tiger Woods practiced with his father at night as a youngster on a US Naval course, where feedback was aided only by the peripheral lights of the base.

It is possible, however, that such dramatic remedies may not be necessary if skills are learned implicitly at least early in the learning experience. Recent work has shown that a brief initial period of errorless learning in golf putting (as little as 150 trials) may provide the learner with the advantages of implicit learning, even if the performer later accumulates a large amount of explicit knowledge. It may be that the initial period of errorless learning is enough to propel a learner irrevocably down a motor control pathway that is disassociated from explicit control of the skill. This finding is of particular applied value, given that it is impossible for a coach to constrain a performer to an entirely implicit learning environment. Control over the learning environment cannot, for example, be maintained during competition, where an umpire (or an opponent) is unlikely to respond sympathetically to requests that the lights are turned off in order to remove feedback. Furthermore, it is very natural for a performer explicitly to work out what is happening when skills go wrong. Indeed, many coaches will argue that performers need to have a foundation of explicit knowledge of the rule structures underlying their skills to fall back on when things go wrong. Although this is not a view held by all skill learning experts, the opportunity to provide the advantages of a consciously accessible knowledge base, while offsetting the negative consequences of reinvestment, by initially learning implicitly, is very attractive.

THE CRAFTY COACH

Another option is to present information to the performer at a level of perception below normal levels of awareness. As an example of just how sensitive the human perceptual system is, we have shown in a series of studies in our laboratory in Hong Kong that a goalkeeper can, simply by standing marginally to the left or the right of the goal center, influence a penalty-taker to direct more penalties to the side that has more space. The goalkeeper can then dive in the biased direction to make a save. This finding is perhaps not vitally interesting until one realizes that, if the goalkeeper stands to the side by a mere 6–10 cm, the penalty-taker will not realize consciously that there is more space to one side. In fact, when asked, penalty-takers are typically very definite that the goalkeeper is standing in the exact center of the goal—nevertheless, they are much more likely to direct their shots to the side with more space.

In other studies we have shown that it is possible to cause implicit learning by presenting feedback regarding the outcome of movements at subliminal levels, such that performers *believe* that they have not seen what happened when they performed the skill. This is typically known as the subjective threshold of awareness, and, although people will claim that they see no information about their performance, if forced to say what happened (e.g. where the ball went or the location of the target), they are usually very accurate. Sophisticated equipment is required to present information at subliminal levels, making such techniques difficult to apply, but there are crafty ways in which a coach can mimic the subliminal presentation of information to change skills without the athlete becoming explicitly aware that they are changing. For example, a volleyball coach may wish to get his players to extend the arm more when spiking. Rather than explicitly describe the changes in technique that he wants to see, the coach might consider increasing the height of the net during practice sessions, in increments so small that the players are unaware of the increased extension of the arm that is required to make a successful spike. Eventually, it will become obvious to the players that the net is higher than normal, but by that time the coach will have achieved his goal implicitly. Alternatively, the coach might consider the 'karate kid' technique, taken from the film of the same name, in which the wise old instructor, Mr Miyage, encourages his young protégé to spend many hours pointlessly waxing his car with the famous line 'wax on, wax off'. In fact, the same movement with which wax on, wax off is achieved, is also that with which a punch to the chest is deflected.

AN UNASHAMEDLY EXPLICIT CONCLUSION

Learners (particularly would-be superstars) actively seek to aggregate explicit information regarding their skills by testing hypotheses and taking instruction regarding the most appropriate way to move. Conscious access to such information is often disruptive to performance, especially when the performer is very highly motivated to succeed. There is evidence that practical advantages are associated with forms of implicit learning that avoid the accumulation of explicit knowledge about the mechanics that underlie the skill.

The coach has substantial influence over the learning environment of the performer. The use of implicit learning paradigms raises practical obstacles that the coach must negotiate, and although he or she cannot always constrain the environment to provide a *comprehensive* implicit skill learning experience, much can be done to discourage a performer from constantly testing hypotheses about the skill and to provide crucial performance information in ways that are not explicit. It is my contention that early skill learning experiences should be maximally constrained to be implicit, the learning environment should discourage active testing of hypotheses about performance outcomes, and any form of instruction that makes possible explicit access to the rule structures that underlie the skills should be strictly rationed.

COACH'S CORNER

Neil Craig

Senior Coach, Adelaide Crows Football Club

Can implicit learning work in practice?

Implicit learning is no doubt something many coaches have utilized in their coaching for many years. Reading this chapter reminded me of a story told by Bob Rotella about Harvey Penick, the coach of golfers Tom Kite and Ben Crenshaw. When asked what technique they needed 'to hit a high lob over a trap and stop it real fast on the green', Harvey directed them to stand behind the bunker and imagine hitting the ball over a tree that was growing in the middle of the bunker. They were told to make the tree grow higher until it was the right height to make the ball sit down and stop near the hole. When both Tom and Ben accomplished this task they were to come and fetch him so he could come and observe their success. And if one of them asked a question about technique for the high lob, Harvey would reply, 'I don't know. Show me again'. After showing him again, he would say, 'It's what you just did'.

There is no doubt we (coaches) can learn to coach more implicitly and in a more systematic manner. Although I understand what implicit learning looks like in its purest form, and agree we learn many skills in this manner, I also feel it cannot be the only way we coach in a high-performance coaching setting, owing to the key constraint of *time and the urgency for successful performance.* Limited preparation time combined with large amounts of information to be learned by players means we have to fast-track learning as much as possible. As a result I see the implicit learning technique as one of the many tools I use in my coaching. What I do like about implicit learning is that it empowers the player in the learning process, resulting in greater understanding and knowledge (even though they don't know they know!) and, most importantly for us, produces skills (physical and mental) that are pressure resistant.

Having said I can't rely solely on implicit learning approaches at the elite level, mainly owing to time constraints, I don't see this as a problem for junior coaches and challenge them to try coaching more implicitly. It would be fantastic for us to recruit players that have come from an implicitly, rather than explicitly, coached background. Currently, when recruiting players, we request their practice histories and examine how much unstructured deliberate play in invasion sports they have completed in their junior years (in my mind, implicit learning practice). If this volume of implicit learning wasn't so interrupted with explicit coaching through a player's teenage years we would be able alter our approach and also become even more implicit and hopefully take the skills of the game to a new level of performance.

Some practical examples of how we use implicit learning

I am a big believer in providing the players with a mental picture of what we are trying to achieve. I think it assists to accelerate their learning. For specific skills we are looking to develop we have found the use of analogies to be excellent in this regard. For example, in order to get players to adopt a low body position and soft hands when attempting to track and then pick up a loose ball rolling on the ground (ground ball), we have asked players to visualize that they are attempting to chase and catch a chicken (chase a chook)! This analogy left an indelible image owing to its novelty, but in terms of skills execution it summarized three or four coaching points into three simple words. In short, the image 'stuck' in the player's memory, made an impact and became a great reference point for the skill.

Teaching game strategies is another area where I think we could benefit from implicit learning techniques, but perhaps in a modified form. Simply to give players the ball and tell them to work out a way to move the ball efficiently from defence into attack, although maybe more implicit than doing a structured drill with the coach yelling instructions, is too undirected and time consuming. We have found that the use of discovery learning and constraints manipulation approaches, although not truly implicit, provide a good compromise. For example, playing our game with 15 vs 15 players instead of the usual 18 vs 18 allows certain movement styles to evolve naturally owing to the larger amounts of free space in specific positions on the ground. In such cases we don't need to tell the players how to move the ball but find that simply the change in numbers produces the required effect.

Another example I picked up from a book called *Blink* by Malcolm Gladwell (2005). He described a psychology experiment where participants were provided with a list of words to memorize. The participants were blind to the fact that the words were all subtly related to aging, for example, gray, Florida, old, etc. After completing the experimental task they were required to leave the classroom and walk down a corridor to submit their results. Unbeknown to the participants, the way they walked in and out of the classroom before and after the experiment was the issue of interest to the researchers. What they found was that the word list had an *implicit* effect on the participants' movement behavior. Compared with how they walked into the room, the participants left walking in a stooped, slow fashion, much like an older person would walk. After reading this I started putting posters up in our change-rooms with words or pictures denoting how I want the players to play. For example, to highlight the importance of precise skill execution, I have a poster with terms such as: precise, focus, hit the target, attention, concentration, care, quality execution, and ball on body displayed. I don't directly refer to the posters but simply put them up from time to time when I think it needs to be a focus. I figure this is implicit.

101

Future directions in implicit learning

Researchers

Go and see. If you want to be a leader in this research field I encourage you to go and spend some time in a coaching environment. This allows you to talk to the coaches and experience the issues that arise in trying to plan a theoretically sound but logistically possible practice rehearsal. Our collective wisdom is sure to produce some new approaches to implicit learning that work at both theoretical and applied levels.

Coaches

There are two critical factors for coaches who want to consider alternative ways of coaching their players:

1. Be inquisitive and want to coach better. To do this you need to ask questions about *why* and *how*.
2. You need time. Time to think things through on an individual level, for example, how I can apply implicit learning in my coaching environment. Then you need to allow time for such strategies to take effect within your team. I don't discard an approach after one practice rehearsal. As Rich indicated, implicit learning approaches do take time, and for some skills I have prioritized that we have the time to wait because the end result will be better.

KEY READING

Gladwell, M. (2005). *Blink*. London: Penguin Books.

Hatfield, B.D., Haufler, A.J., Hung, T. and Spalding, T.W. (2004). 'Electroencephalographic studies of skilled psychomotor performance'. *Journal of Clinical Neurophysiology*, (21): 144–56.

Liao, C. and Masters, R.S.W. (2001). 'Analogy learning: A means to implicit motor learning'. *Journal of Sports Sciences*, (19): 307–19.

Masters, R.S.W. (1992). 'Knowledge, knerves and know-how: The role of explicit versus implicit knowledge in the breakdown of a complex motor skill under pressure'. *British Journal of Psychology*, (83): 343–58.

Masters, R.S.W. and Maxwell, J.P. (2004). 'Implicit motor learning, reinvestment and movement disruption: What you don't know won't hurt you?'. In Williams, A.M. and Hodges, N.J. (eds) *Skill Acquisition in Sport: Research, Theory and Practice*. Routledge: London.

Masters, R.S.W., Polman, R.C.J. and Hammond, N.V. (1993). 'Reinvestment: A dimension of personality implicated in skill breakdown under pressure'. *Personality and Individual Differences*, (14): 655–66.

Masters, R.S.W., van der Kamp, J. and Jackson, R.C. (2007). 'Imperceptibly off-centre goalkeepers influence penalty-kick direction in soccer'. *Psychological Science*, (18): 222–3.

Maxwell, J.P., Masters, R.S.W., Kerr, E. and Weedon, E. (2001). 'The implicit benefit of learning without errors'. *Quarterly Journal of Experimental Psychology*, (54A): 1049–68.

Poolton, J., Masters, R.S.W. and Maxwell, J.P. (2005). 'The relationship between initial errorless learning conditions and subsequent performance'. *Human Movement Sciences*, (24): 362–78.

Poolton, J.M., Masters, R.S.W. and Maxwell, J.P. (2007). 'Passing thoughts on the evolutionary stability of implicit motor behavior: Performance retention under physiological fatigue'. *Consciousness & Cognition*, (16): 456–68.

Reber, A.S. (1993). *Implicit Learning and Tacit Knowledge: An Essay on the Cognitive Unconscious.* New York: Oxford University Press.

Chapter 8

Performance pressure and paralysis by analysis: research and implications

Robin C. Jackson and Sian L. Beilock

INTRODUCTION

> Human beings under pressure are wonderfully unpredictable; their nature is a puzzle
> to us all. . . When human beings are placed in an arena, and their hopes and fears
> exposed in front of thousands of observers, they are likely to do extraordinary things.
> This is especially true if someone has told them, 'Don't let us down now'.
>
> (Patmore, 1986: 7)

By definition, elite athletes execute their chosen skills with a very high level of precision.
Yet often these same athletes perform poorly in pressure situations. Performing poorly in
spite of high motivation and incentives for success has been termed *choking under pressure*.
There are numerous examples across sports in which performers fail at crucial moments to
execute successfully skills that have been performed perfectly time and time again in practice
situations: routine golf putts and rugby place-kicks are missed, basketball free throws hit the
rim, tennis players serve double faults on critical points, and soccer penalty kicks are ballooned
over the crossbar. A frequently cited example of *choking* is that of the golfer Greg Norman
who led by six shots going into the final round of the 1996 US Masters, one of the four major
golf championships. As the pressure of the final round built, Norman's lead was whittled
away until, finally, there was an eleven-shot difference between his score (78) and that of
the winner, Nick Faldo (67). Although such instances may grab the headlines, poor
performance in pressure situations is far from unusual. For example, researchers have found
that the probability of major-league baseball players scoring a hit was approximately twenty
per cent lower when failure to do so would result in the end of that inning (i.e., there were
already two outs). When the pressure to keep one's team in the inning is highest, the
performance of the very best athletes may be lowest.

At the outset, it is important to highlight a difficulty faced by both researchers and coaches:
how does one distinguish between normal or random fluctuations in performance and an
abnormally poor performance? In Norman's case, his experience was clearly out of the
ordinary. He was interviewed for *Golf Magazine* almost a year after the event and said 'Never

in my career have I experienced anything like what happened . . . I was totally out of control. And I couldn't understand it'.

Although it might be convenient to label any instance of poor performance as a *choke*, meaningful scientific use of the term requires corroboration, either through introspective self-reports on the part of the athlete (such as by Norman above) or statistical analysis indicating that the observed poor performance is unlikely to be explained by random fluctuations in performance. This is especially important given that people can be poor judges of what random fluctuations in performance look like and are also not great at distinguishing between a chance occurrence of an event and genuinely unusual patterns. For example, researchers investigating the validity of the 'hot hand' in basketball (i.e., the notion that a player is more likely to make a given shot if it is preceded by a run of successful shots rather than by one or more misses) found little evidence to suggest it was a genuine phenomenon. Researchers compared the probability of NBA players being successful following a series of hits or misses and found that they were no more likely to be successful following one, two, or three previous hits than they were following a series of misses. In fact, when analysing the individual members of the Philadelphia 76ers basketball team, only one player appeared to be influenced by the outcomes of previous shots. But rather than having a *hot hand*, the player was more successful after one (71 per cent), two (73 per cent), and three (88 per cent) misses than he was after successful shots (57 per cent, 58 per cent, 51 per cent, following one, two, and three hits, respectively).

In this chapter we concentrate on instances of poor performance in sport and the implications for coaches and performers. We consider relatively short or acute instances of poor performance rather than more prolonged or chronic *slumps* in performance—as the causes of this latter class of performance failure are complex and multifaceted and do not necessarily stem from a heightened sense of perceived pressure or desire to perform at an optimal level. Along these lines, we also try to distinguish between random fluctuations in performance and pressure-induced failure. We apply the term *choking under pressure* only to those instances of less-than-optimal skill execution that have a clear connection to heightened importance and performance pressure in a given situation.

We present research that has attempted to uncover why choking occurs through examining ways in which pressure-filled situations change how individuals think about and attend to skilled performance. We believe that understanding *how* crucial moments affect the attentional processes supporting high-level skill execution can be used to develop training regimens and performance strategies designed to alleviate skill failure. In the first section of the chapter, we summarize what research tells us about the dangers of *thinking too much* when executing well-learned and highly practiced motor skills. We then consider factors that might moderate or trigger this process. In the second section, we consider the implications of this research for designing strategies to prevent skill breakdown under stress.

RESEARCH ON THE DANGERS OF THINKING TOO MUCH

Why does choking occur in well-learned and highly practiced skills such as the tournament-winning putt or the all-important penalty shot? Several researchers have suggested that pressure situations raise self-consciousness and anxiety about performing correctly. This focus on the self is thought to prompt performers to turn their attention inward to the specific processes of their performance in an attempt to exert more skill control than would be applied in a non-pressure situation. For example, the basketball player who makes eighty-five per cent of his/her free throws in practice may miss the game-winning foul shot because, in trying to ensure an optimal outcome, they monitor the angle of their wrist or the release point as they shoot the ball. After many thousands of hours of practice, these components of performance are not something that our basketball player would normally attend to. And, paradoxically, such attention is thought to disrupt well-learned performance processes that normally run largely outside conscious awareness—*paralysis by analysis*.

In support of the above ideas, work in our laboratories and others has demonstrated that, for well-learned and highly practiced skills, paying too much attention to task control and guidance (what we call skill-focused attention) may actually disrupt execution. Just as thinking about how and where we place our feet as we rush down the stairs may result in the disruption of well-learned walking movements and a fall, attending too much to skill processes that generally run off without conscious awareness can disrupt performance and cause skill failure in sport. For example, in one study in our laboratories, we asked skilled soccer players to dribble the ball through a series of pylons while paying attention to the side of their foot that most recently contacted the ball. This instruction was designed to draw attention to performance in a way that does not normally occur. Dribbling performance was worse (i.e., slower and more error prone) when the soccer players were asked to attend to performance in comparison with a condition in which they dribbled without any instructions. Similarly, in another study, when soccer players were asked to set themselves a goal to maximize success, those who chose to focus on elements of soccer technique (e.g. 'keep loose with knees bent') performed worse than normal.

Similar results have been reported in an investigation of baseball batting. When highly skilled university-level baseball players were asked to perform a hitting task and, at the same time, attend to a specific component of swing execution in a manner to which they were not accustomed, their performance suffered. Here, baseball players heard a randomly presented tone and were instructed to indicate whether their bat was moving downward or upward at the instant the tone was presented. Biomechanical swing analyses revealed that the observed performance failure was at least partially due to the fact that skill-focused attention interfered with the sequencing and timing of the different skill components involved in swinging.

The above research suggests that paying too much attention to highly practiced skills disrupts performance. However, it should be noted that skill-focused attention may sometimes be necessary, for example, when making changes to a well-learned technique. High-level performers will probably have to slow down and unpack automated processes in order to change their technique, which may result in temporarily poor performance (e.g. Tiger Woods' and Nick Faldo's less-than-optimal performance while making changes to their golf swings). Ultimately, of course, these changes are made so that skill execution more closely mirrors desired outcomes. A critical part of this process involves progressing to a level in which the newly learned technique can be performed automatically or with minimal conscious thought. This is far from easy when making fundamental changes. For example, it took the best part of three years for Faldo to retain and then surpass his previous level of performance after remodelling his swing. Others are less fortunate. In searching for more shot distance, the Australian golfer Ian Baker-Finch made changes to his swing and suffered a dramatic loss in form and confidence that eventually led him to withdraw from tournament golf. This was only five years after he won the British Open, arguably the most prestigious of the four 'major' championships.

TRIGGERS OF FAILURE

Now that we have attempted to describe why the failure of well-learned and highly practiced motor skills occurs in pressure situations, we turn to potential triggers of such failure.

Thinking and imaging failure

Although one might assume that people in general (and most certainly highly disciplined athletes) are good at controlling their thoughts and performance-related images, it turns out that athletes *do* report thinking about the possibility of skill failure. Moreover, research has demonstrated that athletes' images of failure and even the mere mention of choking can result in less-than-optimal performances.

One of the first studies to examine this idea investigated the impact of negative imagery on dart-throwing success. It was found that combining dart-throwing practice with negative imagery (i.e., imaging the dart landing near the edge of the board rather than in the center) led to a decrease in dart-throwing accuracy in comparison with combining dart throwing with positive imagery (i.e., imaging the dart landing near the center of the target). Additional evidence that pre-performance negative imagery can impair skill execution comes from recent studies exploring the effects of positive and negative imagery on golf putting. Golf putting accuracy declined when individuals employed negative imagery (e.g. thinking about missing the hole) prior to hitting the ball.

Thus, the ability to control one's thoughts and images prior to and during skill execution seems to be a crucial determinant of successful performance. Both negative self-talk and negative imagery immediately prior to performance may harm execution. Why? One possibility is that thinking about a negative outcome causes individuals to try and control their skill in an attempt to ensure that this negative performance outcome will not come to fruition. Ironically, as we have described above, such added control can backfire, disrupting well-learned and automated performance processes.

Audience factors

In the 1980s, the possibility that the crowd might trigger choking attracted considerable interest. Most intriguingly, psychologist Roy Baumeister proposed that, in critical matches, choking would be more likely when performing in front of a *supportive* audience. He hypothesized that the pressure of performing in front of home supporters who had high expectations of success would cause players to try to control aspects of their skills that are normally controlled subconsciously. That is, players would employ skill-focused attention

107

in a manner that might disrupt or slow down automatic aspects of performance. To investigate this possibility, Baumeister and colleagues analyzed archival data on the home field advantage in the sports of NBA basketball and major-league baseball during world series or championship matches. Examining instances in which the home team was one game away from winning the series, they found that the home teams won just 38.5 per cent of decisive seventh games in baseball and just 37.5 per cent of basketball games in which they had a chance to clinch the championship. Analysis of player errors in baseball and free-throw percentages in basketball suggested that the results were mostly due to poorer home team performance rather than improvements on the part of the away teams.

Some researchers have questioned the generality of the home field *disadvantage* phenomenon by presenting evidence that it only applies to certain clubs. In addition, reanalysis of the baseball data to include the subsequent ten years, a period in which the home team won all of the decisive seventh games, indicated that the data in support of the home field disadvantage fell below the standard criteria for statistical significance. However, this reanalysis may have been confounded by a change to the rules. Nevertheless, other laboratory-based studies have demonstrated that the nature of an audience can indeed affect performance. For example, Baumeister and colleagues compared performance in front of supportive and neutral audiences in a video game task. They found that participants were more prone to focus on themselves and their skill execution in front of a supportive audience than a neutral audience. Participants also performed more slowly and with less accuracy in the supportive audience condition. In spite of this, individuals who performed in front of the supportive audience rated the experience as far less stressful than those who performed in front of the neutral audience. Thus, skill-focused attention need not necessarily be preceded by anxiety or perceived performance pressure.

MODERATORS OF SKILL FAILURE

Skill level and type

From one's reading of the chapter thus far it might be tempting to conclude that the *only* way in which a skill can fail under pressure is by performers attempting to monitor and control skill processes that should be left alone. However, although this may be the case for well-learned and highly practiced sport skills, this may not extend to all types of task or all skill levels. For example, novices asked to attend to how they were executing their skill in both a baseball batting task and a soccer dribbling task (the same tasks described earlier) did not show performance decrements in comparison with normal execution conditions. Unlike experts, novices just starting to learn a skill must pay attention to skill processes and procedures in order to ensure an optimal outcome. As a result, novices are not hurt by conditions that draw attention to performance—and, in fact, often improve with such added attention (although see Masters, Chapter 7).

Given that novice performance is not hurt when individuals are prompted to monitor execution, one might wonder whether novices are impacted by pressure at all. We have found some support for the idea that novice performers are not harmed by performance pressure in the same way that skilled individuals are. Individuals learned a golf putting skill to a high level and were exposed to a high-pressure situation both early and late in practice. Early in practice, pressure to do well actually facilitated performance. At later stages of learning, performance decrements under pressure emerged. This finding is consistent with the fact that most of the evidence for choking under pressure has been derived from highly skilled athletes.

Nonetheless, there are probably well-learned components of sport performance that still require a significant amount of attention and effort for optimal performance and thus may not be harmed when performers attempt to control execution. For example, strategizing, problem solving, and decision making (having to consider multiple novel options simultaneously and updating information in real time) can, at times, require considerable attention and memory resources (also see Farrow and Raab, Chapter 10, and McPherson, Chapter 11). These skills then may not fail when performers concentrate on what they are doing, but instead may fail if performers are distracted from the decision-making task at hand. This area is ripe for research, and we speculate that the time available for making decisions may be an important factor here. For example, if there is plenty of time to make a decision or plan a strategy, then pressure may have little impact on the quality of the final decision. In contrast, in skills requiring rapid decision making, it is possible that pressure to perform well will lead to slower, more analytical decision making that harms performance.

Dispositional self-consciousness

So far we have explored the idea that one way in which failure under pressure occurs is when performers attempt to control their skills consciously. Paradoxically, this can result in poorer levels of performance than if individuals had spent less time and effort thinking about skill execution. One obvious question is whether certain individuals are more likely to try consciously to control their movements than others. To explore this question, researchers have focused on an individual's level of self-consciousness, determined by responses to a scale in which they rated statements such as 'I'm aware of the way my mind works when I work through a problem', and 'I'm concerned about what other people think of me'. One proposal was that people who rated such items as characteristic of themselves (i.e., highly self-conscious individuals) should be less prone to choking because they would be more used to performing in the type of self-aware state that pressure creates. Conversely, others have argued that scoring highly on such items would indicate susceptibility to thinking too much, such that highly self-conscious individuals would be more prone to skill failure under stress.

Overall, the weight of evidence currently favors the latter prediction: highly self-conscious individuals appear more prone to skill failure, certainly in sport skills. Indeed, Rich Masters and colleagues devised the Reinvestment Scale specifically to predict the process of *reinvesting* conscious control in motor skills, incorporating many of the items used to assess self-consciousness. Researchers using this scale have indicated that high scores predict skill failure. And, research involving players from university squash and tennis teams has even indicated that high reinvestment scorers are rated by their team captains and presidents as being more prone to choking under pressure (see Masters, Chapter 7).

109

THEORY INTO PRACTICE: TECHNIQUES FOR PREVENTING PARALYSIS BY ANALYSIS

If thinking too much can disrupt the fluid, automatic qualities of a highly practiced skill, a key question is how to prevent this from happening. Clearly the solution is not easy because there remain many instances of poor performance under pressure. Nevertheless, there are a range of techniques that have proved effective in the laboratory setting and, although such studies are unlikely to recreate the levels of anxiety experienced in competition, they help provide the theoretical basis for interventions in the field. Broadly speaking, interventions can be divided into those that relate to how a skill is learned and those that focus on how to prevent failure when a high skill level has already been obtained.

Learning factors

The relationship between how a skill is learned and the likelihood of subsequent skill failure under stress is covered in more detail in Masters, Chapter 7. Here, we simply note that there is a growing body of research indicating that if performers can learn skills with minimal knowledge of the underlying rules related to the performance of the skill then such skills are less susceptible to breakdown under stress. This line of research has evolved to explore practical means of minimizing explicit problem solving during learning. These include attempting to minimize errors during learning and using analogies or *biomechanical metaphors* as a substitute for a number of explicit instructions given by a coach. The results to date indicate that skills acquired in these ways demand less attention, generate a smaller pool of explicit knowledge, and are more robust under psychological and physiological stress.

'Acclimatization' strategies

An alternative to changing the way we learn skills is to try to minimize the impact of factors that trigger conscious control processes or skill-focused attention. The logic behind acclimatization strategies is that exposing a performer to conditions that heighten self-awareness during training will acclimatize or adapt them to performing in that state. This, in turn, should inoculate the performer against the negative impact of situational pressures that heighten self-awareness. There are only a few studies exploring the efficacy of this approach to date. Nevertheless, there is some evidence from two separate studies of golf putting that participants who practiced the task while being videotaped subsequently performed better under pressure (induced by financial incentives and peer pressure) than did those who did not receive adaptation training. The participants receiving adaptation training were told that the videotape would be used to examine their movements as they learned the putting task.

It is also possible acclimatization training may serve another purpose in addition to, or instead of, adapting individuals to monitoring execution. Namely, it may adapt individuals to the pressure situation in general. To the extent that athletes become accustomed to performing under pressure, a high-stakes situation may not represent much that is new to them. And, in turn, when this type of situation arises, they may not feel as much pressure as non-adapted individuals, and sub-optimal skill execution may be avoided. Nonetheless, some caution should be expressed when attempting to generalize from the results of the above studies because they involved novice individuals trained to a high putting skill level, rather than expert players with several years of golf experience.

Minimize thinking time and pre-performance routines

The more time one has to execute a skill, the better the performance, right? We have all heard the adage 'haste makes waste'. But, is this really true, especially with respect to the performance of well-learned and highly practiced skills? If thinking too much about how to perform a skill disrupts performance, then having a lot of preparation time to think about a technical skill performed with a small margin of error might actually result in a worse rather than better performance.

Recently, Beilock *et al.* (2004) found that skilled golfers performed better when instructed to execute their putts as quickly as possible than they did when instructed to take as much time as needed. Thus golfers were more accurate when given minimal time to think about and prepare for the putt than when they were allowed to perform the task using as much time as they chose. It should be noted that Beilock's study used only short putts of up to 1.58 m. Whether it pays to minimize thinking time on more difficult putts that require the player to *read* the different slopes and judge the speed has yet to be established. Nonetheless, the finding lends support to anecdotal evidence from skilled golfers who believe that significantly reducing preparation time can improve accuracy. For instance, professional golfer Aaron Baddeley has a relatively short pre-putt routine in which he has a *four count* from the moment he grounds the putter to the moment he strikes the ball and is consistently rated as one of the best putters on the US tour.

The issue of preparation time is closely aligned with the routine pattern of thoughts and behaviors a performer engages in prior to executing their skill. In examining these routines, other researchers have found that the overall length of the routine is unimportant, as long as the relative frequency of different behavioral components of the routine remains consistent. Jackson analyzed pre-performance routine times of rugby union goal kickers during the World Cup and found no evidence that better kickers had shorter (or longer) routine times. Indeed, analysis of the data from each kicker revealed large individual differences in, for example, the time they stood still concentrating just before initiating their run-up. Some kickers spent just 4 or 5 s, while others spent over 20 s. In contrast to perceived wisdom, there was also no evidence that better kickers had more consistent routine times. Instead, routine time varied systematically with the difficulty of the kick: the more difficult the kick, the longer the players took standing over the ball before running up to take the kick. It seems that the critical thing for performers is to have a routine that enables them to execute the skill with a *quiet mind*. The total length (or indeed consistency) of the routine appears less important than having skills that facilitate this process. Toward this end, if stressful situations prompt performers to try and control execution in a way that alters their normal routine, then limiting the time available to do this (as Beilock and colleagues did) may help individuals get back to their well-practiced pre-shot routine.

111

Distraction strategies and visual cues

Attention directed internally toward monitoring the process of performance can cause a breakdown in the automaticity or fluency of that performance. But telling performers not to do this, rather like telling someone not to think of a pink elephant, is not particularly effective at suppressing the inappropriate focus of attention. There are, however, active focusing strategies that appear beneficial to performance. Again, researchers in this area have mainly focused on self-paced skills such as golf putting and basketball free throws and have proposed a five-step strategy or pre-performance routine that has proved beneficial to performance. The steps consist of readying (preparing for the act), imaging (visualizing the movement), focusing (on a meaningful cue), executing (with a quiet mind), and evaluating (the effectiveness of each of the previous steps). From an attentional perspective, the key steps are focusing, with effort, on an external visual cue, and executing as if on autopilot. The external visual focus might be the dimple pattern or manufacturer's name on a golf ball, or the seams on a rugby ball. For example, rugby union goal kicker Jonny Wilkinson focuses intently on the precise point of the ball that he wants to strike. This is combined with a very specific target focus in which, rather than focus on the posts, he aims to kick the ball to a particular person in the crowd.

Attentional cues have also been used to cure cases of the yips in golf. For example, verbal cues were used in an intervention for a golfer who had difficulty initiating his down swing, performing numerous false starts on the golf course in which he froze at the top of his back swing. The intervention that proved most effective was to have the golfer say a three-syllable word to match the timing or rhythm of his golf swing (the player used the song title 'Edelweiss' from *The Sound of Music*). Thus, the player said Ed-el-weiss to correspond to initiation of his back swing, the top of his back swing and the point of contact with the ball.

Recently, we have found that distracting performers from the process of execution is facilitative under pressure-inducing conditions. Specifically, we have demonstrated that the performance of skilled golfers under conditions designed to increase feelings of performance pressure and anxiety was actually improved when they were forced to perform a second task concurrently while putting. In one study, Beilock and colleagues had golfers listen to a series of words being played on a tape recorder. Every time they heard a specific target word, they had to repeat it out loud. The process of drawing golfers' attention away from their own performance benefited overall execution under pressure.

Overall then, there appear to be two elements to the successful use of verbal or visual cueing. First, the technique helps focus the performer's attention on a task-relevant activity (e.g. visual fixation on the target). Second, there appears to be an element that occupies the performer's mind such that it prevents or distracts them from focusing on the automated process of performance, allowing such skill processes to run off with minimal conscious involvement. In tennis, coach and author of the *Inner Game* series of books, Tim Gallwey, talked of this process when recommending a strategy in which he encouraged players to say 'bounce' at precisely the moment the ball landed on the tennis court, and 'hit' at the moment it made contact with the player's racquet.

Strategy focus

Many skills require effective decision making as well as technical precision. This is particularly true of *open* skills such as open court play in racquet sports, and open play in team sports such as soccer, basketball, and rugby. If skill failure is the result of trying to control well-learned processes involved in the execution of skills then focusing on *what to do* (strategy) rather than *how to do it* (technique) might help prevent skill failure. Moreover, because strategizing generally requires one to take in and think about multiple pieces of information at a time, this type of focusing may have the added benefit of improving one's decision-making process (see Farrow and Raab, Chapter 10, and McPherson, Chapter 11). Recently, Jackson and colleagues (2006) conducted a study in which skilled soccer players set themselves goals prior to completing a task involving dribbling the ball between a series of cones. The participants were told to choose a *process goal* that they felt would help maximize their success on the task. Results showed that some of the participants set themselves goals that related to the movements or technique required to perform the task well (e.g. 'keep loose with knees bent'), whereas others set themselves goals that related to more strategic or positioning elements of the task (e.g. 'keep the ball close to the cones'). Those who set themselves goals relating to movement or technique subsequently performed worse, whereas those who focused on strategy maintained the same level of performance. These findings were not affected by pressure: participants focusing on strategy still maintained their performance under high pressure, whereas those focusing on technique continued to perform more poorly. Again, this highlights the *paradox of control*: performers may focus on elements of performance they believe will help them to maintain or enhance that performance but which in fact can result in poorer performance.

CONCLUSION

There is a growing body of research examining attentional processes underlying skill failure. Evidence from a wide range of studies points to the idea that the failure of well-learned and highly practiced athletic skills occurs when performers try consciously to control elements of performance that normally run off automatically. This paradox of control, in which the desire to ensure that performance does not fail actually triggers skill failure, provides a challenge to performers and practitioners alike. We have given a brief summary of some of the research that examines this process and considered the implications of this work for the development of effective intervention strategies (see Figure 8.1). Of course, although science is useful for providing a theoretical framework for interventions, no single intervention strategy is likely to be effective for all performers and all skills. The challenge for the coach and sport scientist is how best to apply the principles from the lab to design interventions that prove effective in the field of competitive sport.

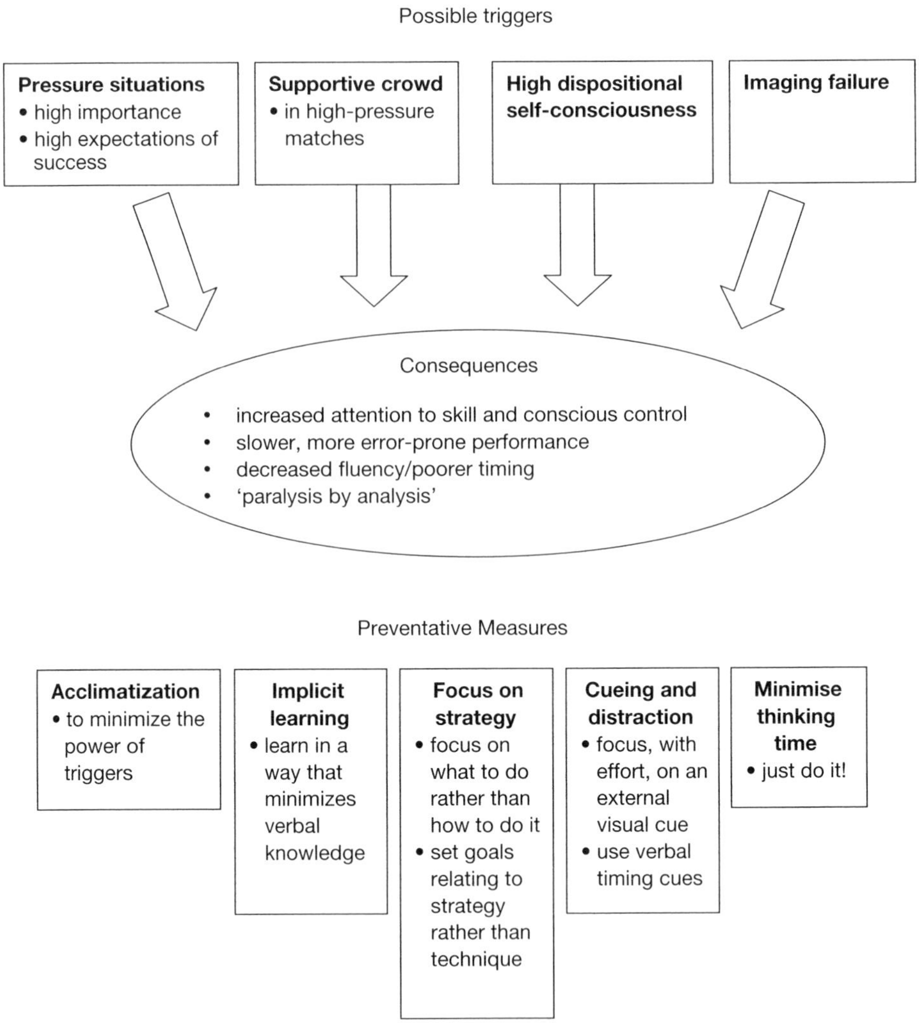

Possible triggers

Pressure situations	Supportive crowd	High dispositional self-consciousness	Imaging failure
• high importance • high expectations of success	• in high-pressure matches		

Consequences

- increased attention to skill and conscious control
- slower, more error-prone performance
- decreased fluency/poorer timing
- 'paralysis by analysis'

Preventative Measures

Acclimatization	Implicit learning	Focus on strategy	Cueing and distraction	Minimise thinking time
• to minimize the power of triggers	• learn in a way that minimizes verbal knowledge	• focus on what to do rather than how to do it • set goals relating to strategy rather than technique	• focus, with effort, on an external visual cue • use verbal timing cues	• just do it!

Figure 8.1 Possible triggers of choking in well-learned skills and associated preventative measures.

COACH'S CORNER

Tim Nielsen

Head Coach, Australian Cricket Team

My sport, cricket, is interesting when identifying opportunities for *the choke* to occur. Although it's a team game, it has a strong reliance on the individual skill execution of the players. Batting and fielding are open (reactive) skills, whereas bowling is a closed (self-initiated) skill. I consistently see examples of both forms of skill being affected (positively and negatively) by pressure. I ask the researchers 'Are there consistencies in each?'

What causes choking

Three things stand out to me in my experience of *choking*, or paralysis by analysis as mentioned in this chapter:

1. Choking: the expectation on the elite athlete of successful execution, heightened dramatically in pressure situations where the result has a finite measure. As identified in the chapter, we should never forget that most *remembered* chokes happen in the biggest arenas—when the outcome is the 'be all' and 'end all': making a duck (scoring no runs) is a blip on the screen in the first innings of the first Test of the series; but making a duck in the second innings of the fifth Test, series drawn 2 all and 2 runs to win is a *choke*!
2. The tyranny of negative thinking, and the inability to distinguish the negative aspect from the positive: the *pink elephant* or *water effect*. For example when I play golf I am always thinking 'don't hit the ball in the water', yet often manage to find it! The authors of the chapter summed this up with their description of the dart-throwing study.
3. The coach: specifically, I feel that the biggest impact a coach can have can be cut into two parts—pre competition preparation, and *in game* environment. Being able to set programs that challenge the athlete to perfect the basics and execute them well under all types of game pressure is paramount in creating the confidence to compete in all situations. The coach having confidence the athlete has *done the work* also helps stop the coach from interfering at important times, which may heighten the pressure on the athlete.
4. The *environment* is a vital component for athletic performance. If the player feels comfortable and supported yet encouraged and challenged always to strive for an improved level, there should be no fear of failure in crunch situations. The coach and athlete will see a high-pressure situation as another opportunity to display what they have worked so hard on, and therefore welcome the position they find themselves in!

How to overcome choking

I feel there are two aspects to overcoming a player's likelihood of choking:

(a) the type of training the players complete in their preparation to play, and
(b) the ability to have mental cues to rely on in the competitive environment.

Preparation

For me, the basic premise of overcoming choking gets back to a core point—ensuring preparation is specific and demanding enough to withstand the rigors of the competitive situation the athlete is exposed to. Right now, our elite athletes commit more time to training than athletes ever did before. Money, technology, and the human resources available to support an athlete's performance grow every day, ensuring that every opportunity is available to the athlete to prepare as well as possible. However, we must never forget that, unless the preparation is specifically aimed at performing at the highest pressure point in the highest level of competition, it is not preparation; it is a level of practice! Practicing to be a club-level cricketer cannot prepare you to perform at the international level.

To this end, personal skill training should offer the specific technical focus and volume that allow for consistent execution under varying conditions and game situations (pressures). The role of the coach plays a massive part here—planning and presenting drills and scenarios that offer the athlete the opportunity to learn the technique his/her most appropriate way (not always what the coach thinks is the best way!), as well as building the confidence to execute the skill when required most. I found this an interesting aspect of the chapter—the need to balance providing technical information to a player and the need for them to forget this information when performing. Similarly, sometimes a drill to create confidence is not the type of drill I would use when focusing on changing an element of their technique.

When the issue of training time/content is discussed, many observers argue that training time is often wasted or *empty*. I feel you need to be careful in saying *wasted*. Although a significant amount of training may not be at competitive intensity, it does help the athlete 'groove' the skill, and create confidence for reactive execution under pressure.

It is also important to remember that all individuals learn by different coaching and learning styles and under different conditions. Where one athlete could thrive on slow, step-by-step breaking down of the skill, another may just *want to do it* over and over and over again as hard as possible. This is one of the skills of coaching—maintaining an individual focus inside the collective environment. Most importantly, the players should feel the coach is not only supporting and educating to assist the player execute, but offering an environment that clearly states that not being successful every time is not failing.

The concept presented in this chapter of distracting the athletes by having them complete a secondary task in training is a good suggestion. However, I also feel that, although we can use all sorts of strategy from a skill and even physical intensity point of view, I am not sure if any elite player ever replicates anything near *in-game* intensity in their training for one key reason—it doesn't matter if you win or lose: there are no short- or long-term consequences from *losing at training*, as the press, supporters, etc. don't judge you on it.

Players should be encouraged to experiment every day in all manner of situations, but most importantly they must be encouraged to experiment in the game environment, in competitive play. Players must understand that as long as they have practiced the core of the skill (or basics) then experimentation in a game setting really involves a different adaptation of these basics. In trying to find a motto for this I have come up with the following: *we aim to perfect the basics so that we can do the more difficult things more easily.*

Preparation, correct preparation, can only be successful if the skill and the heightened awareness of the result is replicated in a competitive setting. One of my experiences with the Australian cricket team illustrates this. Australia won three Test matches in Sri Lanka in February/March 2004, after trailing on the first innings in all three matches played. Our ability to overcome a first innings deficit played a critical role in the success of a drought-breaking series win in India later that year. Innately, in times of stress, the group and the individuals had a preparation (experience) to draw on, one that was of equal if not higher intensity than that offered in India. This tour was used as a physical, mental, technical, and tactical benchmark in the planning and execution of the win in India, by all involved.

A good lesson to be learned here is that not all preparation, in fact a small percentage, takes place on the training track—this is practice. Competitive experience—utilising the skills practiced in training—is a major contributor to overcoming the fateful choke, to see the positive opportunity and trust oneself to get the job done when it counts most.

Having cues to rely upon in competition

As highlighted in the chapter, in the heat of battle when a player's performance starts to deteriorate I think it's vital that the player has cues (routines) to rely on. I encourage all players to develop a pre-ball routine that will assist in getting them subconsciously *into gear* each and every delivery of the game. This routine will help to relax the player in times of higher stress (*crunch time*—when the choke is most likely!) by bringing a feeling of regularity to irregular circumstances. These routines assist the player to maintain focus on what they know they can do (have trained and practiced for), and focus on the process involved with executing the skill rather than worrying about the final result they are so desperate to achieve.

In sum, do what you know, what you have identified works for the individual through practical experience and quality preparation and can deliver with efficient excellence. Then, and only then, will a vision of success be supported by a player ready to deliver it!

KEY READING

Baumeister, R.F. and Steinhilber, A. (1984). 'Paradoxical effects of supportive audiences on performance under pressure: The home field disadvantage in sports championships'. *Journal of Personality and Social Psychology*, (47): 85–93.

Beilock, S.L. and Carr, T.H. (2001). 'On the fragility of skilled performance: What governs choking under pressure?'. *Journal of Experimental Psychology: General*, (130): 701–25.

Beilock, S.L., Bertenthal, B.I., McCoy, A.M. and Carr, T.H. (2004). 'Haste does not always make waste: Expertise, direction of attention, and speed versus accuracy in performing sensorimotor skills'. *Psychonomic Bulletin and Review*, (11): 373–9.

Beilock, S.L., Carr, T.H., MacMahon, C. and Starkes, J.L. (2002). 'When paying attention becomes counterproductive: Impact of divided versus skill-focused attention on novice and experienced performance of sensorimotor skills'. *Journal of Experimental Psychology: Applied*, (8): 6–16.

Gallwey, T. (1974). *The Inner Game of Tennis*. London: Pan Books.

Gilovich, T., Vallone, R. and Tversky, A. (1985). 'The hot hand in basketball: On the misperception of random sequences'. *Cognitive Psychology*, (17): 295–314.

Gray, R. (2004). 'Attending to the execution of a complex sensorimotor skill: Expertise differences, choking, and slumps'. *Journal of Experimental Psychology: Applied*, (10): 42–54.

Jackson, R.C. (2002). 'Pre-performance routine consistency: Temporal analysis of goal kicking in the Rugby Union World Cup'. *Journal of Sports Sciences*, (21): 803–14.

Jackson, R.C., Ashford, K.J. and Norsworthy, G. (2006). 'Attentional focus, dispositional reinvestment and skilled motor performance under pressure'. *Journal of Sport & Exercise Psychology*, (28): 49–68.

Patmore, A. (1986). *Sportsmen Under Stress*. London: Stanley Paul.

Thomas, P.R. (1999). 'Psychomotor disability in the golf swing: Case study of an ageing golfer'. In Farrally, M.R. and Cochran, A.J. (eds) *Science and Golf III*. Champaign, IL: Human Kinetics.

Chapter 9

Organizing practice: the interaction of repetition and cognitive effort for skilled performance

Jae T. Patterson and Timothy D. Lee

ORGANIZING PRACTICE

Sporting excellence is unquestionably a consequence of many hours of practice. Expertise theorists have predicted that a cumulative investment of at least 10,000 hours (e.g. 10 years) of practice is a minimal requirement to achieve a sport-specific level of expertise (see Baker and Cobley, Chapter 3). Inherent within this commitment to practice is the completion of an enormous number of repetitions. A repetition is the lowest common denominator within the practice schedule, but is believed by many to have the greatest impact on skill acquisition. But, not all repetitions contribute equally to the attainment of expertise. Skill acquisition researchers have suggested that it is not only how much the performer practices (i.e., the absolute number of repetitions of a skill such as a tennis serve), but how the performer practices each repetition that is the more important variable in the contribution of practice to skill acquisition. In fact, researchers often classify practice as *repetition without repetition*, because it is not the mere repeating of movements over and over again that is most effective for learning. Rather, successful practice requires that each repetition *build upon* what was learned in the previous repetition. Therefore, each subsequent repetition is something that tries to explore the nature and consequences of the previous one.

Often overlooked by coaches are the strong links between the amount of cognitive (information-processing) effort that a learner puts into practice and the level of skill expertise developed. This relationship means a number of factors should be considered:

- the practice context must optimally challenge the cognitive and motor capabilities of the performer;
- the performer must be able to understand relevant task-related feedback;
- the performer must be provided with the opportunity to engage and learn how to detect when errors have occurred, why they have occurred, and how to fix them.

As such, a single practice repetition (for example, a single tennis serve) has been viewed as a problem-solving process in which the practice repetition should not only reflect the perceptual–motor component of motor skill performance, but the cognitive processes as well. This emphasis on problem solving is congruent with the notion that many motor skills are highly cognitive in nature. Many experts, in addition to motor skill proficiency, also demonstrate superiority in the cognitive processes required for monitoring, planning (e.g. retrieval of information) and interpretation of motor performance (see also McPherson, Chapter 11). For example, interviews with experts reveal that they invest considerable conscious effort in the planning, execution and interpretation of their movements.

The ability of the athlete to consistently and reliably produce the required motor skill at the appropriate time suggests to the coach that the athlete has learned the motor skill. In fact, an important component of skilled behavior is the capability to reproduce the correct motor action in specific competition contexts, independent of instruction from the coach. Skill acquisition researchers examine the impact of specific practice factors (e.g. frequent feedback) on motor skill reproducibility by utilizing tests that are designed to mimic competition (called retention and transfer tests). These retention and transfer tests occur *after* a series of practice repetitions (e.g. minutes, days or weeks) and typically require the learner to perform the motor skill *without* assistance or cues from the coach, as in most competitive situations. Performance of the retention and transfer tests offers clues to evaluate which practice factors were more or less successful in *facilitating* the learning of the task. The purpose of this chapter is to highlight those practice factors that facilitate the cognitive components required for skilled, reproducible motor actions.

The importance of the time before and after a practice repetition

The organization of the practice session can be considered as two separate events, differentiated by the cognitive processes engaged in by the performer before and upon completion of a skill. Before completion of a skill, factors such as the predictability of the repetitions, the use of demonstration, and the use of instructions regarding the athlete's attentional focus are specific practice factors that all have the ability to influence how an athlete *plans* an action. Upon completion of the skill, the performer is engaged in the thought processes required for understanding what went wrong and how to fix it on the next repetition. Practice factors such as the *frequency* of providing feedback regarding motor skill success, as well as the *method* of presenting task-related feedback have been found to facilitate error detection and correction. Researchers agree that a practice session should be organized with the following aims in mind:

- to facilitate the performance of skills at an appropriate level of cognitive and motor difficulty;
- to augment motor performance with informative feedback;
- to encourage the performer to improve their abilities at error detection and correction.

Engaging the learner in a practice context that optimally challenges their motor and cognitive skills required for motor planning and error detection facilitates autonomy and independence in the performer, essential for the attainment of expertise.

Factors that facilitate planning a motor response: consistency or variability in the repetition schedule?

The amount of variation in practice repetitions has a significant influence on how much planning a performer is required to engage in and can subsequently have a dramatic effect on skill acquisition. A classic skill acquisition study found that practicing three variations of a single motor skill in an unpredictable repetition schedule (e.g. random practice) was superior for learning compared with a rote type of practice condition where the performer merely tried to repeat what was done on the previous attempt (e.g. blocked practice). Although the numbers of repetitions were the same in both blocked and random practice schedules, for the blocked condition all repetitions of one motor skill were completed before trials were undertaken on either the second and third variations of the motor skill. Consequently, a movement that had been developed for one particular task was essentially recycled for performance on many subsequent trials. This was not so for the random schedule, in which trials of all tasks were interspersed during practice. Under such a schedule the performer is required actively to think about the current skill goal as a unique experience. The results of this research were rather surprising—performance in the blocked practice condition was superior to that in the random practice condition, *but* only during the practice phase of the experiment. When learners returned later for retention and transfer tests (which provide measures of relative amount learned), the findings were reversed. Learning had been facilitated more by random than by blocked practice.

These findings were considered counter-intuitive to skill acquisition theory at the time—how could a factor that depressed performance during initial practice result in more permanent learning of a skill? More recent research has generalized these effects outside the laboratory, to numerous sport settings. For example, college varsity baseball players who received extra batting practice sessions to hit curveballs, fastballs, and changeups showed superior hitting proficiency of these specific pitches when presented in a random order compared with a blocked order. The benefits of *non-repetitiveness* in the practice sequence have been attributed to the active cognitive processes engaged in by the performer during *motor planning*. For example, the predictability of the practice repetition sequence determines the decision making required by the performer to plan their upcoming movement. As shown in Table 9.1, when the performer is aware of the upcoming required movement, the decision making, or planning is low, because the performer is required simply to repeat the most recent movement. However, as the practice trials become unpredictable with regard to the required upcoming movement, the decision processes in the athlete are heightened.

The theoretical reasons for such counter-intuitive findings have been interpreted by two distinct, yet complementary theoretical models. In both theoretical models, the performer is actively engaged in the cognitive processes required for motor planning. The *reconstruction hypothesis* suggests the performer is investing cognitive effort to construct the required motor plan on every trial during a random practice schedule. As a result, the memorability and retrievability of the motor plan are strengthened, which facilitates performance in later tests of the motor skills. The *elaboration hypothesis* suggests the performer maintains each of the motor plans in *working memory* and is therefore investing cognitive effort in establishing the notable differences and similarities of the motor plans. The result of these cognitive processes

121

Table 9.1 *Repetition predictability and degree of decision making during motor planning as a function of repetition schedule characteristics*

Repetition schedule	Characteristics of repetition scheduling (e.g. thirty repetitions of three different types of baseball pitch)	Predictability in sequence	Decision making during motor planning
Blocked	ten repetitions of fastballs, then ten repetitions of curveballs, then ten repetitions of knuckleballs	high	low
Serial	fastball, curveball, knuckleball; exact sequence repeats ten times	high	moderate
Random	fastball, curveball, knuckleball, curveball, knuckleball, fastball; performance repetitions are not repeated on subsequent trials throughout the practice session	low	high

is a strengthening in memory of the representation and retrieval capabilities of the motor plan. Considerable research exists to support both of these theoretical predictions. The key message for coaches is the notion that the performer is actively investing cognitive effort in *planning* the action that, as a consequence, enhances reproducibility of the motor plan.

USING DEMONSTRATIONS TO FACILITATE SKILLED PERFORMANCE

The use of demonstration has been shown to be a valuable practice factor that emphasizes the cognitive processes of the performer during motor planning. Coaches commonly use demonstration as a method of initially teaching a motor skill. For example, the dance instructor will commonly demonstrate the required dance steps of a movement sequence to their students. Researchers have identified specific factors that discourage the performer from simply *imitating* the motor goal but rather encourage them to become an active participant in the demonstration trial, thus facilitating a *cognitive representation* of the motor goal. During a demonstration, researchers suggest the performer cognitively retains the required movement pattern as a template that is utilized by the performer for error detection and subsequent correction on upcoming practice repetitions. Factors such as the *skill level* of the demonstrator (e.g. expert or learner), as well as the interspersion of physical practice with demonstrations, have been shown to be two important factors that facilitate the problem-solving processes of the performer during motor planning.

The use of a skilled model to demonstrate movement-related information to the athlete is a common strategy utilized by coaches. Based on the skill level of the observer, researchers suggest important pre-practice considerations for the coach. First, for performers learning a movement pattern (e.g. proper form for a soccer kick), researchers suggest that learning is facilitated when verbal cues are used in combination with the visual demonstration. For example, while watching the video of a skilled soccer player, the observer is told 'the plant foot should be pointed in the direction of the intended pass'. Therefore, the coach's use of verbal cues assists the performer in attending to the critical components of the task required for attainment of the required movement pattern. For observers that already have a degree of proficiency with the sport, research suggests that observation facilitates acquisition of new movement *strategies* not previously learned by the athlete and the *sequencing* order of a series of motor skills (a gymnastics sequence or a dance sequence). In both of these examples, the use of demonstration is not redundant with the pre-existing skill of the athlete (for example learning a specific movement form) but is a method to augment and enhance the already existing skill of the performer.

Research examining performers observing an unskilled model who is also learning the motor task has revealed interesting results. A novice watching another novice learning a skill has been shown to facilitate a practice context whereby the observer sees the consequences of a motor plan as well as the strategies utilized by the demonstrator to accomplish the goal of the motor task in upcoming trials. Additionally, the observer can identify the strategies that were *effective* for the demonstrator and those that were ineffective. In this context, the observer has the opportunity to accelerate their motor performance by only selecting those movement strategies that were previously observed to be successful.

With regard to scheduling demonstrations within the practice session, research has examined the interspersion of observation trials accompanied by the performer physically practicing the motor task. Interspersing demonstrations with physical practice facilitates the performer's cognitive skills in identifying the characteristics of the movement components that resulted in a specific movement outcome. In fact, research has shown that replacing fifty per cent of physical practice trials with observation trials is equally as beneficial in motor skill attainment as physically performing all trials. During a demonstration, the observer cannot feel the sensation of the movement that has been produced by the demonstrator. Therefore, the importance of physical practice is to provide the performer with the opportunity to calibrate the motor system to the outcome of the action plan. In fact, the beneficial effects of observing a demonstration are often latent, and are not obvious until the performer has had the opportunity to interact physically with the task.

Another method used by researchers to examine the optimal schedule of demonstrations within the practice schedule is to allow participants to control the *frequency* of the demonstration. Within this practice context, the performer is presented with a choice as to whether or not they wish to receive task-related information, in the form of a demonstration, to assist in their motor planning processes. Therefore, the performer, as opposed to the coach, is self-controlling the *frequency* of the demonstrations during the practice period. The evidence suggests that performers self-structure the practice by requesting demonstrations frequently at the beginning of a practice period, then decreasing the frequency over the remainder of the practice period. The cognitive mechanisms underlying these effects reflect a strategy whereby the performer can accurately introspect about their own specific needs. As a result of physical practice combined with feedback regarding the success of an action, the performer can identify where they require more task-related information to calibrate future actions and where to look for this information in future demonstrations.

Motor skills that require a close approximation of a specific movement pattern, such as a specific diving technique, a gymnastics roll, or a dance step, are examples of motor skills that are effectively augmented by demonstrations. Such motor skills are generally performed in a closed (i.e., predictable) environment that will not affect the planning of the movement, and therefore the same motor pattern can be repeated. However, in an open (i.e., unpredictable) environment, the performer is unable to plan for the required action completely in advance. In most instances, the goal within an open environment, such as a soccer game, hockey game, or football game, is to score points by invading the opponent's zone. A recent surge in skill acquisition research has examined the impact of providing the performer with instructions that focus attention on the effects of one's movement in the environment (termed an *external focus* of attention) or instructions that focus attention on the movements themselves (*internal focus* of attention). Compared with an internal focus of attention, research has clearly shown that, for motor tasks that have an outcome-related goal (e.g. chip shot in golf), an external focus of attention is the superior instructional strategy in facilitating the attainment of the task goal by the performer. To account for these findings, the *constrained action hypothesis* suggests that, when performers actively attend to their body movements, they *consciously interfere* with normally unconscious processes required for controlling movement to achieve the task goal. In summary, the results from this research suggest that instructions that focus the athlete's attention away from the movement pattern for motor skills that are *outcome related* (e.g. scoring a goal in hockey), compared with movement pattern related (e.g. dance maneuver), is an instructional strategy that facilitates skilled performance (see also Jackson and Beilock, Chapter 8).

FACTORS FACILITATING ERROR DETECTION AND CORRECTION

From every performance repetition, the athlete is potentially interpreting two different, yet complementary sources of feedback from an action. Sensory feedback is inherent in all motor tasks and is a consequence of information arising from performing the action (e.g. the diver being aware of where their body is in space while approaching their entry into the pool). Augmented feedback is verbalizable, post-action information utilized by the coach to supplement information already available from intrinsic sources (e.g. telling the diver that the upper body was slightly bent forward on entry into the water), and provides information to the performer regarding the approximation of the task goal and the performed movement outcome. Augmented feedback outlining discrepancies between the *generated movement pattern* and the *required movement pattern* is defined as knowledge of performance (KP). Augmented feedback regarding the discrepancy between the *generated motor outcome* and the *required motor outcome* is termed knowledge of results (KR).

Skill acquisition theories in the 1970s suggested that augmented feedback must be provided to the performer as often as possible (e.g. after every movement) and as immediately as possible after the completion of a movement, in order to maximize the potential benefit to

124

learning. In fact, augmented feedback was perceived as a practice factor that was essential to the acquisition of skill, and without it learning and skill acquisition would not occur. This is not entirely untrue—next to the amount of practice, feedback is essential for skill acquisition. However, what the research tells us is that the method of organizing the provision of augmented feedback during the practice schedule has a dramatic impact on learning. In fact, frequent provision of augmented feedback has been shown to create a *dependence* on this form of information to guide error detection and correction. In this situation, the performer learns to depend on the coach-provided feedback to correct their motor response for upcoming attempts. As a consequence, the performer does not use intrinsic feedback to augment error detection and correction. Skill acquisition research has clearly shown that practice contexts that reduce *dependency* on augmented feedback and engage the performer in the processes required for *intrinsic feedback* facilitate the cognitive processes required for accurate and automatic error detection and correction.

Research examining the provision of augmented feedback suggests that practice repetitions should be organized to facilitate the cognitive processes required for error detection and correction. Therefore, every movement repetition should be structured to engage the participant cognitively. Commonly used methods found to facilitate learning include:

- decreasing the relative frequency or absolute amount of augmented feedback during the practice session;
- decreasing the provision of feedback over trials as the performer increases skill proficiency (e.g. a feedback-fading schedule);
- withholding feedback for a certain number of trials, such as five, ten, or fifteen trials, then presenting the performer with a summary of the feedback (either verbally or graphically);
- presenting augmented feedback once every five performance attempts (reduced relative frequency).

The premise behind these different augmented feedback schedules is that, during the trials where the coach does not provide augmented feedback, the performer is required to engage in error detection and correction utilizing *sensory feedback*. As a consequence, the *dependency* of the performer on augmented feedback from the coach is reduced. Verbal reports from participants receiving decreased frequency of KR have reported greater attention to the intrinsic components inherent within a motor task. These differences are evident in superior motor skill performance when the augmented feedback is no longer available and the performer is required solely to depend on the sensory sources of information for error detection and correction.

Athlete-determined augmented feedback schedules have also been shown to be an effective method to organize a feedback schedule within a practice session. For example, in a *bandwidth feedback* paradigm, a predetermined error tolerance is generated such that, if the performer attains the task goal within the error tolerance, the performance is perceived as correct, as no prescriptive feedback is provided to the performer (e.g. qualitative information). If the performance is outside the bandwidth (e.g. error tolerance), augmented information is then provided to the performer regarding the deviation from the task goal (e.g. quantitative information). Theorists suggest that in the early stages of learning the performer requires prescriptive, quantitative information to guide error detection and correction (e.g. you were 2 minutes faster on your 10 km run). However, inherent in a bandwidth schedule is that, once the performer becomes more skilled at accomplishing the task goal, the precision of the feedback changes from quantitative (e.g. prescriptive) to qualitative (e.g. verbally stating 'that was a good run, you really maintained your pace' to the athlete). This method of organizing the feedback schedule within a practice context has proven to be an effective method of preventing augmented feedback dependency for error detection and correction, and facilitating independent error detection and correction.

In addition to performance-based feedback schedules, skill acquisition research has also shown that empowering the performer to control *when* they receive feedback in their practice schedule has proven to be more effective than coach-determined feedback schedules. Similar to the discussion earlier regarding self-regulation of practice schedules, this recent trend in research to examine the effectiveness of self-regulated feedback has been described as a decision-making process that requires the performer to be an active participant in the factors that support learning. Results from research examining participant-determined feedback schedules have found that feedback is requested frequently in the early stages of the practice session, but that it is gradually requested less frequently as the performer becomes more skilled. Researchers suggest the benefits of performer-determined feedback schedules are attributed to the notion that performers are provided with the opportunity to implement and individualize a feedback schedule that is most beneficial to their specific needs and current level of information processing. Methods of providing task-related feedback to facilitate independent error detection and correction in the performer are outlined in Table 9.2.

Table 9.2 Description of feedback schedules that facilitate independent error detection and correction processes in the performer

Feedback schedule	Description
Summary feedback	augmented feedback about a set of repetitions (e.g. five) after the set has been completed; summary feedback can be presented visually or verbally; athlete is required to interpret their own sensory information from the practice repetitions during the no-feedback trials
Bandwidth feedback	performer is provided with detailed quantitative feedback (e.g. 16 s too fast) only when performance falls outside an agreed upon error tolerance range (e.g. bandwidth); performer is provided with general qualitative feedback (e.g. correct!) when performance falls within the bandwidth
Faded feedback	decreasing the frequency of feedback provision over a series of practice trials; for example, augmented feedback is presently frequently at the beginning of practice and presented less frequently over practice trials
Performer-regulated	frequency of feedback provision determined by performers' requests upon completion of a practice trial
Performer estimation	performer estimates their error upon completion of an action; the coach then provides the actual error demonstrated by the performer

Adapted and expanded from Williams and Hodges 2005: 644.

THEORY INTO PRACTICE

Suggested applications for the organization of practice

Based on the reviewed research, the specific organization of practice factors to facilitate motor skill proficiency is not entirely intuitive. We base this on the research that emphasizes the organization of practice contexts where the performer is engaged in practicing not only the motor components of the task, but also the cognitive components. The requisite cognitive components of motor performance have been identified as the processes actively engaged in by the performer during motor planning (e.g. retrieval of a motor plan from long-term memory), as well as the error detection and correction (e.g. interpretation of intrinsic task-related information). Researchers have suggested that practice contexts should be organized specifically to facilitate the cognitive processes of the performer. In fact, these processes are predicted to require the investment of cognitive effort by the athlete. Some researchers have suggested that practice should be organized to facilitate the *decision-making* processes of the athlete—that decisions should be practiced in a manner that is similar to the demands of a competition, and given the same emphasis during practice as the motor component of the skill itself (see Chapter 11 by McPherson). In this way, practice *repetitions* are problem-solving events, with each repetition cumulatively facilitating the independent decision-making pro-cesses of the athlete (Figure 9.1). The remainder of this chapter will provide the coach with an evidence-based approach to organizing a practice schedule to facilitate the physical and cognitive components of motor skill proficiency.

Practice factors facilitating motor planning: suggestions for the coach

A coach's challenge when organizing a practice session is to identify a balance between a practice context that facilitates accurate motor planning by the athlete (e.g. blocked repetition

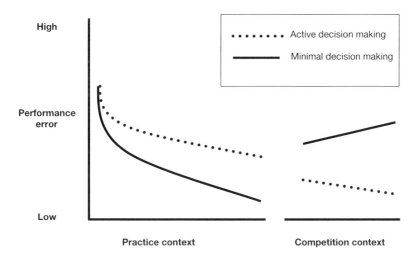

Figure 9.1 *Typical relationship between performance error and active decision making of the performer during the practice context indicating depressed practice performance during practice with increased performance during competition.*

127

schedule) and a practice context that emphasizes the cognitive processes required for independent motor planning (see also Masters, Chapter 9, for an alternative view). Some researchers suggest that the practice session should be organized to encourage independent decision making with respect to retrieving the correct motor plan from memory, or anticipating the action of an opponent, or planning an action under pressure (e.g. completing the movement in a limited amount of time). The decisions made by the athlete during the practice should be similar to the decisions required in the athletic event. Further, the athlete should not only be able to plan and accurately produce the correct action, but also understand *why* they planned the action in that particular way.

The Challenge Point framework predicts that a practice schedule should be organized to *facilitate* the cognitive processes required for *successful motor planning*. During the initial stages of skill acquisition, the athletes are getting the idea of the cognitive and motor requirements to perform the task successfully. For motor skills that require the exact replication of a *movement pattern*, frequent demonstrations of the required movement pattern at the beginning of initial motor-planning trials has proven to be an effective method of augmenting motor planning in the athlete. However, once the athlete knows what to do, the frequency of the demonstrations should be decreased in order to encourage the athlete's dependence on their own cognitive resources to support motor planning. For motor skills that require a specific movement outcome, such as successfully scoring a basket from a basketball jump shot performed from three different distances on the court, a *blocked repetition schedule* may be considered an effective beginning strategy. In this context, the athlete practices planning the same action over a series of trials (e.g. shooting a jump shot 10 feet from the basket for ten consecutive trials before progressing to a new distance). Athletes typically demonstrate quick performance success during a blocked repetition schedule. To increase the cognitive demands required for motor planning, researchers suggest the transition to a serial repetition schedule. In this context, the athlete is required to plan a different motor action on each trial; however, the order of the repetitions is predictable. In a final progression, the athlete practices in a random practice schedule where the upcoming required motor action is non-repeating and unpredictable. For example, the athlete practices a jump shot from 10 feet, then 15 feet, then 10 feet again, then 20 feet, etc. In this context, the order of the repetitions is non-repeating and unpredictable. The underlying impetus of the Challenge Point framework is that once an athlete knows what to do, the problem-solving demands required of the performer within the repetition schedule should be adjusted to impose additional demands on motor planning. Further, the motor-planning demands required during practice should replicate the motor-planning demands inherent within the specific athletic event.

Demonstration is a technique commonly used by coaches to augment the motor-planning processes of the athlete. Research suggests that for demonstrations to be effective, a *verbal cue* must accompany the demonstration to focus explicitly the athlete's attention on the essential components of the movement pattern. This methodology has proven to be effective for the athlete acquiring a specific co-ordinated pattern and strategic knowledge about how best to perform the movement. Further, research suggests that a practice context organized with an *interspersion* of physical and demonstration trials is superior to those practice schedules that utilize all demonstrations before any physical attempts at the motor task. The utility of interspersing physical trials with demonstration trials is beneficial for two reasons. First, during

128

a demonstration trial, the athlete is able to focus on the co-ordination pattern and/or the various movement strategies, but not while physically performing the task. Second, demonstration trials allow for a recovery period between physical practice trials during practice. Moreover, recent research has shown that self-empowering the athlete to select when they require a demonstration to augment their motor planning is a very effective strategy in regulating the frequency of the demonstrations. In fact, research suggests that the need for demonstration may be as infrequent as six per cent of the total practice trials!

An important caveat for coaches is the speculation that, for motor skills requiring the attainment of a specific *outcome* (e.g. open skills such as scoring a goal in soccer), and not a requisite movement pattern, the utility of demonstration is questionable. In fact, some researchers concede that demonstrations place unnecessary *constraints* on the movement pattern of the performer trying to achieve a specific outcome goal. Therefore, a *one movement pattern fits all* for this type of motor task is perhaps not desirable. In fact, athletes should be encouraged to explore actively and discover various movement solutions (e.g. movement patterns) to the given movement problem that are most suitable for the current skill level. Further, instructing the performer to attend explicitly to the *outcome effects* of their movement (e.g. distance from the hole after a 60-yard chip shot) compared with cueing the athlete to attend to the *movement pattern* that produced that outcome has been shown to be an effective method of augmenting motor planning.

Provisions of augmented feedback: suggestions for the coach

In previous times, the advice given to the coach regarding how to organize the provision of augmented feedback during the practice schedule could be characterized as promoting a *guiding* function. That is, coaches were encouraged to provide augmented feedback in such a way as to guide the learners toward the correct motor solutions as quickly as possible. To achieve this, they were told to provide augmented feedback often and as soon as possible after an action was completed. This advice was based on the observable behavior of performers who were demonstrating what appeared to be rapid and efficient motor skill learning *during* that period when the augmented feedback was being provided. However, when the performer was placed in a context where augmented feedback was no longer available, and they were left to their own sources of information to detect and correct errors (e.g. in competition), there was often a rapid decrement in performance. Today, the frequency and time interval between the completion of an action and the provision of augmented feedback are considered critical to facilitate independent error detection and correction mechanisms.

The ability of the athlete independently and accurately to detect and correct their own errors is a direct consequence of the cognitive processes engaged by the performer during the feedback delay interval. In fact, researchers recommend that feedback schedules should be organized to engage the performer in active error detection and correction upon the completion of every action. A commonly used method is to reduce the *frequency* of augmented feedback during the practice schedule. Reducing the frequency of augmented feedback is predicted to circumvent the dependency on this information by the athlete for error detection and correction. In one example, augmented feedback is not presented to the athlete until a certain number of physical trials are completed. On trials where augmented feedback is not presented, the athlete is encouraged to interpret the various sources of sensory information,

129

inherent within performance of the task, to form their own hypothesis about the success of their action. After the completion of the predetermined number of no-feedback trials (e.g. five), the coach then presents augmented feedback about the just-completed trials, either verbally or graphically. This *summary* method of augmented feedback provision has proven to be effective in facilitating independent error detection and correction methods in the performer.

Gradually reducing, or *fading*, the provision of augmented feedback over the practice period is another effective method of facilitating the cognitive processes required for independent detection and correction of errors. In this schedule, the frequent provision of augmented feedback during the early stages of learning the motor skill guides the performer and calibrates the error detection and correction mechanisms of the performer to the goal of the task. However, over trials, the frequency of augmented information is systematically reduced, thus requiring the athlete to depend on their own error detection and correction mechanisms on trials where augmented feedback is not presented. Interestingly, a fading feedback schedule is often found in practice contexts where the performer *controls* when they are provided with augmented feedback.

An interesting variation of the above approach is the so-called *bandwidth* feedback method. In this method the provision of augmented feedback by the coach is dependent upon the *observable* performance of the athlete. The coach and athlete mutually establish an error tolerance, or bandwidth. If the athlete's performance is within the bandwidth, the feedback provided to the athlete is *qualitative*, such that it conveys very little information with regard to how to change the upcoming action. For example, the athlete is verbally told 'correct'. However, if the athlete's performance is outside the bandwidth, the feedback presented to the athlete is *quantitative*. This information is considered *prescriptive*, based on the fact that the athlete understands exactly what to do to change the action on the next trial (e.g. too fast by 5 s, 5 cm from the pin, etc.). Inherent within a bandwidth feedback schedule is the notion that, as the athlete becomes more skilled, the amount of quantitative (e.g. prescriptive) feedback decreases and qualitative feedback increases, thus decreasing dependency on augmented information to support error detection.

An effective method for the coach to infer the accuracy of the athlete's error detection and correction is through the utilization of verbal reports of the athlete's perceived error. In this context, the athlete is encouraged to provide a verbal approximation of movement correctness based on the interpretation of various sources of sensory information, such as the feel of the movement (e.g. the co-ordination of the upper body and lower body in a baseball swing), visual observation of the movement effects (e.g. the trajectory of a tennis ball), as well as the auditory consequences of the movement (e.g. hockey puck hitting the goal post). This information is presented to the coach *before* the athlete receives augmented feedback. Importantly, once the athlete has provided an estimate of their movement success, it is imperative that the coach then provide augmented feedback as a method of calibrating the discrepancy between the athlete's perceived error and the error reported in the coach's augmented feedback.

CONCLUSION

Engaging the athlete in the cognitive processes required for motor planning and error detection and correction results in a *skilled behavior* that is *not readily observable* by the coach or the athlete. In fact, improvements in performance are often enhanced, albeit delayed, when methods are used by the coach to engage the performer in the cognitive processes required for accurate motor planning and error detection and correction. The significant contributions of organizing a practice context that is cognitively effortful during motor planning and error detection and correction are demonstrated when the athlete is required to perform these activities, independent of the coach, in a game situation.

Recent findings from skill acquisition research suggest very specific guidelines for the coach organizing a practice context. Perhaps the most salient recommendation is that practice environments should be organized to encourage active participation of the athlete in the cognitive processes required for motor planning as well as error detection and correction. The decisions made by the athlete during practice with regard to motor planning as well as error detection and correction should closely approximate the decisions required of the athlete during competition. A consequence of organizing practice where cognitive effort is embedded within physical practice trials is that athletes are practicing the skills required to be automatic in their motor planning and error detection and correction. The practice factors outlined in this chapter offer a specific evidence-based methodology for the coach organizing a practice schedule for the athlete just beginning to learn a motor skill, or for the athlete who is considered an expert within their sport-related domain (see Figure 9.2 for a summary).

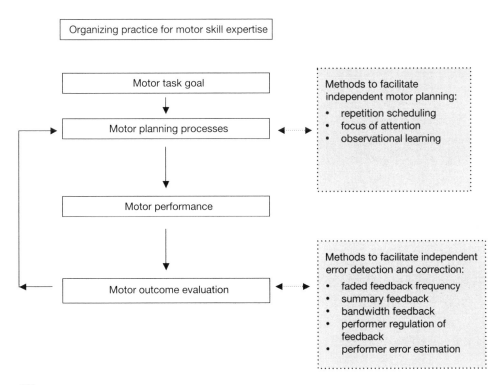

Figure 9.2 *Evidence-based method of organizing practice to facilitate the independent cognitive processes required for motor planning and error detection and correction for the attainment of motor skill expertise. They gray boxes represent optional methods of organizing practice for the coach.*

COACH'S CORNER

Darren Balmforth

Assistant Coach, AIS Women's Rowing Team

What repetition means for rowing

The concept of repetition and mental or cognitive effort is interesting when applied to rowing. Unlike many discrete skills, such as a kick or hit, the rowing stroke is continuous in nature. So although I would define one stroke repetition as from the catch (oar enters the water) until the same point on the next stroke, in reality there is no real start and end point. The precision of the placement of the oar in one stroke will affect the ability to accelerate the boat and will affect the time to come forward, thus impacting on subsequent stroke repetitions. As a result, this has implications with regard to the way we go about coaching the skill. For example, how might we apply random and blocked practice approaches?

I certainly believe in manipulating blocked and random practice methods. As a general rule we use a blocked approach when we are looking to make small technical adjustments as we approach, or even when we are at, a regatta. Changing the type of drill that our rowers are completing is the main way we try to increase the mental effort required. Obviously, unlike sports such as tennis, we can't change between strokes to create randomness. We do, however, manipulate our stroke rates and may ask the athletes to complete one piece with an eighteen stroke rate and then the next piece with a twenty rate.

The other element that requires continuous cognitive effort from a rower is the monitoring of boat speed through feel. The most common instruction or piece of feedback I give generally starts with the phrase 'Just see if you can feel. . .'. The ability of an athlete to feel their rhythm and its impact on boat speed is what separates the best from the rest.

My role as a coach, essentially, is to teach the rower to become their own coach. In other words, I teach them to develop the ability to identify and fix the difference in feel between good and poor strokes. A related skill that becomes important is for the athletes to be able to select the right drill to put in place to correct any flaws they feel they have when the coach isn't present or pre-race. A coach can't communicate with the athletes from the time they hit the water to race, so one of the rowers in coxless boats or the coxswain must be able to set the required rhythm and equally implement a particular drill to exemplify a particular feel or technique required.

Use of video feedback

We use a lot of video feedback in our coaching. Again the logistics of rowing mean that most video feedback is completed after the session is over and the rowers are back on land.

This delay between skill execution and video feedback is both a positive and negative. The positive is that we certainly don't create a dependency on video feedback after a set or piece. However, there is no doubt there are occasions where the ability to use video on the water might speed up the learning process. It was interesting to read in the chapter about the use of skilled or unskilled models. Given that I am working with elite athletes, we obviously don't view unskilled models. However, we will often get specific athletes to model their technique on another crew member who may be executing the stroke component as we require. Equally we will ask rowers what is wrong with a particular stroke. We find video an essential tool because the difference between a good and poor performance is sometimes very difficult to discern with the naked eye, albeit the feel may be strong for the athlete. Hence, to use frame-by-frame analysis and then feedback to show, for instance, incorrect oar entry angles is of great value.

Feedback timing

Reflecting on the feedback section certainly got me thinking. All boats are fitted with a tool called 'StrokeCoach'. This device is fitted to the front of the boat and acts much like a car speedometer. Specifically, it provides the rowers with their rating (strokes per minute) as well as time and speed. Rowers are very reliant on this information, and coaches encourage the usage of this information to regulate the quality of training sets in terms of physiological effort or work. The usage of 'StrokeCoach' is permitted in competition and as such athletes can rely on it to help them set their pace. However, from a skill-learning perspective, I do wonder whether our reliance on this feedback device is taking something away from our athletes' ability to develop a strong self-awareness of their own performance. Certainly, when rowing at maximal effort, even elite rowers demonstrate signs that their perception of boat speed is not as accurate as what we might expect. It is quite common for them to report that they have maintained a consistent boat speed over the course of a race when in actual fact they have slowed.

The future

As technology continues to evolve I can see it having a real impact on the way we provide feedback in rowing. For instance, the ability to decide whether to use instantaneous or delayed feedback about stroke kinematics in the form of graphic overlays, video, and numerical displays will continue to challenge the processing abilities of our rowers. As coaches, we need to be careful about how much, how often, what sort, and how precise our feedback is. Assistance in developing guidelines on such issues is certainly an area where applied research would be most welcome.

KEY READING

Guadagnoli, M.A. and Lee, T.D. (2004). 'Challenge point: A framework for conceptualizing the effects of various practice conditions in motor learning'. *Journal of Motor Behavior*, (36): 212–24.

Hodges, N.J. and Franks, I.M. (2002). 'Modeling coaching practice: the role of instruction and demonstration'. *Journal of Sports Sciences*, (20): 793–811.

Lee, T.D., Swinnen, S.P. and Serrien, D.J. (1994). 'Cognitive effort and motor learning', *Quest*, (46): 328–44.

Salmoni, A.W., Schmidt, R.A. and Walter, C.B. (1984). 'Knowledge of results and motor learning: A review and critical reappraisal'. *Psychological Bulletin*, (95): 355–86.

Schmidt, R.A. and Bjork, R.A. (1992). 'New conceptualizations of practice: Common principles in three paradigms suggest new concepts for training'. *Psychological Science*, (3): 207–17.

Schmidt, R.A. and Lee, T.D. (2005). *Motor Control and Learning: A Behavioral Emphasis*, 4th edn. Champaign, IL: Human Kinetics.

Vickers, J.N., Reeves, M., Chambers, K.L. and Martell, S. (2004). 'Decision training: cognitive strategies for enhancing motor performance'. In Williams, A.M. and Hodges, N.J. (eds) *Skill Acquisition in Sport: Research, Theory and Practice*. London: Routledge.

Williams, A.M. and Hodges, N.J. (2005). 'Practice, instruction and skill acquisition in soccer: Challenging tradition'. *Journal of Sports Sciences*, 23(6): 637–50.

Wulf, G. and Prinz, W. (2001). 'Directing attention to movement effects enhances learning: A review'. *Psychonomic Bulletin & Review*, (8): 648–60.

Wulf, G., Raupach, M. and Pfeiffer, F. (2005). 'Self-controlled observational practice enhances learning'. *Research Quarterly for Exercise and Sport*, (76): 107–11.

Section 3

Through the eyes and thoughts of an expert

Chapter 10

A recipe for expert decision making

Damian Farrow and Markus Raab

The technical and tactical proficiency and physical prowess of an athlete are often used as a means of distinguishing the elite from their less-skilled counterparts in fast-paced interceptive and team sports. Not surprisingly, then, a large proportion of training time is spent refining these qualities. However, there is also a less-obvious quality that is of equal importance to performance that can distinguish between differing skill levels. Decision-making skill[1] is the ability of a player to quickly and accurately select the correct option from a variety of alternatives that may appear before the ball is hit or kicked or an opponent moves. Colloquially, decision making is often referred to as *reading the play*. Some team sport coaches operationally describe a skilled decision maker as the player who is 'a good driver in heavy traffic'—the player who seemingly knows what is about to occur, two passes before it happens. Although such players may not be the fastest around the court, their ability to accurately forecast a game's future means they always seem to have all the time in the world. Although reading the play is a cinch for players such as Australian footballer Chris Judd, ice-hockey star Wayne Gretzky or basketball legend Michael Jordan, for us mere mortals it's more like reading Latin.

This chapter is concerned with first highlighting the key facets of decision-making skill and then, importantly, reviewing how this skill can be improved through training. In order to outline the key underlying components of the decision-making process we discuss those components that separate the best from the rest. Second, we detail the common developmental pathways followed by expert decision makers as a means of identifying potential practice activities that may develop the key components of decision-making skill. Two aspects of decision-making training are then discussed. First, whether decision making can be enhanced through video-based simulation methods completed outside the usual training context. Second, we review methods that can be used in a physical practice setting to increase the skill of players to make both *what* (what movement is to be carried out) and *how* (how a movement is to be carried out) decisions (see Chapter 11 by McPherson for additional discussion of these ideas).

A RECIPE FOR BECOMING AN EXPERT DECISION MAKER

What are the key ingredients to becoming an expert decision maker? From a scientific perspective there is a seemingly never-ending debate about the different perceptual–cognitive competencies an expert athlete should possess. The reason for the absence of a straightforward answer lies in the problem itself. An expert in sport needs to possess excellent perception, attention, memory, skill execution, and many more competencies. Before we discuss some of these concepts in more detail, however, it is necessary to outline the phases of the decision-making process. One model that is commonly used to describe the decision-making process is illustrated in Figure 10.1.

In order to describe this model we offer a brief example from soccer to illustrate each of the seven stages. Imagine a striker in soccer who is dribbling towards the goal and is approached by a defender. At this point, the decision problem has *presented* itself: what action should the ball player take in response to the approaching defender? The striker *identifies* the constraints on his behavior (e.g. he cannot pass offside) and prioritizes his goals (e.g. retain possession, but score if possible). In light of these, he *generates* possible options that he may undertake, such as shooting at the goal, passing to a wing player, or dribbling away from the defender. He *considers* these courses of action, perhaps by ranking them according to their likelihood of achieving his primary goal (retaining possession). Then, he *selects* an action; this is likely to be the one with the highest rank. He *initiates* the action by physically performing so as to bring about the action he selected (e.g. physically dribbling the ball to the right). In doing so, he buys time for the wing player to streak towards the goal, where he passes the ball and assists in a shot on goal that results in him positively *evaluating* his decision.

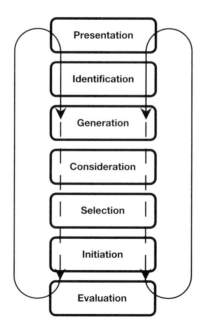

Figure 10.1 *The route to decision-making skill in sport.*

Expert decision makers have learned to progress through these stages very quickly and efficiently, resulting in intuitive performance in the most complex of situations under high pressure. How do they do this? To answer this question, we now describe some of the components that are acquired on the road to decision-making excellence.

Components of expert decision making

Expert decision makers differ from their less capable peers in a number of capacities, as detailed throughout this book. Of particular interest to the current discussion is the expert player's ability to *read the play*, technically referred to as pattern recognition and anticipation. Interestingly, pattern-recognition skill was first investigated in the game of chess. Research demonstrated that chess grandmasters were able to sum up a board in one quick glance. Provided with five or ten seconds to look over a specific chess situation, the best players could accurately recall the exact location of ninety per cent of the pieces. Less-skilled players could only remember fifty per cent. The researchers concluded that the grandmasters could *chunk* the pieces on the board into fewer, larger chunks of information that were more easily remembered and subsequently recalled to produce the required pattern. This is similar to the way we all remember frequently used telephone numbers as one block of numbers rather than eight individual numbers.

Sports science has subsequently demonstrated that elite team-sport players also possess the analytical mind of a chess master. Watching a team sport such as netball is a classic example of watching a continuously changing pattern. Interestingly, although the pattern may look meaningless to the untrained eye, that is, fourteen players sprinting and dodging in all directions, to an expert player (or coach) it can all look completely logical and can inform them in advance as to where the ball is about to be passed. This is quite a handy skill to have if your job requires you to intercept as many opposition passes as possible. It is thought that elite players have developed the ability to rapidly recognize and then memorize patterns of play executed by their opponents. Importantly, this capability to recognize an opposition team's attacking or defensive patterns is not because the elite players have a bigger memory capacity than the rest of us. Rather, their memory of sport-specific attack and defense strategies is simply more detailed than ours and can be recalled and used in a split second.

More recent research has also revealed that the ability to recognize patterns of play may transfer across team sports that possess a similar structure of play. Bruce Abernethy (see Chapter 1) and his colleagues examined expert decision makers from the Australian basketball, netball, and hockey teams and compared their performances on a pattern-recognition task with less-skilled athletes from the three sports. Consistent with previous work, the experts recalled patterns from their sport better than their less-skilled counterparts. However, of interest was that when the experts from one sport (e.g. netball) were tested on other patterns (e.g. basketball patterns), their recall was still better than the less-skilled athletes from that sport (i.e., the non-expert basketball players). Such findings imply that elements of pattern recognition are general in nature and can transfer between sports. This has important implications for the development of decision making, as discussed in the next section on the developmental pathways of expert decision makers.

139

It has been reasoned that superior pattern-recognition skill provides a player with an awareness of what a team-mate or opponent is likely to do next. The outcome of effective pattern recognition is anticipation or the capability to prepare a response in advance based on the information provided early in an event sequence. The capacity to anticipate is particularly valuable in time-stressed sports for a number of reasons. First, in a situation such as the tennis return of serve, it may be necessary to begin moving before an opponent has even struck the ball in order to successfully intercept it. Second, it provides a player with more time to prepare a response, which may increase the likelihood of executing a successful response. Finally, anticipation may also effectively reduce the expert's information-processing load. In sum, the net result of being an expert decision maker is to create the appearance of *having all the time in the world* with which to prepare and execute a response in time-stressed situations by efficiently travelling through some or all of the stages of the decision-making process previously described.

Developmental histories of expert decision makers

A recent research strategy to understanding decision-making skill has involved interviewing elite decision makers and asking them to detail retrospectively the types of activity they completed in their childhood and adolescent years. It is thought that such information may shed some light on the types of activity that should be practiced if one wishes to become an expert decision maker.

The same athletes that Abernethy and colleagues tested on pattern-recognition skills also completed developmental history profiles. Although there are too many findings to detail here (see also Chapters 2 and 3), there a few that are pertinent to the current chapter. Of particular interest was that the athletes accumulated far less sport-specific practice (less than 4,000 hours on average) prior to reaching expert levels than the 10,000 hours that would be deemed necessary by the theory of deliberate practice (see Chapter 3 for more information on this theory). In explaining this finding, it is critical to note that the number of different sports these athletes participated in as a junior was inversely related to the number of practice hours required to become an expert player. For example, one netball player only detailed 600 hours of netball-specific practice before being selected for the Australian team. However, she participated in fourteen other sports as a junior.

Based on such findings, it has been reasoned that participation in a variety of sports before specializing can be advantageous to one's development of expert decision-making skills. Importantly, as highlighted in some research on Australian football, it's not just any sport. Rather, participation in sports that are conceptually similar to the one in which a child wants to excel is more likely to generate the transfer of pattern-recognition skill previously described (as well as other capacities such as physical fitness). For example, expert decision makers in Australian football were found to participate in a significantly greater number of secondary invasion sports relative to non-expert decision makers. Invasion sports are those, much like Australian football, that involve players running freely on a field or court and being able, in some way, directly to challenge their opponents for possession of a ball. This includes sports such as soccer, hockey, and basketball.

DECISION-MAKING TRAINING APPROACHES

Off-court training

The time available to train players in team sports such as basketball and soccer is limited owing to their physical demands. Inevitably these time constraints mean important skills such as decision making are not practiced enough. As a result, researchers have been interested in devising methods both to test and then, importantly, to improve the decision-making skill of athletes outside the normal training environment. In order to be considered a credible training approach, specific conditions must be adhered to:

- The decision-making skill to be developed must be a limiting factor to sport performance; that is, if it isn't a quality that separates experts from the rest then there is little reason to focus on it in training (for example, generalized visual training as described in Chapter 1).
- Suitable training regimes are those that supplement physical practice and selectively enhance the specific perceptual capacity.
- Most importantly, any improvements in decision making arising from training must translate to improved sport performance.

The following section will review some of the training initiatives examined to date with the above criteria in mind.

General visual vs sport-specific training

A key issue when selecting off-court training programs is the notion of whether you are actually training the specific limiting factor to decision-making performance. A variety of training methods have been employed that have been broadly termed *visual–perceptual training*. The research literature investigating visual–perceptual training programs in sport can be separated into generalized visual training programs and sport-specific perceptual/decision-making training programs. Generalized visual training programs have typically originated from within a clinical optometry setting, where behavioral optometrists in particular have prescribed visual training exercises designed to improve the vision of children with reading difficulties. The key tenet behind these training programs prescribed by behavioral optometrists is that improved visual capacity will translate into improved sporting performance. Alternatively, sport-specific perceptual/decision-making training programs have emerged from sport scientists seeking to train the visual–perceptual capacities known to distinguish the performance of experts and novices in the specific sport of interest. These programs have typically involved video-based approaches focusing on early postural cue identification or the reading of patterns of play. Both general and sport-specific approaches aim to increase the speed and accuracy of a performer's perceptual response to an opponent, albeit via very different training stimuli and activities (see Abernethy, Chapter 1, for more discussion). This chapter will focus on sport-specific perceptual/decision-making training as it is likely to provide a more fruitful avenue for the development of decision-making skill. Unlike generalized visual training methods, sport-specific training attempts closely to replicate or simulate the decision-making conditions of the natural sport skill.

Sport-specific decision-making training

POSTURAL CUE TRAINING

The solid empirical evidence demonstrating that expert performers use postural information sources such as an opponent's movement pattern to anticipate likely ball flight (e.g. direction of a tennis stroke or soccer kick) provided researchers with a logical starting point for the design of sport-specific decision-making training approaches. Currently, one of the most promising methods for training anticipation is via the use of video-based temporal occlusion training. These approaches generally involve the video presentation of a performer executing a particular action from the player's perspective, with this vision then edited at a point just before the occurrence of a particular cue (Figure 10.2). Participants are asked to respond by predicting the outcome of the full play sequence. For example, players watch a tennis server from the receiver's perspective, and, as the server reaches the top of the ball toss, the vision is occluded or paused so that no more cues are provided. The participants then report their estimate of the direction and spin of the serve. The participant is then given feedback on his or her prediction either verbally or, more typically, by being permitted to view the post-occlusion action. This procedure has been used in an experimental setting and has in some instances successfully improved the perceptual speed, and/or accuracy, of sports performers.

In relation to racquet sports, a number of studies have been conducted where typically beginner to intermediate level participants have been perceptually trained. The training activities have involved a combination of temporally occluded video footage of particular strokes (i.e., tennis serve and passing shots) and specific instruction (guidance) concerning the relationship between the various perceptual information sources and subsequent ball flight direction (e.g. an instruction such as 'a ball toss placed over the server's head indicates a topspin service is likely'). Improvements in perceptual skill have subsequently been examined via film- or video-based tests that utilize movement initiation time or non-sport-specific perceptual accuracy measures (e.g. pen and paper response grids, vocal reaction time or a button-press task) as an indication of decision-making speed and accuracy. Results commonly reveal that the perceptual training groups make faster and/or more accurate responses, relative to a control group and a placebo group, when such groups are included in the experimental design.

In more recent times, the above perceptual training approach has been used to compare the relative effectiveness of various instructional approaches. For example, traditional, explicit instructional approaches that directly inform the player what cues are most informative have been compared with more indirect approaches such as implicit (subconscious) learning where the player doesn't necessarily realize they have made such connections (see Masters, Chapter 7). A number of innovative approaches of this nature have been studied, such as providing task-related, goal-irrelevant instruction. For example, a player is told to predict the speed of a tennis serve rather than its direction. The logic behind such instructions is that attention to this information might indirectly facilitate the player's service prediction performance, as

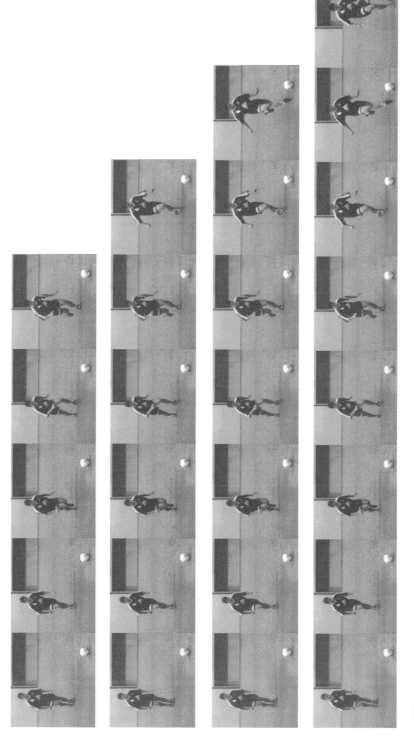

Figure 10.2 Temporal occlusion schematic depicting a progressive increase in pre-kick information for a soccer penalty kick.

they would *implicitly* establish relationships between the service kinematics and resultant service outcome, without necessarily consciously processing such information. Interestingly, results of such studies have generally found that perceptual learning can occur in the absence of direct instruction about the relationship between a specific cue and its resultant action, although it should be noted that the complexity of the decision-making task is a key mediating factor in the use of implicit techniques and will be discussed in a later section. Nonetheless, coaches are encouraged strongly to consider such indirect approaches over direct instruction (Masters, Chapter 7, has a more detailed discussion of this topic).

PATTERN-RECOGNITION TRAINING

Whereas postural cue training is more localized toward understanding the movement mechanics of the opponent, pattern-recognition training is concerned with teaching players how to recognize and subsequently anticipate the outcome of familiar patterns of play as they evolve, as seen in a wide variety of team sports such as basketball. Although there has been less experimental work directed toward examining this issue relative to postural cue training, again, the available evidence is generally positive. Improved decision-making performance has been reported in pattern-based situations such as defending or initiating offensive football (gridiron) plays, initiating offensive basketball plays and selecting the best option in soccer situations.

A typical example of pattern-recognition training can be highlighted using the sport of basketball. Players' decision-making skill was examined by having them physically respond to near life-size video-based simulations of typical offensive basketball situations presented from the players' perspective. Their task was to decide what to do next by choosing one of four available response options (e.g. pass to the top of the key, pass to the base of the key, shoot, or dribble). Training consisted of short sequences of play taken from professional matches that were *frozen* on screen at a critical decision point. Players were asked to imagine that they were the player in possession of the ball and make a decision of whether to pass, shoot, or dribble, as quickly and accurately as possible. They were then shown an un-occluded replay to provide knowledge of the result. Both implicit and explicit instructional groups improved their decision-making accuracy from pre- to post-test by around fifteen per cent. In comparison, a general visual training group and a control group did not significantly improve. No meaningful differences in decision time were observed. In addition to highlighting the value of training players' recognition of common patterns of play, these data again confirm and extend previous research findings indicating that participants do not always require explicit instruction to promote the learning of perceptual regularities in the environment.

Future directions of off-court training

A key issue that remains unresolved with video-based decision-making training is the degree to which the learning transfers to the on-field setting. Only recently has research focused on this issue and, pleasingly, available evidence suggests transfer does occur, although the exact conditions guaranteeing its success are not entirely clear.

One of the factors that require further consideration is what specific features of the natural task need to be replicated in a simulation for any of the perceptual improvements commonly demonstrated in the laboratory to transfer to performance in the natural setting. One framework for examining this issue is through the concept of fidelity. Fidelity refers to how closely a simulation accurately reproduces the real-world setting. In examining the research on simulation and subsequent transfer, the issue of what degree of fidelity is necessary for learning to occur obviously needs to be considered. Traditionally, simulators have been designed to reflect the real-world task as closely as possible. Fidelity has been manipulated in a number of ways, including physically, functionally, and psychologically. Physical fidelity relates to the *look* of the simulation relative to the performance context. Functional equivalence/functional fidelity relates to the similarity in *feel* between the simulation and real task. Psychological fidelity refers to how real a participant *perceives* the simulation to be. When video-based decision-making training is considered, there are two areas that are of interest to scientists and coaches alike. First, whether video-based perceptual training is enhanced when linked in some way to the sport-specific physical responses. Second, whether a three-dimensional (3D) simulation method is superior to a standard two-dimensional (2D) simulation owing to the addition of depth information.

A small number of studies have been conducted to examine the importance of linking decision-making training with on-court training. For instance, a longitudinal examination of the serve reception skill of elite volleyball players found that a variety of video and on-court gaze behavior skills such as ball detection and visual tracking improved the player's serve reception performance. More recent research evidence has demonstrated that, for beginner tennis players learning how to anticipate a tennis serve, it did not matter whether the perceptual information was presented in a perception-only (no physical response required) or perception–action coupled manner (player required to return the serve). Both learning modes were superior to a group being provided with technical instruction about serve mechanics. What remains unresolved from such work, and certainly requires greater investigation, is whether this effect is consistent across all skill levels and types of skill.

The logic behind research examining differences in 2D and 3D simulation approaches is that, if the players feel 3D is more realistic than 2D, they will perform more naturally, and any video simulation training they complete will better transfer to actual on-court performance. Recent experimental evidence from a basketball simulation task was equivocal. Players interacted with life-size video of offensive game situations filmed from their perspective, in both 2D and 3D formats. The basketball players were required to watch an offensive pattern of play unfold, just as they would in an actual game, and then make a decision by actually executing a pass, shot, or dribble (Figure 10.3). The players' response to each situation was filmed so that the accuracy and speed of their decisions could be analyzed later through video analysis. Despite most players reporting that they felt the 3D display was more realistic than the 2D display, their decision-making performance did not differ greatly whether it was projected in 2D or 3D. One notable exception was in situations where the players needed to use depth information to make their decision, such as when executing a long pass across the court. In these situations the 3D condition produced superior decision-making speed. Given the amount of team-sport situations that require this perception of depth, this is a potentially important result and warrants further examination of this concept.

145

Figure 10.3 *Example of a basketball player completing a 3D visual simulation training exercise.*

Summary

Although there are many unanswered questions concerning the application of video-based simulations to develop decision-making skill, there is also enough evidence to support continued investigation and usage of such approaches. Unanswered questions include:

- what is the appropriate intervention length?
- what skill level of player benefits most from such training?
- what type of instructional approach is most effective, and how tight should coupling be to the physical response?
- will a virtual reality approach provide further training benefits beyond those already gained through video-based approaches?

However, there is equally as much evidence to offer encouragement to coaches in the field. In particular, video-based training simulations offer advantages that don't typically exist in the normal training environment. For instance, players who need to do extra decision-making training can do so without needing the remainder of their team-mates to be there to execute the team's patterns. Regular visual simulation sessions could be added to the usual practice week as a low-impact workout for injured athletes or simply to add a new and enjoyable method of training to enhance performance without increasing the physical demands on the player. Finally, the general opinion of athletes exposed to such training approaches is that they are a valuable addition to more traditional training methods.

On-field decision training

On-field decision training plays a key role in daily training. In this section we will demonstrate how decision training can be improved based on the current state of research. Although the importance of decision-making skill in ball games is recognized by many coaches, what still needs to be resolved is how optimally to develop the quality of training to refine these skills.

We distinguish decisions about what movement is to be carried out (*what decisions*) from decisions about how this movement should be carried out (*how decisions*). For instance a table tennis player needs to decide between a forehand or backhand drive (*what*) and if this stroke is played cross-court or baseline, short or long, with spin or without spin (*how*). *What* decisions are often trained in isolation in tactical training and, similarly, *how* decisions are trained in isolation in technical training sessions. In the following sections we will provide evidence for, and examples of, practical interventions for *what* and *how* decisions in isolation as well as when integrated. The main conclusion is that *what* and *how* decisions should be combined quite early in the learning process or early in a season for higher-skilled athletes (also see Chapter 11 by McPherson for related discussion).

What decisions

Four factors that are important for the selection of movements will be discussed, namely: *situation complexity*, *if-then rule use*, *creative decisions* and *option generation*.

SITUATION COMPLEXITY

Some tactical training approaches follow the logic of the traditional technical training model of a simple-to-complex progression of skill development. For example, basketball players are first presented with a two vs two situation containing two choices for the ball player, such as pass or shoot. The situation is initially conducted with quite inactive defense and always from the same distance to the basket, and then complexity is progressively added such as a more active defense, more variable situations, and the addition of more choices by increasing the number of players involved. Alternatively, some approaches propose to start quite complex so that players need to adapt quickly to the ever-changing situations such as those present in pick-up games that are two vs two or three vs three. This hard-first strategy seems of some advantage and is therefore recommended for higher-skilled players.

IF–THEN RULE USE

Another important factor of *what* decisions is the use of if–then rules. For instance, in a two vs two situation in basketball coaches may present two if–then rules through verbal instruction or a whiteboard. Rules such as: IF the defensive player opposed to you is too far from you and your partner is closely defended THEN shoot. The second rule may be formulated as: IF your partner is in a good position and the defensive player is too close to shoot THEN pass to your partner. Of course labels such as *good position* or *defensive player is far enough away to shoot* depend on the skill level of the players in that situation. As an alternative, a coach could also implicitly develop more shooting opportunities by setting up a slower defensive player in one set of plays and more passing opportunities by setting up a good and fast defensive player for the ball player deciding between these options. Based on research conducted to date, it appears that in quite simple situations that involve two to four options each defined by one if–then rule, better and faster choices can result from adaptive behavior that can be picked up directly by the player and may only be interfered with or slowed down if the if–then rules are coached explicitly beforehand. However, if the situation is more complex such as a full five vs five situation with a number of rules and cues that may require a player's attention to make a good decision, then coach instruction may be required to focus the player's attention on the key aspects of the situation.

CREATIVE CHOICES

A third and less researched aspect of training *what* decisions is that of creative choices. Whereas training of if–then rules results in one good choice for a given situation or set of situations, it does not allow adapted choices to be made during the course of a game. Therefore, there are some methods that consider not only each choice in isolation but train choices in sequences and how people should react based on previous choices. One famous example is the 'hot-hand' phenomenon that suggests that a player has a higher chance to succeed if he or she has previously been able successfully to shoot two or three hits compared with a situation in which he or she previously missed the last two or three shots. The empirical evidence is not clear-cut, however, that playmakers use such information for ball allocations. Using the belief that someone is hot can lead in some situations to better performance (e.g. if individual performance is variable) and in others to worse performance (e.g. if an opponent can gain an advantage of the increased allocations to one player). Therefore, structuring training to require playmakers to remember previous hits/misses of their team-mates becomes a possible training activity. In sum, it is important to train the selection of different choices that can be conducted in the same situation so that an opponent is left uncertain about potential changes in the play.

OPTION GENERATION

Another mode of training refers to the cognitive development of different choices within the same situation, called option generation. For instance, one strategy used by coaches is to require players to play the same option over and over again, but using a different choice each time. For example, in basketball, a specific routine for the playmaker may result in a pass to the left wing player, then a pass to the center player or to the right wing player. Research indicates that training such option generation results in better choices if players use a spatial strategy. That is, generate all options on the left side first and then options on the right side, rather than using a functional strategy that searches first for all passes over the court and then for shooting and dribble options. The advantage of a spatial strategy lies in the reduced number of options generated, which leads to a faster choice. Additionally, expert players are well guided if they rely on their intuitive first choice, because these choices often generate the highest success given a specific situation.

How decisions

The *how* decision, for instance in tennis, is to choose the exact parameters of a backhand down-the-line return. The process of such a *how* decision follows the *what* (e.g. forehand or backhand drive) decision by only a matter of milliseconds and, as a result, can be changed later than changing from a backhand to a forehand stroke for example. There are at least three factors that are important for the production of movements: game-like situations; use of pre-cues; and the type of instruction.

GAME-LIKE SITUATIONS

Practice sessions should replicate actual game events and phases of play, with the coach ensuring players are educated concerning how the training activity used reflects the decisions and processing speed required in the competition environment. A well-known skill acquisition expert, Judith Rink, summed it up best when she said:

> Transfer of practice to the game environment depends on the extent to which practice or training resembles the game. If the athletes do not practice in game-like scenarios, they will not play the game well, yet, if practice is too game-like, it may be too difficult to integrate and perform the emphasized skills. The resolution of this implication is that practice needs to occur at a level that incorporates as much of the game as the players can successfully manage.

The adoption of this philosophy is evident in well-publicized coaching approaches such as 'Teaching Games for Understanding', 'Gamesense', or 'Play Practice'. A central tenet of all these approaches is that the decision-making elements of the task are given priority, at least initially, over the instruction of technique.

USE OF PRE-CUES

Coaches use pre-cues to enable faster *how* decisions. For instance, they provide probabilistic information such as 'eighty per cent of the opponent's topspin balls will be played to the backhand'. As a result of such a pre-cue, the player can focus more on their backhand and then choose either cross-court or down the line based on the relative positioning of himself and his opponent. Another technique is for the coach to direct their player to use perceptual information that changes very late in an event before making the *how* decision. For example, an opponent's movement to the left should result in an attack to the right. The time needed to react on such information in *how* decisions depends on the movement planned. For instance, in an attacking phase of play in soccer, information presented by the approaching attacker at the very end of his run will determine whether the goalkeeper should jump to the left or right corner.

TYPE OF INSTRUCTION

Additional aid is often given by instruction. For instance, instructions about *how* decisions can be given verbally in quite different formats. Based on recent research it seems that indirect information preceded by analogies (e.g. 'move your racquet as you would pull it from a backpack' when serving in tennis) has advantages over direct information about the movement

149

itself if players need to use such movements in competitive situations. In addition, instructions that focus a performer's attention on the effects of a movement can have additional benefits for subsequent performance (see Chapters 7 and 8).

CURRENT LIMITATIONS

We see systematic on-court decision-making training as still in its infancy and therefore we want to draw attention to some limitations that can be overcome by further research and best practice. In regard to coaching *what* decisions, further work is required to develop a method that allows coaches to know how to select between different tactical training methods to generate an optimal outcome given a specific team, situation and task. The application of if–then rules as tactics seems a limited approach for teaching creative decision making and situation-based decisions. Furthermore, how to teach players about what kind of information to attend to when making their choice is not yet commonplace in real-world training environments. For instance, in penalty situations such as in soccer, the information that helps a goalkeeper distinguish between a left or right corner kick may be quite different at the start of the kicker's approach relative to just before foot-to-ball contact.

In regard to *how* decisions, even in laboratory research where significant amounts of data are accumulated about instructions, feedback, and other parameters that influence performance, we still do not know exactly when to combine the *how* decisions with the *what* decisions in early learning or across seasonal training plans. For instance, coaches need to decide when in pre-season training an adjusted skill is ready to be tested in more complex tactical situations. Similarly, it remains unclear how to combine instructions and feedback of *how* and *what* decisions in complex training schemes. The individual limits of athlete information-processing, emotional and cognitive abilities are not yet integrated into guidelines for coaches.

CONCLUSION

What does the research tell us about how to train decision making in the field of play? The best answer we are able to provide to coaches is that decision making is very situation (sport) specific and depends on both athlete abilities and the task at hand. Far from providing a comprehensive set of decision-making aids, we have presented some principles for the development of *what* and *how* decisions that are general enough to be applied across different sports and situations, yet specific enough to provide guidelines to choose between different training alternatives.

COACH RECOMMENDATIONS

Expert decision makers are not born, but made through a combination of their developmental experiences as children and then through quality coaching that provides on- and off-court decision-making training opportunities. The on- and off-court training methods discussed here can be coupled with other learning approaches as detailed in the other chapters. A common question is how much each of these training types should be used. Naturally this question is difficult to answer in a general sense; however, our observations of current practice indicate that off-court training should be used far more frequently than is currently the case. Too often any off-court training completed is simply a coach-led preview and review of a competitive match, which, although of some educational value, certainly does not proactively train the players' decision-making capacities. It is our belief that off-court decision-making training should be conducted in a similar manner to a weight-training program. That is, the training principles of volume, frequency, intensity, and overload are manipulated so that a progressive training effect is generated over time. The recipe for becoming an expert decision maker, in our opinion, is systematically to combine on-court training focusing on the execution of *what* and *how* decisions with off-court training. That is, all steps of the decision-making process, particularly the components of *generate*, *consider*, and *select*, should be part of both types of training, though not necessarily presented in an explicit manner.

COACH'S CORNER

Barry Dancer

Head Coach, AIS and Australian Men's Hockey Team

Insights from the developmental history of players

There is certainly a link between the research findings presented in this chapter concerning the background experiences of better decision makers and what we see in hockey. A large proportion of our talent emerges from the regional centers (rather than big cities), and the players have played a variety of other team sports that allow them to develop generic decision-making skills that we find valuable in hockey. In the early stages of our talent identification programs intuitive decision making is one of the key factors we use in identifying potentially elite players. At later stages of a player's development pathway qualities such as mental toughness and commitment become more critical indicators of a player's potential to progress.

Training decision making off the field

We have trialed a number of off-field decision-making training programs with our national team with mixed success. Similarly to the research examples presented in Figure 10.2 relating to the development of anticipation skills for the soccer penalty kick, we attempted to improve the anticipatory skills of our goalkeepers when defending a penalty corner. However, the results seemed to take us down the wrong path in this instance. Through video occlusion training, we attempted to assist the goalkeepers to pick up early cues from the flicker. However, because the opportunity for deception is so great with the penalty flick (flicker is in contact with the ball for over 1m, so there is a long contact time relative to a kick or hit in other sports), this training strategy backfired. Instead goalkeepers are now advised to wait as long as possible before initiating their response to the flick. Although scouting of specific opponents is certainly of value, the need for temporal occlusion type training isn't for this particular skill.

Where we have found a great deal of success is in the use of match reviewing to develop the pattern-recognition skills of our players. After international matches we regularly pick out key situations through the use of Sportscode (game analysis software) and ask the players questions such as 'why did you run here?'. These questions are as much about off-the-ball movements as they are to do with the player who possesses the ball. Generally we use vision filmed from one end of the field as we have found this to be the most valuable for completing this type of review.

These review sessions can be completed in a number of formats that encourage different types of learning to take place. Individual feedback sessions, small groups (sometimes based on playing positions) and whole team sessions are all used. Two video review formats that differ slightly to the standard team review have proven very effective. In the first we often set up small working groups and require the players to review some specific match situations and then ask the working groups to go away and workshop some solutions that they bring back and present to the remainder of the squad for discussion. This type of problem-solving approach has been valuable as it gives the players ownership of the tactical solution developed and generates increased cohesion. A second approach has been to provide a number of computers with the game footage in the treatment/physio room. In this situation accidental and sometimes planned reviewing takes place with a team-mate or two. On occasions it may be players who have related roles on the field. Players who mingle in the video/treatment room can regularly get directly involved in reviewing match situations. We also encourage mentoring between senior and newer squad members, which can assist with the fast-tracking of the newer athlete's understanding of team principles and structures. This situation can also generate learning for the more experienced player who is taking on more of a teaching role in this situation.

ON-FIELD DECISION-MAKING TRAINING

It is very important that we develop training drills and structured mini-games that demand fast decisions at a similar level to that in an international match. A large portion of our training is small-sided invasion drills or games that involve around ten players in a segment of the field that is related to match situations. This training is concerned with on- and off-ball decision making, which goes hand in hand. Certainly the *what* and *how* decisions are constantly integrated in this type of practice. This complements isolated and repetitive skill practice.

One of the points that coaches focus on in technical skill development is body position off the ball and ball-carrying position while in possession. These technical attributes are crucial to maximize a player's awareness and their ability to make appropriate decisions. It is important for our coaches to focus on developing a player's early recognition of movement of team-mates and opponents and the communication of team-mates.

I feel it's particularly important to require players to shift their focus of attention between broad and narrow and back to broad again. A term we use with our players is 'rubber necking', which is about a technique players use off the ball to maintain a broad field of vision. We emphasize the use of body position and rubber necking in scrimmage-type activities to develop a player's ability to shift their focus of attention between narrow and broad. This is particularly valuable for a player in improving his capability to deal with transition situations when the ball is about to change hands between the two teams. Good body position and rubber necking will assist a player off the ball who has to transfer from having a defensive responsibility and very quickly must shift to an offensive role.

FUTURE DIRECTIONS

For me two areas stand out as elements we can do better. First is a greater and more systematic application of off-the-pitch training programs. For instance, increased pattern-recognition training, particularly for our injured players, is an area where improvements can occur. Second is our ability to use feedback on the pitch more effectively. Given the complexity of the decision-making process that our players are constantly involved in, we as coaches need to continue to explore how best to summarize and capture the essential elements of their performance as the training session unfolds.

KEY READING

Abernethy, B., Côté, J. and Baker, J. (2002). *Expert decision-making in team sports*. Research Report to the Australian Sports Commission.

Adolphe, R., Vickers, J. and Laplante, G. (1997). 'The effects of training visual attention on gaze behavior and accuracy: A pilot study'. *International Journal of Sports Vision*, 4(1): 28–33.

Berry, J. and Abernethy, B. (2003). *Expert game-based decision making in Australian football: How is it developed and how can it be trained?*. Report to the Australian Football League Research Board.

Farrow, D. and Abernethy B. (2002). 'Can anticipatory skills be learned through implicit video-based perceptual training?'. *Journal of Sports Sciences*, (20): 471–85.

Gorman, A. and Farrow, D. (2005). 'Training the decision-making capacity of skilled basketball players: The effects of direct and indirect instructional techniques'. *Proceedings of the 11th World Congress of Sport Psychology: Promoting Health & Performance for Life*, International Society of Sport Psychology, Sydney, Australia.

Raab, M. (2003). 'Decision making in sports: Influence of complexity on implicit and explicit learning'. *International Journal of Sport and Exercise Psychology*, (1): 406–33.

Raab, M., Masters, R.S.W. and Maxwell, J.P. (2005). 'Improving the "how" and "what" decisions of elite table tennis players'. *Human Movement Science*, (24): 326–44.

Starkes, J.L. and Lindley, S. (1994). 'Can we hasten expertise by video simulations?'. *Quest*, (46): 211–22.

Williams, A.M., Ward, P. and Smeeton, N.J. (2004). 'Perceptual and cognitive expertise in sport: Implications for skill acquisition and performance enhancement'. In Williams, A.M. and Hodges, N.J. (eds) *Skill Acquisition in Sport: Research, Theory and Practice*. London: Routledge.

NOTE

1 A variety of terms are used to describe decision-making skill. These include perception, cognition, and perceptual–cognitive skill. These terms are used interchangeably throughout the chapter.

Chapter 11

Tactics: using knowledge to enhance sport performance

Sue L. McPherson

When watching televised sports, we often hear remarks from fans, coaches, or sport commentators about the quality of players' tactics or decisions during competition. For instance, a tennis commentator (and former professional player) observing a match during the 2006 French Open made the following remarks regarding a player's decision skills: 'Doesn't she see the pattern? Why does she continue to go to her forehand? Her opponent is driving it down the line today; she can't miss!' This ability to see a *pattern* of behavior in an opponent, and make decisions based on it is what this chapter refers to as tactical skill. Whereas other chapters discuss decision making as more of a case by case skill, tactics, in this context, is the use of information in an ongoing manner, as a game or competition develops.

Elite players who possess high levels of tactical skills are often described as the 'playmakers' or 'students of the game'. Although recent evidence suggests developing this type of brain power requires just as much effortful practice as other aspects of player development, our knowledge about how coaches and players go about developing such skills is limited. For the most part, players' tactical skills are often reported anecdotally rather than examined in a systematic way. That is, most statistics about players' performance behaviors describe motor skills, using measures such as ball speeds or averages of goals, errors, assists, or serves. There is some work, however, by sport expertise researchers who have examined tactics in players at various age and expertise levels in a number of different sports.

This area of inquiry utilizes video recordings to examine the accuracy of players' decisions (e.g. shot selections) as well as audio recordings to examine their rationale for such decisions during competitions. For example, a basketball player's decision to go for a three-point shot would be examined as well as her rationale for selecting this shot. Her rationale or thought processes about this and other decisions made during competition are termed tactical knowledge and cognitive skills. Tactical knowledge and cognitive skills encompass all aspects of a player's knowledge about a sport, including offensive and defensive play patterns, past competitions, etc., that are stored in memory. Various parts of our tactical knowledge and cognitive skills are used during competition for a vast array of purposes such as anticipating an opponent's shot selections, etc. Thus, the decisions we observe players make (e.g. shot selections) are only one of the many products of their thought processes utilized during competition. This chapter will present the major findings from this work and the implications for coaching.

By studying the use of tactics and broader decision-making skill, sport scientists have begun to understand how athletes develop a knowledge base in their sport, and what makes experts better than novices. The aim of this chapter is to:

- show how experts differ from novices and
- present activities designed to promote tactical skills of players.

First, I will introduce terms and ideas about how tactical knowledge and cognitive skills develop. This section will be followed by activities designed to enhance tactical knowledge and cognitive skills.

HOW TACTICAL KNOWLEDGE AND COGNITIVE SKILLS DEVELOP WITH EXPERTISE

Several studies have examined players' tactics in a variety of sports and performance contexts. Before findings from these studies are considered, it is important to address the performance context, as tactics may vary according to type of sport, goals of the task, the situation, etc. For example, in tennis, the ability to interpret an opponent's serve tendencies may or may not lead to an accurate return of serve. Or, the decision to hit a forehand with topspin deep to an opponent's backhand may or may not lead to the ability to successfully execute this shot. There is a difference, then, between being able to decide what to do, and being able to carry out the decision.

A framework for examining tactics and performance skills

In response to these issues, I developed a framework (see Figure 11.1) to describe the various types of sport and performance context that need to be considered when we examine players' tactics and performance skills.

In Figure 11.1, the left-to-right arrow at the top represents the demands on the athlete, moving from response selection (decision skills) to response execution (motor skills) aspects of performance. Thus, in ball sports such as soccer or tennis, players need abilities in both areas of decision and motor skills. For example, in soccer you need to be able to decide that the best option is a shot on goal, and then be able actually to make that shot on goal. In contrast, in sports such as gymnastics or figure skating, players need abilities that primarily involve motor execution skills. A gymnast, for example, has a set routine to perform and does not need to make any major decisions to choose what actions to perform. Of course, the nature of the sport or drill context and player's role (e.g. a goalie or forward) will influence the demands on the athlete as well. For example, if a practice drill involves a prescribed shot then the player's demands regarding shot selection are minimized.

Decision skills and motor skills also include two types of knowledge. One type is termed declarative knowledge and the other type is termed procedural knowledge (noted by two top-to-bottom arrows). Declarative knowledge is knowledge of what to do or how to do

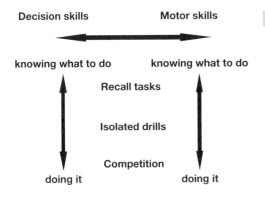

Figure 11.1
A framework depicting various
levels of analysis and performance
contexts in sports.

something. Procedural knowledge is the ability to carry it out. The task carried out may be a decision or motor skill or both, depending on the demands of the sport or sport situation. Thus, a coach examining a player's declarative knowledge about decision skills (left side of the framework) might pause a video and ask a player, 'would you pass, shoot, or dribble?' to determine if this player understands what to do or how to make a decision in this situation. This coach may continue to examine this player's decision skills by observing her decisions in similar situations during practice drills or actual bouts of competition. In these latter situations, procedural knowledge is being assessed. Motor skills (right side of the framework) may be examined via a similar process. For example, a coach could ask a player to critique another player's jump shot to assess her knowledge of how to do this skill. This coach could continue to examine her jump shot skills by observing her ability to execute jump shots during practice drills or actual bouts of competition.

To date, few observational tools have been developed to examine players' accuracy of decisions during competition. One such instrument was developed for tennis and is presented in Table 11.1. Similar versions of this instrument have been developed for basketball, baseball, volleyball, and badminton. Another tool that has been used is to record players' thoughts in these performance contexts. Typing out and later reviewing these thoughts have helped in assessing tactical knowledge and cognitive skills. Several suggestions on how to examine players' tactical knowledge and cognitive skills will be presented later. Ultimately, players and coaches should collaborate to develop instruments that are user friendly and provide the type of information they desire.

What do we mean by tactical knowledge and cognitive skills?

In order to understand a player's tactical knowledge and cognitive skills, it's important to measure what they know about the sport, or their *sport-specific knowledge base*. Sport-specific knowledge bases can be thought of as a specialized system of units of information (or concepts) that are stored in long-term memory (LTM) and accessed when needed. Sport-specific knowledge may also contain cognitive skills that help us read a play pattern, predict a pitcher's pitch, or gather and collect information about an opponent. For example, I may know that it is important to develop knowledge about my opponent's behavior during competition. As a result, I will use a process of updating my ideas about this particular opponent's tendencies

Table 11.1 *Summary of the decision rules for coding components of tennis performance during the serve and game play following the serve*

The serve

Control: Did the player gain and maintain control of the tennis ball?
    Coded as 1: if the server stood close to the center mark and contacted the tennis ball that enabled selection of an action.

    Coded as 0:
    (a) if the server stood far from the center mark and served the ball to the opponent's strong side or to the middle of the service court
    (b) if the server served off balance and without control due to a poor toss.

Decision: Did the player make an appropriate decision in the context of a given situation?
    Coded as 1: the selected action considered the player's and opponent's position:
    (a) any attempt made to serve the ball with depth, spin, speed, or placement in order to force a weak return
    (b) any attempt made to serve the ball to an open area of the service court due to the opponent's position, into the opponent, or to the opponent's weak side in order to force a weak return.

    Coded as 0: a weak decision if the player made a poor decision in the context of a given situation. The selected action considered only the player's position:
    (a) if the server placed the ball in the court in a soft lobbing manner that allowed the opponent to return the ball offensively
    (b) if the server attempted a first serve with erratic power, followed by a soft pushing second serve
    (c) if the server did not attempt to serve to the open area of the court or weak side, which allowed the opponent to return the ball offensively.

Execution: Did the player execute the decision successfully?
    Coded as 3: a serve that was successful and forcing owing to placement, speed, spin and/or depth that usually placed pressure on the opponent.

    Coded as 2: a serve that was successful, yet not forcing owing to lack of placement, speed, spin and/or depth that placed little pressure on the opponent.

    Coded as 1: an unsuccessful serve that was ruled long or wide.

    Coded as 0: a netted serve.

Game Play

Control: Did the player gain and maintain control of the tennis ball?

    Coded as 1: if the player contacted the tennis ball with the racket that enabled a selection of an action (stroke).

    Coded as 0: Actions such as missing the tennis ball, illegal contact (e.g. body parts, carrying the ball) or inability to control the ball from an opponent's good shot or the player's poor footwork, which did not allow the player to select an action.

Decision: Did the player make an appropriate decision in the context of a given situation?
    Coded as 1: a strong decision was coded as selection of an appropriate action (offensive or defensive) according to the player's position, the opponent's position, and the position of the ball. The action usually placed pressure on the opponent, which forced the opponent to move (e.g. sideways, up or back), to play the weak side (e.g. placing the ball to the player's backhand), and/or to stay behind the baseline (e.g., placing the ball deep); also, if the action enabled the player to recover position (e.g. a defensive lob).

Coded as 0:
(a) a weak decision was coded as selection of an inappropriate action according to the player's position on court, how much angle was available, and the opponent's position on court (e.g. a groundstroke returned to the opponent at the net without any attempt to pass, lob or use other strokes that placed pressure on the opponent), which usually allowed the opponent to play an aggressive shot.
(b) Selection of an appropriate action but only within the context of the player's position with the goal of putting the ball 'in play', without consideration of the location of the ball and/or the opponent's position. This action usually allowed the opponent to return the ball with minimal effort.

Execution: Did the player execute the decision successfully?
Coded as 3: a forcing shot that usually moved the opponent (e.g. playing to the opponent's weak side) and placed pressure on the opponent forcing a weak return.

Coded as 2: a shot that placed little pressure or non-forcing actions on the opponent (e.g. the opponent had the opportunity to set up a strong return with minimal effort).

Coded as 1: a forced error that consisted of a point lost as a result of the opponent's good shot.

Coded as 0: an unforced error that consisted of a point lost as a result of the player's mistake rather than the opponent's good shot.

by watching how they behave in certain game situations. In this manner, I create a *profile* of my opponent that I can update. Of course, if I have created a player profile before and done this often enough and I have been exposed to a variety of opponents, my ability to develop a profile about a player's behaviors is more efficient and effective compared with other players' who don't have experience doing this.

Also, only a portion of a player's sport-specific knowledge is typically used during problem solving or task performances. For example, a beginner may be concerned with several general goals to get the ball over the net (e.g. 'hit it over', 'keep it in bounds') between a point during competition with minimal regard for anything else. Thus, to this player, this situation is represented as a limited set of goals. In contrast, a more advanced player may be concerned with selecting a variety of shots based on more specific goals such as keeping his/her opponent behind the baseline, and involving more detailed information such as player and ball locations, and the tendencies of his/her opponent. Thus, to the advanced player, this situation is represented as a set of specific goals with a variety of solutions that make use of the current context and knowledge about an opponent. The performance context and goal of the task may also influence the type of tactical knowledge and cognitive skills utilized by players. For example, a penalty kick drill in soccer might allow a player to focus only on aspects of executing this skill with minimal regard for a goalie if the drill does not include one. In addition, some players may elect to achieve goals other than those defined by the coach or context. To explore these issues, Thomas, McPherson, and French and their colleagues examined players' thought processes (via audio recordings) in a variety of performance contexts. This illustrates the knowledge they are using as they perform. Each player's thoughts are examined according to the concepts that they are linked to. Five major concept categories are used to show what players are thinking about as they perform. Players can use goal concepts, condition concepts, action concepts, regulatory concepts, and do concepts. These categories are important for coaches to understand because they reflect the nature of players' tactical knowledge and cognitive skills.

When players' thoughts are categorized as using goal concepts, they are thoughts that reflect the means by which the game is won, or the purpose of an action selected, or an objective referring to the game's goal structure. For example, in tennis, phrases such as 'win the point' or 'keep the ball in bounds' reflect the games goal structure or means by which the game is won. Other phrases such as 'keep my opponent behind the baseline' may be linked to specific actions to accomplish this goal such as 'hit my groundstroke deep to his backhand'. Players use *condition concepts* when they identify that they are in a particular situation or circumstance or talk about when or under what circumstance to apply an action or patterns of action to achieve the goal. Condition concepts may reflect *explicit cues* available in the game environment or *implicit cues* available through tactical analysis and/or retrieval from LTM (e.g. in tennis, player's own strength or weakness, opponent tendencies). For example, a tennis player may use the explicit cue of an opponent's position on the court, stating, 'If she stays back on the baseline, then I will stay back'. The same player may also use an implicit cue by remembering that she has a strong serve, and her opponent has a tendency to hit to her forehand as she approaches the net.

Action concepts specify an action selected or patterns of actions that may produce goal-related changes in the context of a sport situation. Action concepts may reflect motor executions such as hitting a forehand down the line in tennis, or moving to the net, or be about perceptual responses such as watching a racquet contact point. An example of a player statement that shows the use of an action concept is, 'I sliced it crosscourt deep'. *Regulatory concepts* reflect the athlete monitoring the results of their actions and specify whether or not an action was carried out (e.g. 'my serve went into the net'). *Do concepts* specify *how* to perform an action (e.g. 'I need to toss the ball higher when I serve').

Once a player's concepts are identified, they can be examined for breadth (total and variety) and depth (detail) as well as linkages to other concepts. Although these measures allow us systematically to analyze the type of knowledge and cognitive skills players utilize during competition for research purposes, a rough version of this system can easily be applied by coaches and players as well. Ideas about how to do this are presented later.

WHAT DOES THE RESEARCH TELL US ABOUT HOW ATHLETES USE TACTICS?

Collectively, studies indicate all players, regardless of competitive level, utilize goals during competition that become more varied and specialized with expertise. For example, in tennis, players at more advanced levels utilize fewer execution goals such as 'hit it over the net' and more tactical goals that involve opponents such as 'keep him behind the baseline' or 'force him to use his backhand'. Also, solutions to goals become more tactical with expertise. That is, condition and action concepts become more sophisticated, varied, and related with expertise. At first, conditions primarily concern the current context (player formations, ball location) and become linked to actions, for example, 'if this situation exists then I do this'.

Other concepts may be used together to form *condition profiles* that contain tactical information. For example, profiles are used to make decisions about shot selections or to update information in the profile that is currently being used, or in other profiles. These profiles are contained in players' thoughts at more advanced levels.

Athletes also combine the different concepts (i.e., goal, condition, action, regulatory, and do) to create more complex profiles in memory. Thus, *action plan profiles* and *current event profiles* develop with expertise. *Action plan profiles* are rule-governed prototypes used to match certain current conditions with appropriate visual and/or motor actions. These profiles contain cognitive skills for monitoring current conditions such as player positions and ball placement, player formations, or coordination patterns of opponents to make accurate response selections. For example, coaches use diagrams and practice drills to develop players' knowledge and cognitive skills necessary to recognize and/or execute offensive and defensive play patterns. These player formations typically contain positioning skills and sport skills (e.g. pass, shoot, screen). Research indicates that elite players generate, recognize, and recall player formations or patterns more effectively and efficiently than their less-skilled counterparts (see also Abernethy, Chapter 1, and Farrow and Raab, Chapter 10). Often sport-specific language or signals are used to communicate plays or situations. For example, in basketball, players generate condition concepts such as 'they are playing man-on-man', 'that's a two on three zone defense', or 'block her out' to communicate a complex sport situation or play. Other cognitive skills used by the athlete include monitoring the success of their own actions or attaching verbal labels or cues to their own movement parameters to enhance motor execution. These profiles may reflect current skill levels, styles, and/or preferences of play. For example, a player learning how to perform a topspin serve in tennis might note an error on a previous attempt (i.e., 'I didn't brush up on that one') and apply a cue to correct this error (i.e., 'brush up, brush up on it'). As this player becomes more proficient in executing a topspin serve they may rely on this cue less often or not at all during a practice drill. During actual competition, this player may once again rely on this label if they experience difficulty with executing this skill or they may opt to abandon this skill altogether. Again, this is why it is important to understand a player's rationale for shot selections or other thought processes in a variety of contexts.

Current event profiles are used to keep relevant information active with potential past, current, and possible future events. These profiles are tactical scripts that guide the continuous building and modifying of pertinent concepts to monitor during the competitive event. A current event profile is built from past competition or previous experiences prior to the immediate competition and from cognitive skills used to collect information as competition progresses. Thus, elite players with well-developed profiles are predicted to have access to more effective and efficient tactical knowledge during competition than their less-skilled counterparts. Table 11.2 presents an example of how a condition profile about an opponent may develop with tennis expertise. In basketball, condition concepts reflecting current event profiles might be noted in phrases such as, 'I keep getting pushed out of bounds when I go for it, she is blocking me out under the basket'; 'on the last two attempts we hung back too far and it is killing us on offensive rebounds'. If players generate condition concepts that reflect only what happened, without any reasoning about why it happened, then chances are they do not have any tactical scripts for diagnosing players or game events.

Table 11.2 *Examples to illustrate how tactical knowledge and cognitive skills about an opponent develop with expertise in tennis (levels represent advancing levels of expertise (1= lowest level; 5 = highest level))*

Level	Tactical knowledge	Cognitive skills
1	conditions about opponent not a part of tactical knowledge; thoughts do not contain this concept	no need to monitor opponent; no cognitive skills embedded in knowledge
2	conditions about opponent reflect general or weak analyses; thoughts at times contain weak concepts about opponent	monitor opponent; occasionally reiterate events; cognitive skills are rarely embedded in knowledge
3	conditions about opponent regard his/her position on court and/or prior shot; thoughts are in the moment thus reflect evidence of rudimentary action plan profile	monitor player positions and shots; concepts about opponent linked to shot selection or reiteration of events
4	conditions about opponent's position and shot tendencies are updated on a regular basis; conditions about opponent emerge from action plan and current event profiles; these profiles become more tactical and associated and are linked to other profiles (e.g. about their own behaviours)	analyses opponent's position and shot tendencies to update profile and develop tactics and shot selections; cognitive skills are highly specialized and may be linked to other cognitive skills in other profiles
5	condition profile about opponent is highly tactical and based on prior knowledge of other opponents' style of play and preferences; action plan and current event profiles become more tactical and associated and are linked to other profiles (e.g. about their style of play and preferences)	same as 4: opponent profile is used to anticipate opponent's tactics

Training and the development of tactics

Longitudinal and coaching studies by Thomas, French, McPherson, and colleagues show that the focus of practice and coaching influences what aspects of tactical and performance skills are acquired by players. For example, a longitudinal study of a team that focused practices on tactics and organization for competitive play showed that child expert and novice basketball players improved basketball knowledge (paper pencil test) and decision making during games, but did not improve basketball skills such as free throws and rebounding. This is in contrast to a longitudinal study of a baseball team where team practices focused on skill execution, and players rarely had the opportunity to practice decisions. The study showed that players were primarily developing motor skills and exhibited weak tactical knowledge and cognitive skills.

Short-term coaching studies examining novices in badminton and tennis indicated that different coaching or teaching approaches produced different tactical skills that affected how performers viewed and interpreted game events. For example, at the end of a semester of instruction in tennis, players exposed to a cognitive-strategies approach exhibited more tactical knowledge and cognitive skills than players exposed to a more traditional motor-skill approach. The next section presents some ideas about practice and other activities that coaches may find useful for developing players' tactical knowledge and cognitive skills.

WHAT TYPES OF PRACTICE AND OTHER ACTIVITY PROMOTE THE DEVELOPMENT OF PLAYERS' TACTICAL SKILLS?

As previously mentioned, research indicates the focus of practice and instruction affects what aspects of performance are acquired, including tactical knowledge and cognitive skills. The intent of the following ideas is to work within your existing practice structure to modify activities rather than add length to practice. Several activities may be performed outside practice as well:

1. When designing practice environments or developing other activities, consider what aspect of the knowledge base you are focusing on:
    a) Are you attempting to develop action plan profiles, current event profiles, or a combination of both? Document what you do in practice and why. Record activities designed to promote tactical knowledge and skills. Is it possible that some drills and activities could be performed outside practice?
    b) The framework (see Figure 11.1) introduced previously may be used to organize practices. This is useful when considering tactics as they are influenced by the performance context, sport, and player position. This framework is also useful for assessing players' tactical skills and performance skills.
    c) Keep in mind that *one size fits all* may not be a suitable approach for developing players' tactical skills. Typically, there are several solutions to one game situation. Whenever possible, tactics should be individualized for each player and should be negotiated between a player and coach, or between team-mates and coache(s) when the tactics concern an entire team or unit. Of course there will be instances when tactics may not vary drastically among players. Let tactics emerge from players as much as possible. Players are more likely to invest in the process of developing tactical knowledge and cognitive skills if they have ownership.
2. Analyze players' performance skills periodically during practices and competitions:
    a) Use videotape of practices and competitions to analyze decision skills. These provide important statistics for you as well as your players. For example, a player may not be aware of their poor decision skills during a zone defense in basketball. Also, a player may abandon a tactic because his/her motor executions are not successful (or highly variable). If a player can't kick from a certain distance, then this is not an option and will be abandoned. Thus, players exhibiting this type of behavior should receive support and/or feedback regarding this issue. You and players should collaborate on solutions to such issues.
    b) Several studies provide complete details of coding instruments. These may be modified or you may decide to develop your own. Players can be trained to use

163

these instruments to develop profiles about their own or opponents' strengths and weaknesses.

3. Reward and reinforce good decision making, not just good skill execution:
   a) Make good decision skills a priority; use the performance skills coding system mentioned previously to reinforce these skills in practice and competition.
   b) Alter scoring systems to reward decisions. Have players help you design new ways to develop point systems. For example, in tennis, a point may be replayed if the shot selected was weak or not the type of shot they were assigned to work on. Also, performance skill tests should assess tactical skills as well as motor skills.

4. Design practice activities that allow (or force) players to make decisions in the context of game play. Develop drills that allow players to make choices regarding their shot selections. Make sure the context simulates game situations that promote the use of tactical knowledge and skills:
   a) As an example, in tennis, have players practice second serves in game situations with opponent returning serves. This develops their monitoring skills concerning current context (players' positions and ball location) and decisions about shot selections (based on game situations, opponent's strengths and weaknesses, etc). In baseball and softball, players should practice with runners on base, different pitch counts, and numbers of outs. This develops their visual search strategies to monitor runners and encoding and retrieval strategies to keep track of pertinent information to use in planning future responses, anticipating actions, and modifying plans based on changing game conditions.
   b) At more elite levels, develop drills that force players to adapt to broken plays or assume roles most often played by other players. Let players play modified bouts of competition over long periods of time; develop tactical drills that have more than one solution per player. During practices, force players to communicate with each other about tactics (upon your signal or during natural pauses). Provide feedback if necessary. You and your players may develop signals (or verbal cues) to serve as reminders to apply a particular tactic.

5. Help players develop current event and action plan profiles during practice activities or while watching videos or scouting opponents:
   a) Have players develop profiles of their opponents. 'What were their opponent's strengths and weaknesses?' 'How could I capitalize "my game" to counter the opponent's strengths?' 'How could I protect "my own weaknesses" against this opponent?'
   b) Have players determine play patterns in the context of game events or have them determine error detection and correction strategies, etc. 'What play did they run in this situation?' 'When did you recognize the pattern?' 'How?' 'Did you use any cues?' 'Why did you do better on that attempt?'
   c) During practice, interact with players:
      • Apply the 'stop, look (both ways) and listen' approach. That is, stop telling them what to do, assess tactical as well as motor skills, and listen to their thoughts. Using this process, you may gain useful information about what individuals are processing and what they are not processing.

164

- Stop play at various points to ask players what they are thinking. Just asking questions can focus attention toward thinking about tactics. Ask open-ended questions. Neutral and open-ended questions are more likely to reveal the problem-solving activities they engage in. Allow adequate time for them to respond, and listen to their responses. To ensure their responses are complete, you might use neutral probes such as the following: 'Anything else?' 'Can you tell me more about that?'
- Listen to what information they are attending to. What environmental cues do they attend to? Do they plan in advance? Are they paying attention and remembering what tactics their opponent may be using during play?
- Use specific probes to reinforce tactical knowledge and cognitive skills. For example, to assess a player's error detection and correction of a motor skill you might ask the following questions: 'How did you do that?' 'Why did you do better on that attempt?'
- Use situation interviews to examine the status of knowledge concerning game situations. In these situations, players look at videos or static diagrams of plays or game clips and respond to various open-ended questions about shot selections or play formations, etc. Several studies have shown a close match between tactical knowledge and cognitive skills during these tasks. If they do not develop a profile of an opponent's tendencies while viewing a video, chances are they will do not develop one during competition!

d) Help players develop their own solutions; provide feedback during the previously mentioned activities only when necessary to ensure profiles are developing appropriately.

6. Introduce players to the idea of *arrested development* developed by psychologist Anders Ericsson. That is, most players are tempted to remain at a certain level of proficiency (e.g. certain aspects of their performance skills are automated and require minimal processing). Once this level is obtained, they will typically resist moving to a higher level of proficiency knowing this would require more effort in terms of practice, lessons, competitions, etc. Research indicates near elite players resist the temptation of automaticity and continue to build tactical knowledge and cognitive skills. So, don't let them rest on their laurels!

   a) All players should be provided with practice and other activities designed to build their tactical knowledge regardless of age or skill level. Of course, these activities should be developmentally appropriate and match the setting (e.g. goals of players or organization).

   b) Define *paralysis by analysis* to help players interpret this idea correctly. Typically, this phenomenon refers to *over-thinking during motor executions* (refer to Jackson and Beilock, Chapter 8, for more information). Tactical skills, if developed appropriately, are designed to complement motor skills. Elite players modify motor executions with discretion and view such events as temporary. However, when a player is learning (or relearning) a motor skill or tactical skill, other aspects of their performance skills may suffer. Thus, it is crucial to allow players in this situation enough practice time that simulates competition to learn how to allocate attention resources, etc.

165

7. Provide opportunities for players to learn how to analyze their own (and others')
    tactical behaviors during performance and how to practice for improvement. Establish
    a mentoring program to pair players who use more advanced tactics with players who
    use less advanced tactics to work on diagnosing an opponent and/or team. Mentoring
    may be useful among beginners as well.

8. Research suggests all players react but experts continue to problem solve. Help
    players understand that errors are part of the learning process and are experienced by
    all players at all levels. Help players learn how to cope with their frustrations and
    how to move on. Time spent venting is time taken away from problem solving. Teach
    players how to interpret their performances in a variety of ways.

9. Enhancing players' tactical knowledge may enhance other aspects of players' sport
    experiences as well. That is, players' levels of motivation and enjoyment in sport may
    increase:

    a) For example, if a player knows that she made a good decision in the context of a
        game situation and others recognized this, then she may not feel as bad or
        defeated if she fails to execute a shot successfully. In addition, she may
        experience more success as she begins to learn to recognize that performance is
        much more than winning a point or executing a motor skill. She may also
        continue to participate in this sport as she interprets success in broader terms.
        Further, she may desire to spend more time practicing decision and motor skill
        drills if she understands that these skills are important aspects of tactics. Her
        motivation to work on underlying skills such as fitness, strength, and agility may
        improve if she understands that these skills may enhance her performance skills
        and tactics. Overall, her motivation to practice various tactical as well as motor
        skills may increase.

    b) Players should be encouraged to develop specific goals related to development of
        tactical knowledge and cognitive skills. For example, goals might include moving
        to the right spot or anticipating an opponent's shots during competition. These
        goals could be measured in terms of percentages or other outcome measures.
        Also, goals may pertain to developing aspects of their problem representations
        over a certain period of time. For example, you and the player may review their
        serve tactics at monthly intervals (e.g. do they reiterate or interpret pertinent
        conditions? what types of serve do they plan?). Also, a long-term goal may be to
        become a mentor for others. Goals should be negotiated between you and the
        player.

10. Teach others (coaches, family members, sport psychologists, etc.) the basic tenets of a
    knowledge-base approach to player development:

    a) Teach others how to differentiate performance skills so that they are able to
        engage in a discussion about other aspects of performance. Teach others to use
        questions that reinforce knowledge-base development (e.g. 'Did you make some
        good decisions during practice today? Tell me about them'.) Teach others that
        rewarding good decisions is important, especially following a failed motor
        execution or when they are defeated.

166

b) In some cases, others may assist in activities designed to promote tactics. For example, they may videotape performances or score decisions for an aspect of play. Also, injured players or those not participating in competition at the moment may take an active role in a variety of tasks designed to enhance their tactical skills as well as others.

c) Solicit advice and help from other individuals working with your player or team (e.g. sport psychologists, strength trainers, athletic trainers). A player's thoughts during one study indicated he implemented a behavior obtained from a sport psychologist. Imagery or relaxation techniques would fit well within a knowledge-base approach and could be monitored (along with tactics) during competition or other activities. Also, issues of fatigue or injury should be incorporated within a knowledge-base approach as tactics could be modified to compensate for these issues.

11. Embrace and utilize technology. Coaches, players, and scientists continue to gain access to equipment that is transportable, low cost, and user friendly (e.g. digital video and audio recorders/players, telemetry devices, virtual reality, editing software). For example, a professional baseball team in the US recently began using hand-held video devices in the dugout to review game clips.

a) Have players record their responses or videotape competition. Use walkie-talkies or cell phones with this feature to obtain players' thoughts or allow communication among players and coaches. Players could develop and store daily logs (via digital recorders) to map their progress. Also, they edit their own video clips for motivation and reinforcement of tactical and motor skills. Overlays on video clips that contain probes or reminders to reinforce tactical knowledge and skills may be developed as well. Several sport science centers or institutes and universities have access to more expensive equipment (e.g. virtual reality training programs) for training. Encourage players to take advantage of such opportunities (see Farrow and Raab, Chapter 10).

b) It is important to note that players will require guidance and training when utilizing technology to reinforce tactical skills. Merely watching videos or talking does not necessarily lead to better knowledge. Also, small notebooks and pencils work well for some players and are used by several professionals in a variety of sports.

CONCLUSION

Obviously, we need to learn more about how to promote the development of tactical skills in sport. Trying to develop players' knowledge too fast or just telling them what to think is not the solution. Knowledge bases are not built overnight. Opportunities to experience activities related to tactics must be promoted and built into practice sessions to develop adequately tactical knowledge and cognitive skills. Research examining instructional interventions suggests that what is learned depends on what is emphasized. Thus, many of the aspects of knowledge-base development in sport domains will be in the control of the coaches and their respective programs. Currently, several player development programs are embracing new ways to create opportunities to develop tactical skills in a variety of sports. Of course other factors (e.g. biological, physiological, psychological, sociological) addressed elsewhere in this book will influence the acquisition of sport expertise. Also, coaches' domain-specific knowledge bases and structure of practices as well as other age-related issues are predicted to impact the development of players' sport expertise. Thus, several factors should be considered when designing practice and other activities.

COACH'S CORNER

Norma Plummer

Head Coach, Australian Netball Team

My knowledge development

My playing history meant that I developed an understanding of tactics from a relatively young age. By the age of 14 years I think I was an astute observer of the game. Being the team's captain also meant I was the coach and would organize team practice. This meant I had to be thinking about our capabilities relative to our opponents and working out ways to beat them. As my playing skill developed and I competed in our National league and then as an Australian representative in Test matches I would regularly come up against the same direct opponent. If a particular player beat me in a given game, I would pride myself on going away and learning from the experience and making sure it never happened again. I think this is a common trait of elite players that they develop extensive knowledge about their opposition and don't just play against them but try to understand them. I try and develop this quality in my players by asking them to tell me about their opponent's strengths and weaknesses. I am often surprised by how many players don't even remember whether they have played against someone before, let alone have a detailed understanding of how they play.

How do you coach tactical knowledge?

I think the critical issue in developing knowledge is repetition. Players pick up information at different rates, which means you need to ensure everyone has enough exposure to be confident they know what to do in a specific situation when it arises. My role as a coach is to identify where there is a weakness in the opposition and then develop a strategy that will take advantage of that weakness. We then develop a drill or mini-game that will allow us to practice this over and over again until the team becomes familiar with it and can handle the situation under competitive pressure. In netball, being able to handle a team that shifts from playing a man-on-man to a zone defense is critical. Recognizing when it happens and then changing your style of play to overcome it requires large amounts of practice and repetition.

Another coaching strategy we use with the National team is to divide the players into their playing areas (e.g. defense, mid-court, attack) and get them to develop a solution to a tactical problem that may have arisen against a specific opponent. Although we as coaches may already have a strong idea about how to overcome the issue, we have found it valuable to let the players have some ownership of this process. If the players feel that they have significantly contributed to developing the solution, they are more likely to implement it with success in a game.

Another issue that arises when coaching a National team is that you select players from all over the country. Different regions have different coaching approaches and subsequently produce players with specific styles of play. Combining these different styles within the one team becomes a challenge. For instance the linkage between the shooters and the center-court players that pass them the ball is one of the most important relationships on a netball court. If a shooter has been conditioned to lead in a particular direction and the center-court player isn't used to passing to that type of lead, problems can emerge. Hence, a lot of time preparing the National team is about getting players to understand each other's playing styles and finding a way to take advantage of that in a tactical sense.

Using technology to develop knowledge

One advantage we have is our relationship with the AIS. As a result we get the opportunity to utilize some of the latest technological advances on offer. One tool that we have found extremely beneficial in developing the tactical knowledge of our players has been a software program called Pattern Plotter. This software allows us to chart the movement of the players and ball throughout the course of a game. Then, importantly from a coaching perspective, we are able to generate reports that summarize the key elements of the game. For instance, we can compare ball movements that resulted in goals with ball movements that were unsuccessful. This information can be presented visually to players and can summarize a great deal of detail in a very simple but powerful manner (see Figure 11.2).

A second technology we have utilized in a variety of formats is video feedback and analysis. On the training court we are able to have a plasma screen set up next to our court that feeds to a camera recording training. If at any moment I wish to reinforce a particular coaching point I can get the players to come to the side of the court and watch an instant replay of our movement (see Figure 11.3). Being able to use video during training is an excellent way of holding players' attention and providing a different medium in addition to verbal instruction for giving feedback or direction. Although you may have been yelling at a player from courtside to reposition in a particular way, it is often not until a player sees the incorrect movement that they believe you and make the change.

Another way we use video is through the use of large screen projections. We ask the players to watch specifically selected patterns of play that we pause at critical moments and ask them to write down what they would do next. We find this is another way of developing their court knowledge but in an off-court environment. Doing this type of training as a group is also valuable as players can share their responses with the squad and debate/discuss why they picked the option they did. I think it is important once you have completed a video session to then get on the court and reinforce the key messages that have been highlighted.

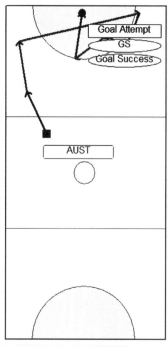

Figure 11.2
A screenshot of the tactical information from netball that can be generated and presented to players from the software program Pattern Plotter.

Figure 11.3 *Norma Plummer coaching with the help of on-court video feedback.*

KEY READING

Baker, J., Horton, S., Robertson-Wilson, J. and Wall, M. (2003). 'Nurturing sport expertise: Factors influencing the development of elite athletes'. *Journal of Sports Science and Medicine*, (2): 1–9.

Ericsson, K.A. (2003). 'Development of elite performance and deliberate practice: An update from the perspective of the expert performance approach'. In Starkes, J.L. and Ericsson, K.A. (eds) *Expert Performance in Sports: Advances in Research on Sport Expertise*. Champaign, IL: Human Kinetics.

French, K.E. and McPherson, S.L. (2004). 'Development of expertise in sport'. In Weiss, M.R. (ed.) *Developmental Sport and Exercise Psychology: A Lifespan Perspective*. Morgantown, WV: Fitness Information.

Gallagher, J.D., French, K.E., Thomas, K.T. and Thomas, J.R. (2002). 'Expertise in youth sport: Relations between knowledge and skill'. In Smoll, F. and Magill, R.A. (eds) *Children in Sport*, 5th edn. Champaign, IL: Human Kinetics.

McPherson, S.L. (1994). 'The development of sport expertise: Mapping the tactical domain'. *Quest*, (46): 223–40.

McPherson, S.L. and French, K.E. (1991). 'Changes in cognitive strategies and motor skill in tennis'. *Journal of Sport and Exercise Psychology*, (13): 40–1

McPherson, S.L. and Kernodle, M.W. (2003). 'Tactics the neglected attribute of champions: Problem representations and performance skills in tennis'. In Starkes, J.L. and Ericsson, K.A. (eds) *Recent Advances in Research on Sport Expertise*. Champaign, IL: Human Kinetics.

Chapter 12

The sport official in research and practice

Clare MacMahon and Henning Plessner

Without a doubt, judges, referees, and umpires are essential components in sport. They are responsible for evaluating athlete performances and enforcing rules. They often have a direct impact on the outcome of a competition, and their decisions can be the center of Monday morning post-game discussions, or, at the worst of times, fan, athlete, and coach abuse. Although a great deal of the information in this book can be applied to the official, there are unique aspects to this role. Despite this, the bulk of sport science research has not addressed the sport official. Although a number of early studies focused on stress and the impact of crowd behaviors, recent work acknowledging this role follows the trends in athlete research by:

(a) assessing the demands of officials
(b) examining characteristics of decisions and the influence of different features on decision making and
(c) tracing the training of elite performers.

In this chapter, we will talk about the research in these three areas. We will show that, for some officials, physical demands are often a priority, which is reflected in their training. We will also show that the research approach to officiating decisions differs to that used for athletes, where officiating decision making often follows a socially driven thinking process. Although factors that influence decisions are sometimes framed as biases, we will show how they are due to the difficulty of the task and simple human nature, and often take place on an unconscious level. Finally, because there is still a great deal of research to be done with officials, we will often ask the questions that remain to be answered. Although there are a variety of different types of sport official, from the basketball referee to the judge in dressage, the research we will review deals mostly with judges (e.g. gymnastics), referees (e.g. soccer, rugby) and umpires (i.e., baseball).

CLASSIFICATION OF OFFICIALS

In order to address a group as complex as that of the official, we must acknowledge the variety of demands faced by different *types* of official. These demands will dictate the relative importance of different research questions, findings, and thus training. To this end, we have identified four dimensions that we feel are the key sources of variation between types of official. These dimensions are: knowledge and rule application, contextual judgment, personality and management, and physical fitness. Of course we acknowledge that all officials need knowledge and rule application, and that physical fitness will always be an asset, however, the volume and complexity of knowledge vary from sport to sport, and some officials must remain stationary whereas others must do a great deal of running and sprinting.

As an extension of this differentiation, Figure 12.1 proposes some general *categories* of officials. These categories are based on two major collapsed dimensions: the amount of interaction with athletes on the playing/competition surface, and the number of athletes or cues that are being monitored. In interaction with athletes, personality and management become important. In some cases, physical fitness is also highlighted. Examples are the soccer referee and the cricket or baseball umpire. With fewer athletes to monitor, the wrestling mat official and the boxing referee are examples of this category labeled as *interactors*. Interactor officials have an impact on the pace of the competition at a micro level, ensuring that the rules and laws are enforced. They are also instrumental in ensuring the safety of the athletes. Most open-sport officials fall into this category.

With little to no interaction with athletes, the gymnastics judge is an example of a *monitor*, who does not determine the pace of the competition (except the head judge who signals the start of a performance), but observes and assesses the quality of performance in relation to a points system. Although monitors most often assess one performer at a time, albeit with

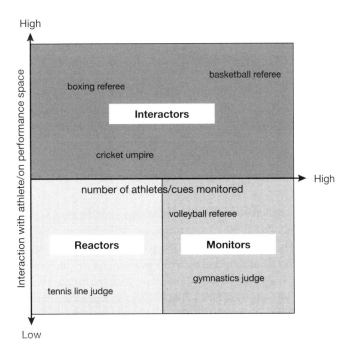

Figure 12.1 *A classification system for sport officials.*

the potential for a great number of cues to consider, synchronized swimming judges are an example of monitors who evaluate a relatively larger number of athletes at once. For this type of official, perceptual–cognitive skills become increasingly emphasized. As we will see, the overwhelming demands to process high-speed action may also lead to some characteristic errors.

Finally, we have identified *reactors* as the type of official who is responsible for only one or two cues and does not largely interact with athletes. An example here is the tennis line judge. The assistant referee in soccer may also straddle the reactor and interactor category. Similar to *monitors*, perceptual–cognitive demands are often highlighted for this group, although there has been little research devoted solely to this type of official.

THE DEMANDS OF OFFICIATING

Considering the dimensions we noted in our classifications, there is no doubt that officiating is a demanding role. When we consider examples of some of the best referees and officials, it is obvious that there is a need for a basic level of fitness and a deep knowledge of the rules. But high-performance officials also display skills that speak to additional demands. The best officials seem to possess *intangible* personal judgment and the ability to manage contests without dominating them. To identify key skills better, a study of rugby union refereeing proposes five cornerstones to performance, of which four resemble the dimensions we used in our classification:

(a) knowledge and application of the laws
(b) contextual judgment
(c) personality and management skills
(d) fitness, positioning, and mechanics, and
(e) psychological characteristics of excellence.

This section will touch on some of these cornerstones again, as we consider the demands of officiating and review both relevant research and areas that may be fruitful for additional study.

Physical demands

Research that quantifies the demands of sport officials has been the most comprehensive when addressing the *interacting* official, who must move about the playing field and interact with the athletes. A soccer or rugby referee must keep pace with up to thirty players, moving about a field that is up to 110 m long and up to 75 m wide. At any moment a kick can move the action 50, 60 or 70 m away. Heart-rate monitors were placed on referees and assistant referees during the final games of the EURO 2000 soccer championships, and the data collected showed that match referee heart rates throughout the game were between eighty and ninety per cent of their maximum. These physical work rates are as high as, if not higher than, those of the players. What's more, the average age of a recent study sample of FIFA and UEFA soccer referees was 41 years, whereas the players being refereed are in their mid to late twenties. As we will consider later, there are declines that accompany aging that have an effect on training and performance. This highlights how hard referees must work to keep pace with players and the action they are evaluating.

Decision making and teamwork

In addition to these physical demands are the large number of decisions that are made throughout a game. From the same soccer study discussed above, researchers watched all of the games from the EURO 2000 tournament and counted the number of observable decisions (e.g. when the referee makes a signal). The results showed that, during the course of a game, the match referee makes an average of 137 decisions. With an estimated sixty or so unobservable decisions, such as deciding *not* to blow the whistle, this puts the average number of decisions up to around three or four *per minute* during a game.

It's also important to consider that the majority of officials do not work alone. Of the average 137 observable decisions during Euro 2000 games, sixty-four per cent were made in communication with the assistant referee. Teamwork and communication are especially highlighted in sports such as Canadian football (gridiron), where a crew of seven officials must co-ordinate throughout the game. In this case, the role and responsibilities of each official are specialized and well-defined, arguably more so than the roles of athletes in many team sports.

This teamwork and communication aspect of refereeing has not been examined in enough detail yet. For example, we can ask whether it is better to have officials specialize as a referee or assistant referee, as in soccer, or have the ability to rotate positions between the referee and touch judge as in rugby union. Is it better to keep a crew of seven officials together for a whole season, or to rotate them among different crews?

Work in organizational psychology that tested how groups learn to assemble a radio is relevant here. Researchers either told every group member how to do every sub-task, or they taught each member a different sub-task. The groups with members each having their own specialized task assembled the radios better and more efficiently. They had developed a shared understanding of how to assemble a radio, and trusted that they only had to complete their sub-task, and that each other member would do the same. If this pattern is shown when learning a skill or task as a group, how will it come through when each member already has experience, as is the case with sport officials in a crew?

Some current work looking at team officiating is using questionnaires among crews of officials to understand their perceptions of how specialized their roles are, how much they trust each member of the crew, and how well they feel they co-ordinate together. For example, after a game, the officials are asked to rate their agreement with statements such as: 'I trusted that other crew members' knowledge about the game and rules was credible', 'Each crew member has specialized knowledge pertaining to their position on the crew', and 'We officiated the game smoothly and efficiently'.

These three things—specialization, credibility/trust, and co-ordination—are seen as components of a shared understanding of the overall task, or a *transactive memory system*. The idea is that when a crew has created a transactive memory system, in which they share a group model or understanding of the task of officiating, performance will improve. The final link, then, is that keeping members consistent and specialized is the best way to create a transactive

175

memory system. As a final note on interaction between officials, although some officials such as a panel of gymnastics or skating judges don't explicitly interact with each other during the judging process, there is evidence that they are influenced by each other's judgments nonetheless. We will show this in the section addressing characteristics of decision making.

Game management and personality

Not only do officials interact with each other, but they interact with athletes and coaches. Officials learn the appropriate hand signals to communicate calls; however, many sports require skill in dealing with players and coaches before as well as after decisions. In most sports, referees and umpires will tell you that one of the most important things is to show *confidence*. Many sports also emphasize spectator appeal and maintaining *flow*, discouraging officials from calling unnecessary stoppages. This often leads to informal interactions and *preventive refereeing*, where an official may instruct a player to prevent them from committing a foul or offense (e.g. 'number 3 get onside!').

Although it's difficult to study or assess things such as personality and management skills, we are making strides. For example, a recent review of psychological and performance demands describes the use of a conflict management style grid in rugby referees. An example of conflict is given when a player addresses the referee by saying, 'Come on, ref, he's offside- that's ridiculous!'. The co-operation and assertiveness used in response combine five different conflict management styles, as shown in Figure 12.2. As the authors of this work point out, there is no research yet that can be used to guide referees on *when* to use which style; however, an awareness of different options is a starting point for the individual referee to experiment.

Judgment

There are times when officials are asked to interpret actions, with many rules based on the intentions of a player. This coincides with contextual judgment as one of the earlier-mentioned cornerstones of rugby refereeing. The ability to read and interpret emotions, both in rule application and dealing with confrontation, and even to predict reactions, is a sub-component of what some psychologists have identified as *empathic ability* or as *emotional intelligence*. For example, it's crucial for a good referee to sense when players are becoming too heated. The stringency of calls may then be adjusted, and captains may be spoken to to avoid a brawl or unnecessary and dangerous fouls.

Although, as we say, this has always seemed to be an intangible skill, researchers can use questionnaires to produce data and examine emotional intelligence in officials. Although the questionnaires have their limitations, we might expect that more successful referees and umpires show greater emotional intelligence, but that the same is not true of sports where the officials do not have as much interpretation and interaction with the athletes (e.g. gymnastics, skating). This is all speculation at the moment, as this work remains to be done. But as one of the best known and most respected soccer referees, Pierluigi Collina, has said:

> If you have good relations with all the players in a match, including the coaches, it's possible to have a better match—the players can do their job, and the referee

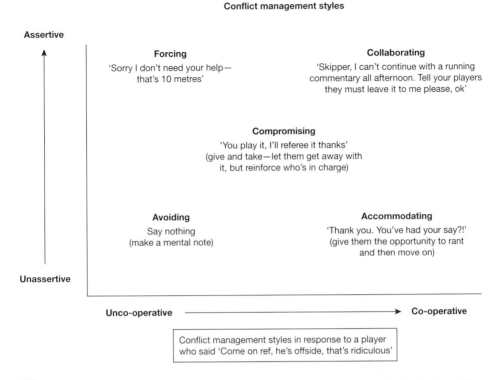

Conflict management styles

Conflict management styles in response to a player
who said 'Come on ref, he's offside, that's ridiculous'

Figure 12.2 *Thomas and Kilmann's (1974) Conflict Management Style Grid adapted for refereeing (from Mascarenhas et al., 2005).*

can control the match better. If the players trust and accept a referee and his decisions, I feel that it makes for a better game of football.

However, it should be noted that this philosophy is not shared by all officials in all sports, and even many soccer referees would insist that it is better for them to be as 'blind' as possible toward the participants of a game. This also highlights the differences we point out in our classification system, where some officials may be more focused on accurate rule application (e.g. in gymnastics) and some on game management (e.g. in basketball).

Perception and information processing

Another reason why emotional intelligence and interpretation are important in officiating is that there is often intentional deception—from the gymnast or skater who tries to cover up a fault, to the catcher in baseball who *frames* a pitch to get a strike call, or the soccer player who uses a little bit of acting to draw a penalty. Although dealing with athletes and coaches can make or break an official, one of the most demanding aspects of the role is that officials must evaluate intentionally deceptive, fast-paced action under time pressure, with very little information. As a result, officials need to gain as much information as possible. In many

177

sports, this is why positioning and mechanics are so important: to get the key information they need, and to deal with deception, officials become aware of typical tactics and practices and counter them by using key cues. As we will see when we discuss training, some of this knowledge is based on personal experiences, both as officials and former competitors or coaches. And even so, there are many situations where task demands overwhelm resources and there is missing information. Because there is a relatively good base of research in this area, the next section of this chapter will deal with perception and show how officials sometimes *fill in the blanks*, which may lead to error. These errors can be categorized according to their source and the point at which they occur during the decision-making process.

DECISION MAKING AS A SOCIALLY DRIVEN PROCESS

Many researchers regard the way we think using a computer analogy. Put in very simple terms, humans are like machines that take in information, process it using existing stored information, and then provide an output. This information-processing approach is also used for decision making, with the stages identified as:

(a) perception (e.g. a referee sees a tackle);
(b) encoding or categorization (e.g. the referee classifies the tackle as legal or illegal);
(c) storage and retrieval (e.g. the particular tackle is transferred to memory, and also compared with other tackles that the referee remembers seeing); and
(d) decision or judgment (e.g. the referee brings together the information from perception, encoding and memory to decide that the tackle is illegal).

   Henning Plessner and Thomas Haar (2006) recently looked at research on sport judgments and the errors that occur. They see sport judgments as an example of how we make sense of other people and ourselves as we go through the four stages of information processing. This is called a social cognitive approach. The errors that have been identified in the research are then placed in each of the processes of perception, encoding/categorization, memory, and information integration. It's important for officials to be aware of the errors that have been shown in the research so that they can counter them. We will give some examples of these errors, but also provide key references at the end of the chapter for further reading.

Errors in perception: the importance of positioning

As mentioned, officials are often asked to make important judgments with partial information. It seems like a straightforward judgment to decide whether a rugby player has touched the ball down to score a try. It's made much more difficult, however, from a distance, with opposition players obscuring the view. In a key study in soccer, Raoul Oudejans *et al.* (2000) showed how positioning of the assistant referee can lead to perceptual errors in judging offside. In soccer, a player is in an offside position if he or she is nearer to the opponents' goal line than both the ball and the second last defender at the moment the ball is played by a team member. In order to judge offside, assistant referees are instructed to position themselves in line with the second last defender. The Dutch researchers found that the high percentage of errors in offside decisions in soccer mainly reflects the viewing position of the assistant referee (see Figure 12.3). Although they should stand in line with the last defender, on average, they are positioned too far behind. By considering the retinal images of referees (i.e., the projection of the scene being viewed onto the eye's retina), the researchers predicted a specific relationship of frequencies in different types of error (wrongly indicating offside vs not indicating an actual offside) depending on the area of attack (near vs far from the assistant referee and inside or outside the defender). In an analysis of 200 videotaped matches, this prediction was confirmed, thus demonstrating that assistant referees' decisions directly reflect the situations as they are projected on their retinas. Similar results were obtained from studies in sports where officials have fixed viewing positions, for example, in gymnastics. The main message from these studies is that even experienced officials are influenced in a predictable way by basic perceptual illusions as they are determined, for example, by their imperfect viewing positions.

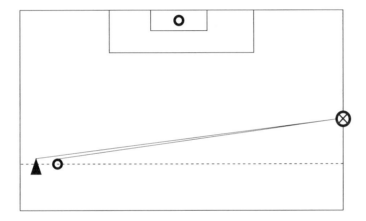

Figure 12.3 *Optical errors in judging offside positions. Positions of defenders are indicated by circles and attackers by triangles. The offside line (in line with the second last defender) is indicated by a dotted line. The typical position of the AR just ahead of the offside line is marked by a circle with a cross. From this position, the attacker furthest away (who is actually onside) appears to be ahead of the second last defender and the AR is likely to commit a flag error.*

On the other hand, there is some evidence that proper feedback training can help partly to overcome limitations of perceptual illusions. In a training study by Gernot Jendrusch and colleagues, electronic devices were installed on a tennis court to assess objectively the point where the ball hits the court. In a training group, line judges received accurate feedback about their decisions during several sessions a week. Their decision making improved markedly in comparison with a control group that did not receive training.

What is most interesting about this study is that, according to all kinds of physical measures, there was no improvement in the perceptual abilities of the training group's line judges. Rather, they learned what to look at to make decisions. That is, they used relatively valid perceptual cues to assess the point at which the ball hit the court—for example, the shape of the flying curve. The message from this work is that creating learning environments that help officials to use multiple valid cues should be an important aspect of developing decision

179

training. In addition, it should be noted that we can figure out the best viewing position for an official by analyzing the details of their perceptual demands. For example, a study in baseball found that repositioning the home plate umpire as suggested in visual perception research literature improved the accuracy of ball-strike judgments.

Encoding/categorizing actions: interpretations are changeable

In other judgments, the input, or perception is not the problem: it's interpreting the action. This interpretation may be based on factors that are not immediately performance-relevant, but are used by officials to help them fill in the gaps of missing information. In figure skating and gymnastics, for example, coaches create an order for their athletes to compete in, putting the better skaters or gymnasts at the end. This creates an expectation for the quality of the performance, based on this order. Several studies have shown this effect: when the same gymnastics routine or skating program is seen later in the order, it is scored significantly better than when that exact same routine or program was seen as one of the first performances.

These expectations are not only created in the often-criticized *judged* sports. For example, baseball umpires are influenced by being told that a pitcher has a reputation as being either controlled or wild (no control over his pitches). In several studies, athletes' and teams' reputations, as well as many other sources of expectancies, such as stereotypes, have been found to influence judgments of sport performance. Although these influences are mostly treated as unwelcome, it should be noted that expectancies that mirror true differences can also improve accuracy in complex judgment tasks.

Taking this work together, the encoding and categorization of a performance have been found to be systematically influenced by the activation of various types of prior knowledge, even when this knowledge has no performance-relevant value in judging an athlete's performance. It is clear that these influences increase in likelihood as judging situations increase in ambiguity. Therefore, officials should at least be aware of potential judgment biases via the activation of inappropriate knowledge. Again, (video-based) feedback training has been suggested by many authors as a measure to improve accuracy in categorization tasks, such as recognizing an offensive pattern in football.

Errors in memory: should judges watch the warm-up?

Unfortunately, there is some evidence that officials' judgments are not only biased by the activation of general memory structures, but also by specific memories of athletes' prior performances. Such influences have been studied in an impressive series of experiments by Diane Ste-Marie and her colleagues. They investigated how the memory of prior encounters with an athlete's performance can influence actual performance judgments. In these experiments, judges first watched a series of gymnasts perform a simple element and decided whether the performance was perfect or flawed. The judges' task was the same in the second phase that followed, except that the gymnastic elements shared a relationship with the performances shown in the first phase. Some of the gymnasts were shown during the second phase with the identical performance as in the first phase (e.g. perfect performance both times), and others were shown with the opposite performance (e.g. first perfect and then flawed). It was found that judgments in the second phase were influenced by the performances

180

in the first phase. For example, a perfect performance in the second phase was less likely to be judged as a perfect performance by the judges if they had seen this athlete with a flawed performance in the first phase. That is, judgments were less accurate when an athlete's performance varied between the first and second phase than if it did not. The robustness of these findings led the authors to the conclusion that judges inevitably rely on retrieval from memory for prior episodes. In principle, the only way to avoid these biases would be to prevent judges from seeing the gymnasts perform before a competition. However, given the limited number of top athletes and the limited number of top officials in most sports, this may be an unrealistic proposal.

Errors in integrating information for a final decision

In the final step of social information processing, information about an athlete's performance that has been encoded and categorized, together with information that has been retrieved from memory, are integrated into a judgment and a final decision. Ideally, officials consider all the relevant information and integrate this information in the most appropriate, analytical way. However, because the human capacities to process information are limited and sport situations often introduce constraints such as time pressure, officials have frequently been shown to use short cuts or heuristics to cope with the complexity of judgment situations. An example of these shortcuts, as mentioned, is the use of prior knowledge, such as the reputation of a pitcher. Unfortunately, little is known about when and why judges in sports switch between more analytic and more heuristic processing. Research on information integration processes in sport performance judgments typically focuses on the more or less deliberate use of information beyond the observable performance. An important question that arises from this research is, how adaptive is the use of this information?

For example, the judgment of an athlete's performance is frequently based on comparison with other athletes, or with prior judgments of other athletes' performance, respectively. In principle, comparisons can be very helpful in order to achieve fair judgments that mirror true differences in performances. However, recent research also suggests that such comparisons can lead to biased judgments. In an experiment by Lysann Damisch et al. (2006), experienced gymnastic judges had to evaluate two routines on vault in a sequence. The two athletes were introduced to the judges as belonging either to the same national team or to different teams. Although the second routine was the same in all conditions, half of the judges first saw a better routine, whereas the other half first saw a worse routine. It was found that the second gymnast's score was assimilated toward the standard when both gymnasts were introduced as belonging to the same team. The opposite effect occurred when the judges believed the gymnasts belonged to different teams. In other words, when the gymnasts were believed to be from the same team, the two routines were scored similarly, but when they were believed to be from different teams, the scores were less similar, or in contrast.

Together, quite a few biases have been identified that occur from different processes of information integration. A first step in order to prevent theses biases is to make officials familiar with them. However, it should be noted that some of these processes work in a rather automatic fashion and are, therefore, difficult to control even if judges are aware of them. In addition, processes such as comparisons can be helpful guides in an uncertain environment. That is, if judges, for some reason, are not able to apply the rules in the supposed way, the use of direct comparisons will bring them much closer to the *true* value of a performance than simply guessing. Therefore, some general advice in order to prevent biases on this step of information processing is the training of accurate rule application that leaves no room for interpretation.

TRAINING FOR SPORT OFFICIATING

There continues to be a great deal of focus on training within sport expertise studies. The most influential research is the theory of deliberate practice, which proposes that, to become an expert in a field, one needs to engage in a large volume of practice—up to 10 years or 10,000 hours. This practice must also be highly effortful, and relevant to improvement, with opportunities for feedback and correction. We will leave the detail on this theory and on training research to Baker and Cobley (Chapter 3), and simply present and make comments on the research findings with officials.

In a recent study, twenty-six elite soccer referees from FIFA, UEFA, and the English Premier League were asked to report the time they had spent in different training activities for their first year of formal refereeing; 1998; and 2003. For example, they were asked how much time they had spent per week in on-field activities such as speed and agility training, high-intensity runs, and recovery runs; off-field activities such as strength training, flexibility and video training; and match or match-related activities such as refereeing league or exhibition games. These three years were chosen to get a picture of practice changes over time, as well as the impact of structured training programmes—which were put in place in 1998, and remained in place in 2003.

The results of the study show that elite officials are unique to athletes from a training perspective. These elite performers were not simply retired players or coaches. They had specialized relatively early as referees, and spent many years training. For example, the fourteen FIFA referees in the group had started formal refereeing at an average age of 18, and it took a little over 16 years on average for each of them to reach the FIFA list. All of the referees reported doing very little weekly training in their first year, but gradually increased both the amount and also the different types of training activities. For example, the referees typically reported that in their first year they would do an hour a week of high intensity running, and perhaps 30 min. in low-intensity running. They would also engage in *other training* such as bicycling for fitness. Over the years, they maintained their focus on high-intensity running, with an average of 1.5 hours per week, but also increased the amount of time spent in other activities such as speed endurance and agility training, recovery runs, video training, and technical skills. At the same time, the *other training* dropped off, showing their specialization in activities that mimic the physical demands of on-field performance.

One of the basic ideas in the theory of deliberate practice is that the most useful practice provides an opportunity for learning through feedback. Feedback is a tricky issue in learning to officiate. Even delayed feedback from assessors is often in short supply for referees, especially as they are making their way up the ranks and acquiring skill. Probably as a result of this, the referees in the study discussed above reported that *refereeing league games* is the most relevant activity for improving performance, even ranked ahead of refereeing exhibition games.

The essential nature of experience is highlighted in a study of rugby union referees that identified the concept of *deliberate experience* as an alternative way to develop refereeing expertise. A number of rugby referees observed and interviewed by researchers felt that traditional training alone was not sufficient to reach expert levels of performance. One ex-international official stated that:

> To be a good international standard referee, you have to referee international games. It's the same for the guys who want to move up to Zurich (a higher level of competition). The games are totally different and you are constantly learning.

The study also acknowledged that experience in other roles contributes to referee proficiency in a *transfer of skills*. The researchers reported that referees feel experience gained from playing helps a referee know how a player thinks. Echoing our earlier statements related to the demands of officiating, the referees also felt that personality, confidence, and assertiveness contribute to refereeing, and that these are often developed in one's occupation, but transferred on to the field.

The fact that skills such as management and assertiveness are developed over time and transferred from other roles, combined with the need for deliberate experience through actual game refereeing, may explain why it took the referees in the soccer study 16 years to reach the FIFA list—a lengthier time than expected by the theory of deliberate practice. On the one hand, sport bodies must acknowledge that development in officials is arguably more complex than that of athletes, with the need for:

(a) the development of officiating skills
(b) the development of a positive reputation, and
(c) the negotiation of the politics of promotion.

This lengthy skill acquisition and promotion process has an impact on the age at which many officials are at their peak. Some officials may thus simultaneously encounter the beginning of age-related declines, and a need for increased recovery from bouts of demanding officiating. We know very little specifically, however, about whether these declines have an impact on performance. For example, although an older official may have less physical capability such as running speed, the experience of knowing where to be and how to anticipate the play may compensate so that there is no loss in performance. In the application portion of this chapter, we make further comments on some issues that become more relevant for the older official; however, there is more research needed in this area.

On the other hand, it may be that officials can shorten the length of time that it takes to become a top performer by increasing or refining their training methods. It seems certain that some sport officials will benefit from an increase in deliberate experience in the form of refereed games. There are limits, however, and it may be unrealistic to expect that a novice official will have access to a large number of games for training purposes. In this case, the official can follow the route used by many injured athletes and use video training. Watching full games can help an official think through specific cases of penalties and fouls and observe the appropriate positioning. As well, isolated clips can be used to train and test rule-based decisions. A few studies have identified potential video-based decision-training tools and their features. For example, a soccer study that had warm-up clips and used video of only one type of action (tackle situations) found that referees performed better than players in identifying the correct call. This finding makes the point that experience of playing may help an official interpret player intentions and spot deception, but rule-based decision-making skill cannot be gained simply by playing, and is somewhat specific to officials (see Farrow and Raab, Chapter 10, for more information on this idea).

Video-based training tools also raise some of the most interesting and hardest questions in officiating research: How do we decide on the *correct* call? And thus, how do we appropriately evaluate performance by officials? In many sports, a video replay of the action does not provide the same point of view that the on-field or on-court official had at the time. Nor can an isolated clip of action provide the context that an official might use to influence decision making. In many areas, the 'biases' used in judgment and decision making can be considered as adaptive and helpful. These factors are what probably contribute to the difficulty in creating sensitive tools to assess and train referee skill. In creating a research tool or test, when an expert panel, which may be composed of coaches, ex-officials, and administrators, cannot agree on the correct decision for a clip of action, we decide that it would not make a good testing item and exclude it. But this may result in a pool of clips that are *too easy*, and does not discriminate between more and less-skilled officials or even officials and players. It also eliminates the types of play that prompt criticism and second-guessing of an official's decision—the *key* decisions. In the *real world* of the referee and referee assessors, key decisions need to be evaluated.

From both a research and an officiating evaluation perspective, there needs to be an acknowledgment that there are, in fact, *ambiguous* actions, for which the call may change depending on the context. For researchers, this acknowledgment opens the door to studying the contextual factors that have an influence through experimental manipulation. Researchers can further use *fuzzy signal detection* to create tests that are more flexible. Rather than viewing each video clip as, for example, a foul or no-foul, we can acknowledge the *fuzziness* of a play by allowing experts to scale their responses. Thus, a rater may indicate how much *fuzziness* there is in the decision for an action by using a scale from definite foul/definite no-foul (1) to borderline foul/borderline no-foul (10). In this manner, we're able to tap in to the *gray* of decisions, rather than impose a black and white measure and miss out on the level of agreement between raters and those being tested.

The acknowledgment of ambiguity and *fuzziness* will also benefit assessors who are concerned with evaluating the performance of an official. Evaluators need to be mindful of, and sensitive to, the fact that they may be assessing an official's decision based on either less (e.g. absence of context), more (e.g. slow motion), or different (e.g. angle of view) information than the official had at the time of making a call or decision. In addition, once officials are made aware of potential 'biases' and factors that have been found to influence decisions, evaluators may look to see if an official has fallen into a judgment trap.

Although it is understandable that assessors may look to create evaluation systems that are objective and quantitative measures of performance, great detail and statistics do not always translate into a great evaluation system. The research that presented the five cornerstones of referee performance for rugby union advises evaluators to avoid diminishing the task into a skeleton of itself. Evaluators should consider the characteristics and skills of several of the sport's top performers, and what skills or qualities are not captured in a ticks and checks evaluation system, and where there are different, but equally successful *styles* of refereeing. An appropriate evaluation should provide the opportunity to cater for an individual, so that it is *meaningful* and provides *specific feedback* on which an official may take action and seek further training and refinement. For example, a referee may be told to reconsider positioning

184

for a specific type of play. The following section will also provide some advice on aspects to consider in evaluating officiating performance.

RESEARCH INTO PRACTICE: ADVICE FOR SPORTS OFFICIALS

In the sections above, we have reviewed research, and also suggested areas for continued research into demands, skill and training of sport officials. Again, there is relatively little research into the sport official. In addition, the demands and skills vary a great deal between different *types* of official, from the smaller differences between the referee and assistant referee, to the bigger differences between a gymnastics judge and a rugby referee. This limits our ability to provide concrete guidelines for all officials. Nonetheless, the general points below should be considered by researchers, sport bodies, and individual officials themselves. We will begin by addressing basic training for officials, and move to issues that may be more relevant as they acquire skill, and resources become more available.

Examine the basic training systems that are in place

The most basic requirement in officiating, on which licensing and accreditation are often based, is knowledge of the rules and laws of the sport. Arguably more so than athletes or coaches, officials are required to have a strong foundation of declarative knowledge, which is often defined as rule-book knowledge. The implementation of the rules is referred to as procedural (how to) knowledge. For both learning of the rules and learning of rule application, most sports provide materials in the form of commentaries and accompanying videos that help the novice official to become familiar with the specific rule system beyond the mere study of the written rules. These materials are important because laws are typically written with the main purpose of being exact and not of being user-friendly. In addition, in some sports learning the rules is already the greatest challenge for the future official. For example, the Code of Points in gymnastics is rather complex and comprises, among other things, a detailed list of hundreds of value parts that need to be recognized in a competition. Accordingly, research has pointed to the fact that in such sports the main differences between novices and experienced judges are due to their knowledge structure. This research argues that experienced judges have specific knowledge that helps them to process performances faster and more efficiently. They know what information is relevant, what to expect, and what the typical interrelations are among variables. Again, it seems that this kind of knowledge is not attained as an automatic consequence of mere experience in a sport—for example as an athlete—but is acquired through specific, structured, and effortful training.

Apart from video materials that can be helpful in order to learn both the rules and how to implement them, officials are also advised to frequently observe and discuss athletes' performances either in training sessions or competitions.

Understand the demands facing the official

Officials are often left out in the cold in terms of a research basis for their training. They are left to rely on what we know about training for the athletes in their sport. For some skills this is not entirely inappropriate. For example, the fitness and physical training of the soccer official should be somewhat similar to those of the soccer athlete. However, we should strive to obtain a clear understanding of the specific demands on the official, keeping in mind that some of these are additional and/or different to those on the athlete. It's also worth mentioning that these demands may differ depending on the level of play that is officiated, and the gender of the athletes. Demands may be assessed by watching a selection of videotapes of performances and coding the action using a number of categories:

- movement patterns (e.g. forward, sideways, backward; sprinting, jogging, walking)
- communication (e.g. length, number of communications with other officials, athletes, coaches)
- number of decisions and type.

Identify the key decisions or typical errors

Once the demands are understood, these can be used to identify key decisions, typical areas of difficulty, and even sources of error. This can be based on noting the source of arguments with coaches and players, discussion with other officials, and even the impact of a decision. For example, a penalty decision has a major impact if it leads to point scoring. The information-processing approach is helpful to identify the stage at which errors have occurred. Thus, for example, positioning may be a large source of perceptual difficulty that leads to error in a particular decision. Once again, key decisions may differ by level of play, and undoubtedly for different types of decision-making system (e.g. panel of judges vs on-field referee). This type of analysis can provide information on common practices, types of system and their influences on decision making. For example, the use of a panel of judges responsible for providing a global mark for an athlete vs split responsibilities (e.g. technical and artistic assessments, as in gymnastics).

As a final comment, knowing the demands and typical decisions at different *levels of play* may help create a smoother transition for developing officials. For instance, a typical rookie error for Canadian Football League officials is to call a player offside believing 'he couldn't have been that fast'. This is an example of how officials need to adapt to the physical capabilities of players at a higher level of competition. They may also encounter different tactics, requiring adapted positioning, and an increased frequency of higher-order skills such as a drop kick during open play in rugby. They may no longer be expected to 'let some calls go', and must now adapt to a new set of *unwritten rules*. These may all be captured through analysis of key decisions and typical errors, and contrasted across levels of officiating.

Cater advanced training to the demands and typical errors

The next obvious step is to use the information gained from an assessment of demands and errors to guide training. In physically demanding officiating, training should build an aerobic base and mimic the on-field demands. Here the training literature provides a great deal more specific guidance. With regard to decisions, officials can now become sensitized to which key decisions require additional focus in video tools, the law book, and positioning. Although training should acknowledge that high volumes of deliberate practice in relevant activities are associated with improving skills, we also encourage officials to increase and maximize their *deliberate experience*, and gain as much *actual officiating* as they can. The influence of context and realistic scenarios must be emphasized. Because these principles are considered in Joan Vicker's work on decision-making training in athletes, we present her guidelines here:

- frame practice events to place decision-making skills at the fore
- design drills that train the decision in conditions that simulate those found in competition
- use the seven decision-training tools of:
    1. variable practice
    2. random practice
    3. bandwidth feedback
    4. questioning
    5. video feedback
    6. hard-first instruction
    7. modeling.

(More detailed information on these seven tools is available in the Vickers *et al.*'s (2004) work, referenced at the end of this chapter. The reader is also directed to Farrow and Raab, Chapter 10, which is dedicated to decision-making research and to Patterson and Lee, Chapter 9, which considers issues in practice design).

In the emphasis on decision making in this system, referee-coaches and officiating trainers play the role not only of evaluators, but of physical and *decision-making* coaches, designing, running, and assessing training activities. General skill-acquisition activities, such as training camps, controlled games, and *shadowing*, where a novice official follows an experienced official, follow these general principles, but may be improved by a clear focus on the features highlighted above.

Develop cornerstones to form the basis of evaluation systems

As we have discussed in previous sections of this chapter, officials face demands that are not necessarily observable or captured by ticks and marks. These skills and their relative importance to the overall proficiency of an official should be communicated to create an assessment, training, and promotion system that is as transparent as possible. For example, the cornerstones of success for rugby referees that we have repeatedly referred to provide specific areas for assessment and skill development. When evaluations are concrete but meaningful, assessors can direct officials to the tools for improvement. Moreover, as we mentioned above, *teams* of officials can be evaluated where appropriate to assess the impact of consistently training and performing together.

A COMMENT ON AGE-RELATED DECLINES

On the practical side of officiating, we have noted that officials are often older than the athletes they officiate, and some may experience age-related declines as they move toward older adulthood. Once again, we lack a specific officiating research base for comments in this area; however, it is worth noting some age-related declines that may have an impact on officiating performance. These abilities should be considered as part of evaluation systems in order to help older officials *remain* at peak levels as long as possible and retain the skills that they have developed over time.

The most obvious impact of age may be the capability to perform and recover from physically demanding officiating tasks such as high-intensity running (sprinting) and speed-endurance running. As well, however, officiating places demands on attentional resources that decline with age: in particular, and of relevance for officials, *vigilance*, *task switching*, and the *inhibition of irrelevant cues*.

As we age, it is more difficult to *sustain* attention over time. Thus, an older official may need to pay particular attention to calls at the *beginning* and *end* of play, or during breaks in play for more continuous sports. Older officials may also begin to have difficulty paying attention to multiple sources of information, such as the position of two players, plus a field marking, and the movements of a third player relative to the ball. Related to this, unimportant but distracting information may become more difficult to block out, such as screaming fans. Physical performance and recovery, and attentional errors or declines can all be traced through evaluation and performance journals. Once officials recognize problems with attention, all that may be needed is some extra effort guided by attentional cues and strategies. Appropriate evaluation systems will help assess skills and provide tools to maintain peak levels of performance. This is preferable to arbitrary age cut-offs for retirement, given the length of time needed to develop in this role.

CONCLUSION

We have shown that officiating is a diverse role within sport: there are many different *types* of official, with different demands. Research has focused on describing these demands, tracing the training of the top performers, and understanding the characteristics of decision making. The official is both similar to, and different from, the athlete in many respects. These characteristics and demands should be understood in order to provide focused training, assessment, and improvement. It should also be noted that demands may change based on the level of play being officiated. As well, age-related declines may need to be considered at present, but perhaps avoided in the future if we are able to short-cut the path to proficiency in officiating by improved training.

There is still a great deal to do in understanding the demands, training, and skills specific to sport officials. Although we have provided some general practical guidelines, just as important are the potential research areas we have highlighted. Although many officials are accustomed to shunning the spotlight, and in fact strive to be somewhat invisible, understanding and improving their skills are areas where they would do well to raise their voices and attract some attention.

COACH'S CORNER

Adrian Panozzo

National Umpiring Development Manager, Australian Football League

There are a number of things that I noticed from this chapter with regard to our practices in the development of AFL umpires. Let me point out a few things that we are doing, and how they coincide with points raised in the chapter.

The transition from player to umpire

It's true that there is some specialization between umpires and players. We have an umpire who made the transition from having played 100 games in the AFL to becoming an umpire. Having been a player created a positive foundation for him. He had empathy for the players, and was good at managing emotions. He could understand, for example, why a player might complain after being penalized a free kick. On the other hand, there was some interference. The stimulation was there for him to be a player—he had to prevent himself from moving to a position where he could receive a pass, and instead concentrate on where to look and where to run *as an umpire*.

Match management

The chapter talks about the idea of 'game management'. This is what we call 'match management'. We don't want match management to conflict with consistency, though. We would say that there is never a case when you would just let a call go. A free kick is still a free kick, but where match management comes in is in how you sell the decision to the players. An umpire's style doesn't come from the decisions, but from how they communicate a call. Our most successful umpire right now is a gardener by trade—he's assertive, confident, and consistent, and the players like him.

We can very easily evaluate an umpire just by looking at his or her body language. The non-verbal communication can be more influential than the actual words that are used. There's a difference between having technical knowledge and selling it from a body language point of view. Does the umpire feel he or she belongs there? The most successful umpires will shake off a mistake and move on, and you won't be able to tell from their body language that something might have gone wrong—it won't affect their next decision or how it's delivered. The chapter presents a figure on conflict-management styles. It's the same thing here: we would never advise on what to say, because it's all just language, and it depends on *how* it's said.

One thing underlying match management is that people target umpires and say that the successful teams get an easier go from them. But that's not really the case. In fact, they looked at successful teams, and they actually gave away *more* free kicks to the opposition.

But they also took more risks, they dominated the game and had more possession. This is part of why we disagree when people say that without an umpire there would be no game. That's not true—but with an umpire, the game is safer, fairer, and more enjoyable. We try to discourage the attitude that umpires have a hard job. They don't. They train for it and, compared with players, they don't get taken off the ground for mistakes. Everyone on the field out there has a personal risk. If umpires keep saying it's a hard job, then no one will try it, and it's not going to help!

Development and training for umpires

I agree that the best place to gain practice is in actual game performance. Even at the elite level, skill drills (e.g. bouncing the ball to commence play) lack the environment, intensity, and motivation from the umpires for any gains. They end up being a waste of time because the skills don't transfer—they aren't enough of a simulation, and the umpires know it, so the motivation isn't there. They get bored.

It has become the responsibility of the sport to help develop the umpires. The attitude should be that, if you want good match officiating, let the umpires come to practice. Use them so that they get good simulations of umpiring and you help create better officials. Make a commitment—don't change your plans at the last minute, or use their attendance as a way to argue calls from the weekend. And the entire league should understand that an umpire practicing with a team does not change any of the calls when that umpire draws a match with that team.

The importance of mentoring

We have also created a mentoring program in AFL umpiring that we very much believe in. It helps umpires learn in competition time. Although we're moving it toward being accepted, at the moment, there is little tolerance for a new umpire to gain real in-game experience. It is common for a new player to get five minutes at the end of the game as he or she is learning. So it should be the same for a developing umpire—the way that you have learner drivers on the road.

We use green shirts for first year umpires, and they are mentored by experienced umpires who they shadow during a game. What this lets us do, for example, is just isolate one call. The learner will be told that he or she should just concentrate on calling marks (when the ball is caught cleanly from the air), and that's all they have to think about. After five minutes on the field they're taken off so that they have time to reflect and get feedback. This is a practical example, which is changing how players think. They now see that umpires have to learn and develop and now they don't expect them to be perfect. And it provides real game conditions for learning.

Age declines and age advantages

We also think that the mentoring program is providing huge benefits beyond just having green shirts in games. The younger umpires are getting one-on-one attention, learning how to treat players, and for the older umpires, we think that they now have a new motivation— they want to see the younger guys and girls they mentor get to the highest level. This helps them take advantage of their skills in a new way. The chapter comments on age-related declines, and we definitely see this in AFL umpiring. Although our umpires are only between 30 and 40 years old, the older umpires can reach a physical threshold while they are still great umpires. With the demands of training and injury, sometimes they just can't get fit.

However, the older umpires can help teach about the subtle advantages that they have over younger and beginning umpires. We see better efficiencies in the older guys. For example, a new umpire working with a veteran will say, 'I know I'm fitter than him, but he's there, he's with the play and I'm not'. With the older umpires, it's about exclusion, and being more efficient. They also have the advantage that the players respect them more. If there's a marginal call, the players will accept it from an experienced umpire, and question it from a young guy. We don't think that you build rapport within one match—it happens over a longer period of time.

Gender

Along with our mentoring program, we are also developing female umpires. Fifty per cent of AFL fans are females, and we think that umpiring is a way to participate in the sport at the top level and to get there on equal footing. The young girls we have going through the umpire training programs have the empathy and the rapport with the little kids they umpire. They're not motivated to do it for the money—they love the game, they love umpiring in a group with their other girlfriends, and we think they're really good at it. We've done focus groups with the girls, and they also like to umpire the boys—we shouldn't just assume that they want to umpire girls' games. They like the sport and to see it played well, and they are motivated to get up to the highest level they can. We try to support their enjoyment so that they will develop into elite umpires, and we're really excited to see them get there. This is another place where we're changing the culture of the sport. When the little kids are exposed to umpiring by girls early on, they get used to it, and it's not going to be a battle to have them umpired by females later on.

Training and research

Our focus right now, above recruitment, is on understanding how best to *coach* umpiring. One of our biggest challenges is getting hard research, and funding for training. We need to invest in the future by looking at where we're spending our money. The attitude at the moment is that if we can pay salaries then we are serving officiating. But this is only short term. We need to be giving our umpires the best training, and move away from the idea that the guys at the top may not necessarily be the most skilled, but are, more than anything, the most resilient.

This is where all of our mentoring and development comes in. We are building up the recognition and support for developing umpires. This is also where the community and changing attitudes come in. We want coaches to help us by telling us what they want from umpires—what do we need to do? In the research, we're really good on the physical demands—we know about heart rate and we've done global positioning, but we need to understand skill and training a lot better—we need evidence-based practices. I think this is where we're heading.

KEY READING

Collina, P. (2003). *The Rules of the Game*. London: MacMillan.

Damisch, L., Mussweiler, T. and Plessner, H. (2006). 'Olympic medals as fruits of comparison? Assimilation and contrast in sequential judgments'. *Journal of Experimental Psychology: Applied*, (12): 166–78.

Helsen, W. and Bultynck, J.B. (2004). 'Physical and perceptual-cognitive demands of top-class refereeing in association football'. *Journal of Sport Sciences*, (22): 179–89.

MacMahon, C., Helsen, W.F., Starkes, J.L., Cuypers, K. and Weston, M. (2007). 'Decision-making skills and deliberate practice in elite association football referees'. *Journal of Sport Sciences*, 25(1): 65–78.

Mascarenhas, D.R.D., Collins, D. and Mortimer, P. (2005). 'Elite refereeing performance: Developing a model for sport science support'. *The Sport Psychologist*, (19): 364–79.

Mascarenhas, D.R.D., O'Hare, D. and Plessner, H. (2006). 'The psychological and performance demands of association football refereeing'. *International Journal of Sport Psychology*, (37): 99–120.

Oudejans, R.R.D., Verheijen, R., Bakker, F.C., Gerrits, J.C., Steinbrückner, M. and Beek, P.J. (2000). 'Errors in judging "offside" in football'. *Nature*, (404): 33.

Plessner, H. and Haar, T. (2006). 'Sports performance judgments from a social cognition perspective'. *Psychology of Sport and Exercise*, (7): 555–75.

Ste-Marie, D.M. (2003). 'Expertise in sport judges and referees: Circumventing information-processing limitations'. In Starkes, J.L. and Ericsson, K.A. (eds) *Expert Performance in Sport: Advances in Research on Sport Expertise*. Champaign IL: Human Kinetics.

Vickers, J.N., Reeves, M.-A., Chambers, K.L. and Martell, S. (2004). 'Decision training: Cognitive strategies for enhancing motor performance'. In Williams, A.M. and Hodges, N.J. (eds) *Skill Acquisition Sport: Research, Theory and Practice*. New York, NY: Routledge.

Chapter 13

The past and future of applied sport expertise research

Janet Starkes

INTRODUCTION

> There is a crack in everything. That's how the light gets in.
>
> (Leonard Cohen)

First, apologies to Leonard Cohen for borrowing these lines from 'Anthem'. I think they are particularly applicable to the message that I'll convey throughout this chapter. In reviewing the area of sport expertise it's important to consider where our cracks have been and what new sources of light there may be. The views expressed in the chapter are personal but reflect on the 30 years I have spent researching high-performance sport.

In the first part of the chapter I'll talk about how technological advances, research, and sport performance enhancements have always gone hand-in-hand. I'll use swimming as a case study and examine the types of technology change that have happened since the first 1896 Olympics, up to and including the Sydney Olympics. I'll illustrate my points with regard to research by showing the kinds of research that have been of interest along the way. Of course, the things that haven't changed during this time are the athletes' passion for their sport, the desire to win, and their commitment to be the best (as discussed in Chapters 3 and 4). The other things that have not changed are a coach's desire to provide the best possible training/competition for their athletes, and the sport scientist's wish to enhance performance wherever possible (see Horton and Deakin, Chapter 6).

In the second part of the chapter I will focus on technology changes since the 1970s that have altered the way we are able to test and examine sport expertise. The advent of microcomputers, 3D movement analysis, and eye movement analysis systems has altered not just what we are able to measure but how we think about sport experts. Most recently technological changes have impacted how we are able to aid athletes in their training.

In the third part of this chapter I'll list what I think we currently know about sport expertise from both a theoretical and a practical perspective. Finally, I'll highlight a few directions we might want to pursue as future directions in sport training.

193

TECHNOLOGICAL ADVANCES IN SPORT AND HOW THEY IMPACT PERFORMANCE: SWIMMING AS A CASE STUDY

An examination of swimming from the first modern Olympics (1896) to the Sydney Olympics (2000) provides an interesting case study of the kinds of technological change during that time period and the subsequent impact on sport performance. In the Athens Olympics of 1896, a young, 19-year-old Hungarian, Alfred Hajos, managed to win both the 100 and 1500 m events. In these events competitors dove off a boat in open water, and swam the event in the Bay of Zea wearing long cotton swimsuits. By the 1912 Stockholm Olympics, organizers had opted for the more controlled environment of an outdoor pool. In the free-style events most swimmers employed the new Trudgen stroke and most wore the newer 'short' swimsuits. Amsterdam in 1928 was the first instance where sport scientists employed high-speed film to assess performance. The Los Angeles Olympics (1932) saw a number of technological changes. By this time events were conducted in an indoor pool, stopwatches were used to time events, and the first ever photo finishes were employed. Significantly, sport scientists had designed lane markers to cut turbulence between lanes. By 1968 (Mexico City), the design of lane markers had been improved, and bubble machines were used in dive events to improve safety. High-altitude training was used for the first time by several teams hoping to gain an edge over those less prepared for the altitude of Mexico City. By Los Angeles (1984), Ron Havriluk had designed the first computerized system to measure swim velocity and efficiency. By 1992 (Barcelona), sport scientists were able to use 3D assessments to measure lift and drag forces of the accelerating hand in the stroke. In 1996 (Atlanta), Speedo unveiled its new suit—the Aquablade. At the same time Omega introduced touch pads for timing and electronic false start devices. By 2000 (Sydney), Speedo's Fastskin suit had taken over the pool, as evidenced by Ian Thorpe's success. Sport scientists were now able to use computational fluid dynamics to measure the acceleration, deceleration, and fluidity of each stroke. Over the roughly one hundred years since the advent of the modern Olympics, swimming moved indoors, lane markers and electronic timing and start systems were introduced, and swimmers took advantage of a number of innovations in swimsuit technology. At the same time sport scientists went from using high-speed film to linked computers to assess the fluid dynamics of a moving limb. Improving technology heralded vast improvements in performance. Although continued practice and good coaching can never be replaced, technological advancements and sport science were critical to these improvements.

The AIS's high-tech pool

In 2006 the ASC officially launched the AIS Recovery and Swimming Center, which boasts a new high-tech ten-lane, 50-m pool integrating a range of performance analysis devices and biomechanical systems purpose-built for the training, testing, and development of Australian swimmers. The $17 million Recovery and Swimming Center is being hailed as one of most technologically advanced pools of its kind in the world. This world-class swimming pool is the product of Australian-made ingenuity, with many of the technological elements custom-built in-house at the AIS. Its uniform 3m depth and high-quality filtration system are designed

194

for fast swimming. In addition, the new hydrotherapy and recovery facilities will greatly assist elite swimmers in recovering from intense training. These include three spa baths with a variety of jets, a plunge pool, a cold-water walk through, and a river for active recovery and stretching.

A range of high-tech performance analysis devices and biomechanical systems have been installed in the new pool and will monitor and measure the technique and action of AIS swimmers over various stages of race distances. These include:

- moveable boom—allows flexibility to change the length of the pool quickly without the need to swap lane ropes for short course and other distances; large lane rope markers will reduce turbulence
- high-quality water filtration—allows for a completely clear underwater view of the full length of the pool, which contributes to underwater filming
- underwater viewing—windows built into the pool base at the end of each lane and in the sides.
- Magnetic Timing System—raised from the floor to measure split times at specific distances that make up key components of a race
- Filming Control Room—air-conditioned environment for computer equipment— allows for all video, data, and voice communications to be patched through to computer facilities to monitor the technique and performance of elite swimmers; two control rooms contain a large plasma screen that swimmers can view without getting out of the pool
- 3D magnetic computerized modeling system—creates accurate 3D skeletal frame model of swimmer actually swimming; this allows for a computerized model analysis of the swimmer's action
- digital displays—future panels will provide read-outs at the pool end to provide instant feedback about the technique and performance of AIS swimmers
- resistance training devices—(i.e., bungy cords) can be fitted to tracks in lanes 2 and 7
- pacing-lights system—to provide a continuous external pacing stimulus for swimmers
- instrumented start blocks—measures the force, acceleration, angle, and timing of swimmers off the blocks
- instrumented wall—concealed behind touch pads on three lanes—provides data on force, acceleration, push off angle, and timing of the swimmer's turns and backstroke starts
- camera tracking—twenty-four cameras above and below the water provide co-ordinated video footage of swimmers; permanent concealed tracks allow camera trolley to move alongside a swimmer
- analysis-data and video images are fed into the video control room linked to AIS IT systems as well as being displayed on the plasma screen as part of the biomechanical analysis process (Figure 13.1).

Figure 13.1 *Real time video and kinematic feedback being delivered to an AIS swimmer.*

TECHNOLOGICAL ADVANCES IN EQUIPMENT RELATED TO SPORT EXPERTISE RESEARCH

In contrast to research on performance improvement, the history of perception/decision research in sport is much shorter, about 30 years. Nevertheless, expertise research has been as dramatically impacted by technological advancements as sports have. Briefly, I'll trace seven areas where I think technology has permitted us a better understanding of what makes an expert athlete:

1. In the 1970s researchers were interested in determining what aspects of superior game performance could be tapped within the laboratory. It was unclear at this point whether expert differences would be largely innate and thus eventually be used for talent identification (see Gulbin, Chapter 5), or whether differences would prove to be acquired through practice and thus be important in the design of training. The earliest research used game information presented in photographic slides for brief periods and asked athletes to recognize, remember, or reconstruct what was happening in the picture. The rudimentary technology involved (Figure 13.2a) comprised paper and pencil, slide projectors to present game information, and reaction timers to assess how fast game-related decisions could be made. To control the amount of game information provided, visual exposure time was limited via a shutter (tachistoscope) attached to the projector. Decision time was recorded by

Figure 13.2a *Circa 1970–1980: paper, pencil, slides.*

various means, although millisecond precision was only recently available and digital accuracy was still in the distant future. Some researchers (Abernethy for example) used high-speed film in the laboratory to gain greater physical fidelity in the laboratory tasks (resemblance to the actual game). Still, high-speed film could only be shot in black and white, and editing involved literally cutting and pasting film.

2. In the late 1970s and early 1980s two major advances assisted sport research (Figure 13.2b). First Apple II microcomputers were available at a reasonable cost, and video was invented (originally in Beta format and much later in VHS). For the first time experimental protocols could be driven by computer, data could be stored and analyzed, and manuscripts could be written in word processing format. Although the earliest microcomputer models were expensive ($3,300 for 48K of hard drive space and 4K ram), as statistical analyses were far easier than on the hand calculators previously used, their longevity was guaranteed! Researchers were overjoyed at the possibilities for physical fidelity in their laboratory tasks that the advent of video presented. Tasks could now be dynamic, and actual game footage could be employed. Research seemed to be limited only by the requirement for a strong videographer (because the camera unit weighed 24 lb) and budget for batteries (as battery life was short). Editing was an extremely laborious process of blackening sections of tape and re-recording.

Figure 13.2b *Circa 1978–1983: microcomputer.*

3. Thankfully, by the late 1980s microcomputers were cheaper and more powerful, and could be integrated with both videotape stimuli and reaction-time peripherals to synchronize all aspects of game simulations in the laboratory. At this point however, a great deal of technical support was still required in order to facilitate the integration of all of the required programming and peripherals.

4. For many years sport researchers had puzzled over how best to present a specified amount of visual information within game simulations. The earliest attempts employed tachistoscopes, but some other inventions included goggles with blinders, or welders' masks that flipped up and down to provide controlled amounts of visual exposure. Paul Milgram's invention of liquid crystal occlusion goggles in the late 1980s (Figure 13.2c) provided a much needed piece of technology. Milgram originally designed the goggles to provide time-limited visual information in his research on driving skill, but sport researchers immediately recognized their value. Now the goggles are routinely employed in on-court/field tasks to train visual perception in athletes (for example by Singer and Farrow in tennis, and Starkes in volleyball).

5. From the earliest days of sport research, coaches and researchers have recognized the value of analyzing skilled movements in three dimensions to understand better how the best athletes perform certain moves (Figure 13.2d). This technology has seen tremendous advancements over the years to become less intrusive to movement, cheaper, more portable, and more precise, to require less memory for storage, and to portray captured movements more realistically. Today the technology plays an important role in analyzing the relative efficiency of skilled movement.

Figure 13.2c Circa 1987–present: liquid crystal occlusion (Plato) goggles.

Figure 13.2d
*Circa 1978–present:
3Dimensional movement
analyses, motion capture.*

6. Early on in sport research there was the hope that by understanding where the eyes were looking we would understand what parts of the visual display during the game are most important for expert performance. Although we now understand that where someone focuses and what they attend to, process, and use are not necessarily equivalent, there is still a great deal to be learned by integrating information about eye movements with what is happening in the visual environment, and the resultant skilled movements of a high-performance athlete (Figure 13.2e). No one has done more to develop integrated technology between eye, video, and movement than Dr Joan Vickers from the University of Calgary. Her research continues to show us the value of multiple methods of monitoring and analyzing eye and whole-body movements.

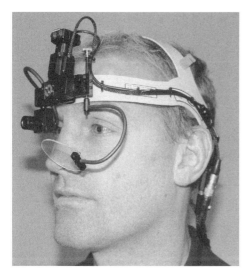

Figure 13.2e *Circa 1980–present: eye movement analysis.*

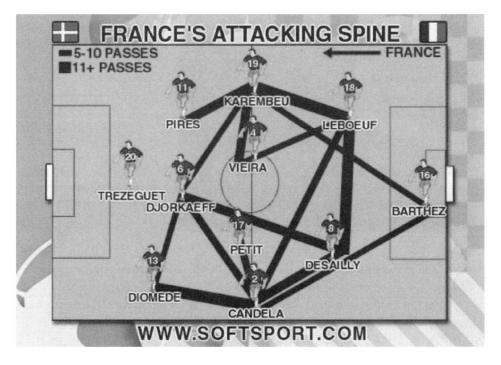

Figure 13.2f *Circa 1980–present: game stats and tactics, computerized notational analyses.*

7. Finally, both coaches and sport scientists have always known the importance of gathering game statistics and their potential use in developing game tactics (see also McPherson, Chapter 11). Digital video, real-time analyses, and relational databases have taken the production of game stats and tactical development to new heights (Figure 13.2f). These systems are now widely employed by both professional and amateur clubs. Although their importance is only likely to increase, their use illustrates the growing digital gap between have and have-not sport associations and countries.

THEORETICAL PERSPECTIVES

Given roughly 30 years of research on sport expertise, it's important to step back and examine where we are now from a *theoretical perspective*.

• First, unlike 20 years ago we realize the value of both laboratory and field research. Few developments in the training of athletes have happened without extensive laboratory testing in advance. But it has also been important to understand how well laboratory findings translate in the field. (Many coaches might argue that we have not done a very good job following through and translating laboratory findings into usable constructs on the court or field.)

- We understand the value of multidimensional approaches to studying sport experts. High-performance athletes are not superior because of one or two skills. They are better because of a multitude of physical, emotional, and perception/decision skills. To tap that expertise we need a range of tasks and measures.

- We realize that a very unique aspect of sport is superior movement skill *under time constraints*. Sport isn't simply a complex cognitive domain, like chess. It is the speed, agility, and grace of movement that make sport special and must be a part of any discussion of expert performance in sport.

- Thankfully, over the past 30 years it has become possible to publish sport research in sport, human movement, and psychological journals. Now we need researchers willing to translate findings in a form accessible to coaches and athletes.

- It is important to consider areas in which we are weak. One issue is that we still don't have a good understanding of perception–action coupling, or how perception is integrated with the movement requirements in sport. This is in part because testing athletes under laboratory conditions often constrains the types of movements that are feasible. It is rare that we are able to test athletes in sport situations where the full range of movement skill, complexity, speed, and grace can be employed and analyzed.

- The encouraging results of early studies using a dynamical-systems approach have not been borne out in the long run. This approach suggests that movements are not programmed or planned in advance; they arise from the natural adaptation of a biological and biomechanical system to achieve a specific movement goal. They have been routinely used to study repetitive movements such as drawing circles or juggling. I would argue that the dynamical-systems approach has aided little in our understanding outside *novel* repetitive or cyclical movements. If you think about it, there are many sports in which skilled rhythmic, cyclic movements are the hallmark of performance: rowing, cycling, pommel horse, uneven bars, running, to name a few. The dynamical-systems approach should assess skill in these sports, but to date few scientists (Keith Davids, Peter Beek, and Raoul Huys being some exceptions) have used this theoretical approach to help us understand those skills that could be most illuminated by this research.

- Currently we have a fairly good understanding of many of the unique skills of experts in various specific sports. Our weakest point is understanding the underlying psychological mechanisms that scaffold expert performance. For example if one chooses to become highly skilled, at some point in development the athlete must move beyond pure reliance on coaches' feedback and be able to analyze/critique their own skills, practice, shortcomings, etc. Elsewhere this has been termed a 'change of agency' from coach to self. When and how this occurs or how it should be fostered have never been examined.

- The last dozen years have shown a much renewed interest in how the microstructure of practice can aid expert performance, in part owing to the popularity of Ericsson's theory of deliberate practice and the interest it has generated in sport research. As Baker and Cobley's chapter suggests (Chapter 3), we need to go further and understand better what this research suggests for the training of individual athletes (see also Patterson and Lee, Chapter 9).

201

- Finally, in spite of many predictions over the past 20 years, we still don't have a general theory of expertise to cover all sports let alone all movement skill. The need for such a generalized theory continues to be a topic of debate.

PRACTICAL PERSPECTIVES

- There are much better working relationships between coaches and sport scientists. There was a time when coaches felt sport scientists were too laboratory-oriented and had little to contribute to the training of athletes on an everyday basis. Likewise, sport scientists were too wrapped up in testing their models with little concern for what their findings meant for athletes and coaches. I sense a closer relationship and recognition that they share a common goal and each can contribute to an athlete's development. The best example of this is the working relationship between coaches and sport scientists at AIS, and their joint role in developing elite athletes.
- There is a lot we don't really know, in spite of the amount of research done to date. We don't know how best to conduct perceptual training or decision training, or how best to use simulations. For example, we don't know what level of skill can benefit most from perceptual training. We don't know the relative trade-off between physical/decision fidelity of simulations and their efficacy for training. Sometimes simulations that have high fidelity (are closer to the actual game context) can be very costly to produce, but are the advantages worth it? Decision fidelity in simulation (being able to make the kinds of decision required in an actual game) may be easier to attain than physical fidelity (having the task physically resemble the game) but is it enough?
- Perceptual/decision training appears to be beneficial, but at the moment few clubs can afford the technology and support staff to engage in this kind of training (see Farrow and Raab, Chapter 10).
- On-line continuous human performance evaluation is now a reality as anyone who watched the 2006 Tour de France will know from watching Lance Armstrong's daily performance. This includes coaches and trainers being able constantly to observe and measure physiological, biomechanical and decision-making performance in real time, remotely. It also provides a record of many aspects of performance for athletes to be able to review in detail following their performance.
- The AIS and some other national training centers are using court/field perceptual-training devices to the benefit of many athletes. This work is discussed in more detail by Farrow and Raab in Chapter 10.
- It is possible to employ virtual displays as part of broadcasts (for example showing first and ten yard lines in American football, or the trail of the puck in ice hockey). Virtual displays/games will become more widely used in perception/decision training, perhaps to show the anticipated result of a decision in advance of it being carried out.
- Sources of information can be readily modified or adjusted for viewer preference. Already some viewers in England can select viewing angle for games, and this option will only increase. Perhaps we will be able to watch soccer games 'through the eyes

of David Beckham', or select an umpire's view to determine the information they really had when an offside was called.

- Increasingly it is possible to have customized, on-line, continuous compilation of game stats and tactics. Everyone knows the influence that the availability of complex game stats has had on sports. In US college football and in professional ice hockey, games are recorded and computational analyses are conducted simultaneously so that coaches have available to them, at any time during the game, stats on how effective certain plays or players have been so far in that game. Game strategies can be altered mid-game or player positions revised as a result.

- Very soon it will be possible to have continuous compilation of video highlights. It is already possible to convert long sequences of game play to digital simulations and rotate these simulations to reflect any point of view on the field. Of course computer memory technology plays a huge role in all of these areas. At the moment it is estimated that every 18 months the memory capacity of the latest chip available doubles. Blu-ray technology is now adding a quantum leap to this estimate. Blu-ray ensures that each CD will hold fifty times the current data. Most people will be able to back up an entire computer system on one disk. This technology is already available.

- Computer memory developments will have significant impacts on the collection and manipulation of broad relational databases for stats, imaging, and potentially sport training. Take an example of a basketball point guard preparing for an important game where he or she will be playing one-on-one against a particular player. Soon it will be easy for that guard to sort through inordinate amounts of recorded game images by simply requesting all instances of that player (for example) beating the defense on a drive, or using picks to help out a high post player. All relevant examples from 2005 to present could be immediately selected and presented in sequence. The player could study the opponent in great detail, without the labor associated with screening hours of game films to select relevant plays.

- Finally, in the not too distant future, tiny, extremely inexpensive chips will be installed everywhere in items (clothing, transport, buildings, food, and places), leading to the 'Everywhere Network' and the opportunity for scientists to capture more on-line performance data than ever before. Unfortunately, what these changes mean is an ever widening 'digital divide' between have and have-not countries, sport associations and clubs. For example, whereas in the US fifty-six per cent of the population are connected to the Internet, worldwide the figure is only four per cent.

WHERE MIGHT WE CHOOSE TO GO IN SPORT TRAINING AND EXPERTISE RESEARCH?

What I have tried to do so far is illustrate by example where we have been in sport and sport-expertise research, and some areas where we are likely to go in the near future. With change happening so quickly, it becomes ever more important to examine some areas where we might *choose* to go in sport training and research.

- Web-casting has become both economically feasible and quite easy technologically. In the future we need to consider web-casting sport conferences, special speakers, and coaching clinics. For individuals who can't afford to go to conferences or coaching clinics, offering them as live web-casts can help coaches, athletes, or anyone else with access to the Internet. A couple of years ago I was a keynote speaker at a hockey summit of professional coaches, athletes, and league administrators. The summit was web-cast live, and time was set aside at the end of each presentation to address questions that had come in via e-mail from the live Internet audience. The questions were enlightening and informative, and would not have been possible without this technology. Web-casting serves a certain democratizing function when it comes to sharing coaching and sport science knowledge. Suddenly coaches, athletes, sport administrators, and parents are able to take part in discussions that heretofore would have been available only to a select few at national training centers or conferences.

- Second, we have a great need for information sharing between coaches and sport scientists. Fifteen years ago when the worldwide Human Genome Project was undertaken, all researchers were invited to share their information and technological advances in pursuit of mapping the thousands of existing human genes. Nay-sayers said it would never work because scientists are too competitive; too isolated in their own little research areas. Thirteen years later some 25,000 human genes have been mapped, and the information is freely available to all researchers worldwide. We should take this as an inspiration, a challenge, and evidence that co-operative research can work. Although international collaboration often exists on a one-to-one basis in sport, we need structures that permit this to happen more readily. 2005 saw the first issues of the *International Journal of Sports Science & Coaching* (www.multi-science.co.uk/sports-science&coaching.htm) and the *International Journal of Coaching Science* (www.icce.ws.journal/). These are two new international journals that focus on the science of coaching, and are clear signs that research on coaching is coming of age and that there is a need for international collaboration. I hope they are successful.

- We need to broaden our vision of what constitutes high-performance sport from the very ageist view we currently hold. Not only is the world population aging, but the fastest growing segment of sport participation is Masters sport. When the World Masters Games were held in Brisbane, 25,000 athletes attended, in Melbourne 24,000. In Edmonton (2006) registration had to be suspended (at 21,000) three months in advance because all forms of accommodation in the city had been booked. All sports that support Masters competition are seeing increases in numbers. By way of example, there are now thirty per cent more senior-level hockey players in Canada than there are youth sport players. Masters athletes are an incredibly motivated group who have often maintained lifelong training and competitive schedules. We owe it to them to help them retain whatever expert performance they have acquired over a lifetime of competition. Along the way we may find (as has already occurred in some sports) that the average age of world record holders is also on the rise!

204

- With the ever-widening gap in sport performances between have and have-not countries, it behooves us to consider ways in which this gap could be narrowed. One possible way is through sport legacies created by major games. Every major games in the world (Olympic Games, Asian Games, Commonwealth Games, PanAmerican Games, etc.) has a bid process to select host cities, and very often part of the bid proposal is a legacy created by the games. Too often the legacies are major stadia or facilities within the host country. If each games association decided that a portion of games funding (say a meagre ten per cent) must be committed as a sport legacy to improve sport development worldwide, this would have tremendous impact. If the legacy commitment had to begin when a host city was announced and led up to the games, it could have an immediate impact on the preparation of athletes for that particular games and the future of sport. One example of a legacy commitment might be sport fellowships to help deserving coaches, athletes, and sport scientists in less wealthy countries work with mentors in the host country to develop sport back in their own community. Another legacy might be travel awards for athletes from have-not countries to travel to international clinics and competitions in advance of the games. A matching funds program could be made available to help developing countries build facilities for training and competition. Sometimes funding for facilities need not be of large magnitude to have great impact. For example, Belize now has its first ever track facility for training athletes. This was the result of a personal donation by Marion Jones, whose mother is originally from Belize. A relatively small personal donation has had a huge impact on sport development in that country.

I hope through this chapter I have demonstrated a few of the places in sport training and research where the cracks may be, but being the optimist that I am, a few of the ways in which the light continues to shine in.

KEY READING

Baker, J., Côté, J. and Abernethy, B. (2003). 'Learning from the experts: practice activities of expert decision makers in sport'. *Research Quarterly for Exercise and Sport*, (74): 342–7.

Côté, J., Baker, J. and Abernethy, B. (2003). 'From play to practice: A developmental framework for the acquisition of expertise in team sports'. In Starkes, J.L. and Ericsson, K.A. (eds) *Expert Performance in Sports: Advances in Research on Sport Expertise*. Champaign, IL: Human Kinetics, 89–113.

Elferink-Gemser, M. T., Visscher, C., Lemmink, K.A.P.M. and Mulder, Th. (2004). 'Relation between multidimensional performance characteristics and level of performance in talented youth field hockey players'. *Journal of Sports Sciences*, (22): 1053–63.

Ericsson, K.A. (2003). 'Development of elite performance and deliberate practice'. In Starkes, J.L. and Ericsson, K.A. (eds) *Expert Performance in Sports: Advances in Research on Sport Expertise*. Champaign, IL: Human Kinetics, 49–87.

Helsen, W. F. and Starkes, J. L. (1999). 'A multidimensional approach to skilled perception and performance in sport'. *Applied Cognitive Psychology*, (13): 1–27.

205

Hodges, N.J., Kerr, T., Starkes, J.L., Weir, P.L. and Nananidou, A. (2004). 'Predicting performance times from deliberate practice hours for triathletes and swimmers: What, when, and where is practice important?'. *Journal of Experimental Psychology: Applied*, (10): 219–37.

Hodges, N.J., Huys, R. and Starkes, J.L. (2007). 'A methodological review and evaluation of research of expert performance in sport'. In Tenenbaum, G. and Eklund, R.C. (eds) *Handbook of Sport Psychology*, 3rd edn. NY: Wiley Publishers.

Starkes, J.L., Deakin, J.M., Allard, F., Hodges, N.J. and Hayes, A. (1996). 'Deliberate practice in sports: What is it anyway?'. In Ericsson, K.A. (ed) *The Road to Excellence: The Acquisition of Expert Performance in the Arts and Sciences, Sports, and Games*. Mahwah, NJ: Lawrence Erlbaum, 81–106.

Starkes, J.L. and Ericsson, K.A.(eds) (2003). *Expert performance in sports: Advances in research on sport expertise*. Champaign, IL: Human Kinetics, 115–35.

Williams, A.M. and Hodges, N.J. (eds) (2004). *Skill Acquisition in Sport: Research, Theory and Practice*. London: Routledge (Taylor & Francis Group).

Index

Page references in italics indicate illustrations.